Management Mastery and Practice Series

Everything You Ever Wanted To Know About Managing People But Were Afraid To Ask

Endorsements

Welcome to the new world! And welcome to a guidebook that helps managers and leaders, their people and organizations, survive and thrive in it. The Covid-19 pandemic is a symptom of the intersectional challenges we face in this world. It is global, unpredictable, opportunistic and stressful. It keeps us on guard and demands that we be stronger and more sensitive to our needs and the needs of others and possibilities for the future. How does a useful book help us meet this challenging new world of work and life? It does just what Stout-Rostron and Taylor have done – manage and lead us by example. They apply the core models and best practices from the past, but reapply them within the new context of our new world. They provide the practical how-to's for day-to-day management with a transformational mindset and the holistic and systemic balance of mind and body, one-on-one relationships, and team and organizational dynamics. Bravo for this practical guide with lessons from the past and a map to use them and new strategies to build your management and leadership expertise for today and tomorrow.

— *Lew Stern, PhD, Leadership Council of the Faith Communities Environmental Network, past Co-Chairperson of The Executive Coaching Forum, Founder and past Director of the Graduate Certificate Program in Executive Coaching at the Massachusetts School of Professional Psychology*

It is always a pleasure to read any new book from Sunny Stout-Rostron and with her co-authors, Michael and Ingra, this exploration of *Everything You Ever Wanted To Know About Managing People But Were Afraid to Ask* does not disappoint. It combines reflection on ideas, challenges we currently face and practical approaches that the reader can consider and apply. It recognises that leaders are also managers and need to ensure they are equipped to deliver through the way they manage. The authors explore some of the breakdowns we are currently facing and the vulnerabilities that have been exposed yet highlight the opportunities to reset our thinking.

This new thinking requires in their view a step up to a new level, a challenge some are struggling with given that it demands significant mental and emotional agility. They attempt to guide leaders to operate in the new world that confronts us. They take the reader on a journey to examine their purpose, concerns, self-care, support and personal and professional development. This practical book provides key tools for that journey and I am pleased to recommend it as a valuable tool to ensure that new thinking can be developed.

— *Professor David A Lane, Professional Development Foundation, UK*

I was struck by Sunny's departure from writing mainly about the field of coaching, to this book which reflects a broader interest in the wider field of leadership and management. This is an ambitious shift, but one that she traverses well. I applaud the emphasis on the integration of leadership and management, when many would express this as a duality. And equally applaud the focus on the emergence of the need for 'hybrid management' in VUCA times.

This book explores ways in which African wisdom informs Western practice. The provocative title invites the reader to explore the challenge, *Everything You Ever Wanted to Know About Managing People But Were Afraid to Ask*, echoing of course the Woody Allen question, 'Everything You Ever Wanted to Know About Sex but Were Afraid to Ask.' I have little insight into the minds of contemporary middle managers, but can believe that there is much fear-based reticence with regard to inquiring into the unknown. I feel sure that this book will help leader-managers find a variety of answers for themselves.

— *Daniel Doherty, Critical Coaching Research Group, UK*

This book provided me with such a rich blend of learning, reflection and fun. I found myself remembering all those occasions on my own management/leadership journey when I would have benefitted so much had I then had the book available, and I very much enjoyed the flow of each chapter from theory to practice to personal experience. I was also delighted to discover how so many accepted management theories and truths evolved from and complement each other!

One could choose to see the work as a reference book, an introduction to management and leadership, or as an engaging guide on a journey in pursuit of management mastery. The abundance of real-world examples, useful activities and oh-so-familiar case studies provides insight and context to the broadest range of management realities, and will help anybody, at any stage in their leadership journey, best embrace the changing, hybrid world of work.

— *Bill Hoggarth, CEO Dataways, South Africa; previous CEO SAS Africa/Middle East*

My excitement when a new Sunny Stout-Rostron book appears is as much gratitude as joy. Gratitude for the beautifully-reasoned, widely-experienced, deeply human offering of her insights for a world that hungers for them. And *Everything You Ever Wanted to Know About Managing People But Were Afraid to Ask* is all of that. Its presentation of the nature of the leader-manager, of their symbiosis, and of their requisite deep self-knowledge is stunning. She and Michael Taylor with Ingra Du Buisson-Narsai have produced an elegant collaboration, both of wisdom and of writing. I hope that leaders and managers everywhere will read this book and live its message. These gifted writers have in turn given us all a gift, one that will fill us with both gratitude and joy.

— *Nancy Kline, Author:* The Promise That Changes Everything: I Won't Interrupt You, *Penguin Random House;* Time To Think: Listening to Ignite the Human Mind, *Cassell Hachette. Founding Director, Time To Think Ltd, UK*

"This book is a terrific addition to the knowledge base for leader-managers, that will have a far-reaching impact. I love the richness of relevant theory and research in *Everything You Want to Know About Managing People But Were afraid to Ask*. With the logical structure and organisation, and the compellingly realistic and pragmatic examples, I will be one of your first buyers!"

— *John Reed*, Managing Director, Quinn Reed Associates, author of Pinpointing Excellence: The Key to Finding a Quality Executive Coach, *Miami, Florida USA*

"The global pandemic has amplified levels of complexity and uncertainty in the past two years, yet there are opportunities to be seized. Real-life experiences have shown that people are at the center of business and it does not matter whether you have people reporting to you - you are a leader and manager. Managers play a critical role in building resilient people and organisations, and in the hybrid work environment transition to management and leadership requires a different set of skills and capabilities. *Everything you wanted to know about managing people but were afraid to ask* provides practical, deeply insightful wisdom, and tools for managers to learn, reflect and refine how they lead and manage themselves, teams and organisations to thrive as lives and businesses continue to evolve."

— *Jeanett Modise, Group Human Resources Director, Sanlam, South Africa*

Management Mastery: Everything Your Wanted to Know About Managing People but Were Afraid to Ask is set to become *the* go-to book for key concepts and practices in becoming a skilled leader-manager. There are nuggets of leadership and management theory that give perspective on the fast-evolving world of management and leadership. It introduces the challenges of a hybrid working environment, where the positive management of employee relationships online as well as face-to-face is a critical competency. The wide range of practical activities, set out by experts in their field, support each topic covered in *Everything Your Wanted to Know About Managing People but Were Afraid to Ask,* from self-awareness and testing levels of emotional intelligence to coaching skills and managing performance. For leader-managers who strive to develop good work habits, self-belief, relationship skills and resilience in the face of risk, I envisage this book being the most well-thumbed reference in a manager's collection.

— *Dorrian Aiken DProf (Executive Coaching), Comensa Master Practitioner, Master Integral Coach, Time to Think coach, Consultant, South Africa*

Everything You Ever Wanted to Know About Managing People But Were Afraid to Ask is well-presented and structured, taking the reader through the challenges of leading and managing people in a fast-changing context. The focus on self-development as a manager is well supported by self-assessment tests throughout, to help managers understand their strengths and weaknesses. Mining material on what is known in important areas such as leadership, neuroscience and coaching, the book provides food for thought and support for the aspiring manager. The focus on honing communication through assertiveness provides practical suggestions for managing people. The final chapters explore further developing one's leadership abilities, and provides a fitting finale to the overall, developmental theme of the book.

— Dr Pauline Armsby, Academic and Consultant in Work and Learning, UK

This book unfolds a very effective process of discovery and well researched key areas for practice in the field of management and leadership. It comes from authors who have a lived experience of leadership, consultancy, research and coaching which makes it highly relevant in our world of shifting landscapes. There is an increasing need of such a resource. The book offers an accumulation of touchstones into very sound theories, models, and reflective exercises that serve to land the pearls of wisdom in this broad field.

I will be recommending this to so many of my clients as many leaders come to their role without management skills, and struggle with what one would think would be part of their preparation and development work. Instead of stepping up, many regress to more doing and taking on of responsibilities which lead to burnout, high anxiety and poor performance. A focus of this book on the inner development facilitates a way to shift from doing to being as a core part of the work as a leader-manager. In my own work as a leadership coach, clients, from across so many industries and professions (ranging from higher education to manufacturing) are grappling with essential management skills and techniques that would alleviate so much of their stress. The cultivation of mastery through the when, where and how in *Everything You Ever Wanted To Ask About Managing People But Were Afraid to Ask* resonates with me and will resonate with so many. I believe that this will act as a resource book for many consultants and coaches to share with their clients. Key to everything is the inside work that goes with the outer work. This book offers an accessible journey through this territory. Well done on this wonderful offering .

— Dr Paddy Pampallis (DProf: executive coaching), Founder CEO of Integral Africa Institute; The (Integral) Coaching Centre (TCC); with co-founder, Dr Dumisani Magadlela of the Ubuntu Coaching Foundation. Paddy was a founding member of COMENSA, the Global Coaching Community, and is on the accrediting board of the Worldwide Association of Coaches, South Africa

Many books on leadership and people management can lose themselves somewhat in theory and consequently can be boring to read and with little practical advice. In contrast *Everything You Ever Wanted to Know About Managing People But Were Afraid to Ask* is easy to read for the busy executive in bite-sized distinct chapters. Where relevant it provides condensed background on some of the leading theories behind management practices and most importantly provides practical and implementable advice on how to deal with or think about people management issues. I highly recommend reading this book.

— *Klaus-Dieter Kämpfer, Managing Director, Commercial Property Finance & Equity Investments, Absa Group Ltd, South Africa*

Sunny and Michael, with a contribution from Ingra, have been able to communicate simply the bedrock of what every manager should know entering the journey of leadership. And indeed, knowledge and insights that many managers have not yet been exposed to in the leadership adventure – although they should have been! Part instruction-manual, part practical-degree and part progressive-insights into a modern way to create impact as a leader, *Everything You Ever Wanted to Know About Managing People But Were Afraid to Ask* is a 'go-to' guide and 'must-have' in your personal leadership library. I appreciate the rigour and care that comes through this work, and recommend all leaders to reach deeply into the value it will bring them.

— *Simon Bold, MD BOLDCOM, Executive and Renewal Coach, South Africa*

Sunny and Co. draw on decades of experience in coaching and developing managers and leaders to produce this essential leader-manager handbook based on solid theoretical principles. This one-stop treasure-trove is filled with a multitude of perspectives and tools to help leaders and managers navigate current times. The "activities" sections are especially useful to help the reader make practical sense of the rich content. Highly recommended for leaders, managers and those involved in developing them.

— *Dr Nicky Terblanche, Head of Management Coaching at University of Stellenbosch Business School, South Africa*

This book firstly digs into the underlying principles and theories of all manner of leadership responsibilities and challenges, providing a solid foundation for those who are entering management or even for seasoned managers who want to fine tune their effectiveness and impact. The accessibility of the practical guides that go with each of the key areas of management combines with the theory to provide a rich and multilayered resource with an easily accessible layout, that can be read end to end and then revisited repeatedly to deepen one's practice as a manager and developing leader. Complexity delivered in a compact, user friendly style and format, bursting with resources.

— *Vicki Crabb, Partner, Workware Solutions, and Senior Consultant, Pique Global, Melbourne, Australia*

Dedication

To Susan Schuurmans

and in fond memory of Theo Schuurmans

First published in 2022.

ISBN: 978-1-86922-944-3 (Printed)
eISBN: 978-1-86922-945-0 (PDF Ebook)

Published by KR Publishing
P O Box 3954
Randburg
2125
Republic of South Africa

Tel: (011) 706-6009
E-mail: orders@knowres.co.za
Website: www.kr.co.za

Typesetting, layout and design: Cia Joubert, cia@knowres.co.za
Cover design: Marlene De Lorme, marlene@knowres.co.za
Editing and Proofreading: Nick Wilkins
Project management: Cia Joubert, cia@knowres.co.za

Management Mastery and Practice Series

Everything You Ever Wanted To Know About Managing People But Were Afraid To Ask

by

Sunny Stout-Rostron and Michael Taylor

with contributing author

Ingra Du Buisson-Narsai

kr
publishing

2022

Management Mastery and Practice Series

Edited by Dr Sunny Stout-Rostron

Context

This series is suited to a range of managers. You might be a newly promoted manager or about to step into a greater managerial role with increased responsibilities. Or perhaps you have been in a management position for some years but have had no formal management training, or you are an executive leader but need to refresh your ideas on the essentials of leading and managing yourself and others. Whichever length of time you have been managing, this series is to help you deal with people management. This includes cultural diversity, systemic issues within the organisation in which you work, and to develop effective communication and coaching skills, the ability to manage conflict, difficult situations, company politics and career development.

The authors look at how to inspire staff and teams, understand motivation and demotivation, manage stress, build better performance with effective communications and well-run meetings, build great teams, and prepare leaders for the future. Each book includes theory, research, case studies, practical exercises, and tips on how to handle challenges – avoiding the pitfalls that can cause managers to fail. Your effectiveness as a leader-manager depends on what support you can expect from your staff, direct reports, and team members. This series will help you to build your skills and competence, developing your own unique signature as a leader and a manager.

Book 1: Management Mastery: Everything You Ever Wanted to Know About Managing People But Were Afraid to Ask

by Sunny Stout-Rostron and Michael Taylor with contributing author Ingra Du Buisson-Narsai

Being a leader-manager requires the skills of both management and leadership. This book covers essential aspects of both: identifying and solving your most challenging people problems quickly, and motivating your people to perform at their highest potential. Understanding when to lead and when to manage, taking a deeper dive into self-awareness and self-management, delegating to develop your team, broadening your range of communication skills in order to inspire and motivate people and managing difficult people and situations. However, the most important competence essential for stepping into being a leader-manager is that of self-awareness, conscious observation and thoroughly understanding yourself in order to lead and manage people. It is critically important that you understand and know how your teams "experience" you – because this is the path towards identifying what change is needed in terms of your own assumptions about yourself and others. It is vital to understand your own thinking, feeling and behaviour. This process is described with clear guidelines, case studies, practical exercises, and self-assessments to move you into greater competence as a leader-manager.

Book 2: *Ubuntu coaching and connection practices for leader-managers: Building a high-performance team in the new normal*

by Dumisani Magadlela, PhD

New leader-managers in the whirlwind digital world do not have the luxury of gathering all the necessary background data that will equip them with information on each member of their new team. Joining an organisation with the task of a new team, or inheriting and leading an existing one, and then growing the team to become what you envision, is a tall task at best even for the most experienced of leaders. Given the fast pace of change and access to information by many employees in the digital age, new leader-managers are faced with the daunting task of integrating the divergent views of their new team members. The task of building a high-performance team in a fast-changing digital world becomes even more complex when the new leader-manager operates from the stance of a KIA (know-it-all). Ubuntu coaching skills, ubuntu intelligence lenses, and many new tools are packed into this book to help equip new leader-managers with essential skills to become agile and versatile in a rapidly evolving environment, and to adopt a "teaming" approach that is team-friendly and helps them to build their new team. This book shares illustrative examples and easy-to-use exercises at the end of each chapter to help deepen a leader-manager's self-awareness, re-humanising a new world of work through their teams and across organisational systems.

Table of contents

List of tables

List of figures

List of activities

Series author biographies

Sunny Stout-Rostron, DProf

An organisational development specialist, Sunny coaches at senior executive and board level. Having worked internationally in the corporate world for 20 years, she also has a wide range of experience in leadership development, helping organisations cultivate collaborative strategies to manage relationship systems, culture change and conflict. Sunny has played a leading role in building the profession of coaching and has created a succession of leadership and management programmes in the corporate, legal and educational fields. Her passion is to deepen the knowledge base for coaching through research and critical reflective practice, as well as fostering an understanding and implementation of genuine cultural diversity in organisations.

Sunny is a director of People Quotient (Pty) Ltd, a Doctoral Supervisor at several business schools, a member of the Management Coaching faculty of the University of Stellenbosch Business School (USB), part-time faculty at the South African College of Applied Psychology, and on the global faculty for Time to Think, Inc. She is a Founding Fellow at the Institute of Coaching at McLean Hospital, a Harvard Medical School Affiliate, and Founding President of Coaches and Mentors of South Africa (COMENSA), and a long-standing member of the Worldwide Association of Business Coaches (WABC).

Sunny is the author of six books including: *Transformational Coaching to Lead Culturally Diverse Teams* (Routledge, 2019); *Leadership Coaching for Results: Cutting-edge practices for coach and client* (Knowres, 2014); *Business Coaching International: Transforming individuals and organisations* (Karnac 2009, 2013); and *Business Coaching Wisdom and Practice: Unlocking the secrets of business coaching* (Knowres, 2009, 2012).

Michael Taylor, MPhil

An experienced facilitator, international management consultant, and master coach, Michael has deep expertise in understanding and implementing culture change, building world-class teams and developing global leaders. He experienced first-hand the excitement of running profitable high engagement businesses, which included managing a team of 25 professional consultants. Michael is managing director of Xponential (Pty) Ltd, a professional services firm he founded in 2006, and a director of People Quotient (Pty) Ltd.

A practice leader for executive coaching and leadership development, Michael is highly regarded as a thought leader in the fields of executive coaching and team effectiveness. He has a wealth of practical experience at both management and executive levels, and inherently understands the challenges leaders face in the current world of complex volatility, uncertainty and ambiguity.

He has been instrumental in facilitating many significant global transformation projects that have seen organisations execute their strategies with greater clarity, insight and inspired leadership in diverse industries such as central banking, financial services, FMCG, information technology, digital media and telecommunications. Michael is a qualified organisational behaviourist and Master Coach and completed his MPhil in management coaching at the University of Stellenbosch Business School (USB).

Dumisani Magadlela, PhD

With over 25 years of human development experience, Dumi is a certified international executive and leadership coach. Based in Johannesburg, he works for the Pan African Capacity Building Programme (PACBP) at the Development Bank of Southern Africa (DBSA). With clients across the African continent, Dumi works as a skills development practitioner and trainer, and a leadership skills development facilitator.

He designs and delivers skills development courses for senior and young African professionals across different sectors, and works with Ubuntu coaching skills, emotional intelligence and Gestalt principles. A senior faculty member at Integral+ Africa Institute and The Coaching Centre (TCC) in South Africa, he delivers a module on "Coaching in the African context". Dumi is part-time faculty at the University of Stellenbosch Business School (USB), lecturing on the MPhil in Management Coaching. He teaches "Team coaching from an African perspective, "and "Culture change with Ubuntu-awareness".

Dumi previously worked for the United Nations Development Programme. He collaborates closely with the African Union Foundation and is a member of the WBECS Global Team Coaching Institute (GTCI). He recently published a chapter on Ubuntu Coaching in *Transformational Coaching to Lead Culturally Diverse Teams* (Routledge, 2019), edited by Dr Sunny Stout-Rostron. Dumi features regularly on the African speaking circuit.

Contributing author biographies

Ingra du Buisson-Narsai, MCom OrgPsych, MSc ProfPrac

Ingra is the co-founder and Director of NeuroCapital Coaching and Consulting, which consults to some of South Africa's leading and most admired companies. She has 20 years of executive-level experience in corporate South Africa, and is a Registered Organisational Psychologist in private practice. Her unique contribution is as a catalyst for change, using integrative organisational neuroscience. Ingra is also an established leadership and executive coach, and is affiliated with the Business School of the University of the Witwatersrand in South Africa, where she supervises and examines the work of postgraduate students in business and executive coaching. Ingra is an Executive Committee Member of the Society for Industrial and Organisational Psychology of South Africa (SIOPSA) and the Chair of the Interest Group of Applied Organisational Neuroscience (AONS). Ingra's academic qualifications include an MCom (Organisational Psychology), PGCNL and Master of Science (MSc) in Neuroscience of Leadership. She is busy with a PhD in Organisational Neuroscience. Ingra is the bestselling author of the newly published book *Fight, Flight or Flourish: How neuroscience can unlock human potential*. Ingra actively pursues the increasing visibility of neuroscientific methods and diagnostics in the study of organisational behaviour.

Preface

by Dr Sunny Stout-Rostron and Michael Taylor

Today managers need to be able to lead people, and leaders need the skills and competences to manage them. Being a leader sounds more exotic than being a manager, and yet executives and managers are often promoted into leadership positions without yet having mastered how to manage people. We need both – leaders need to manage, and managers need to lead.

This is more important than ever with the outbreak of COVID-19 and the subsequent lockdowns in most countries around the world which have impacted us all. While it has exposed vulnerabilities in our governance and management philosophies, and tested our levels of trust in others, it has also highlighted courageous and visionary global leadership and management practices. While some prominent business leaders are predicting a total global economic "reset", have you considered the readiness of yourself as a business leader and manager to leverage the opportunities that this represents?

Times of crisis expose weaknesses in our leadership. They illuminate the fault lines in those who think arrogance, dogma and historical success will carry the day. Rather, the leadership and management that will take us through tough times requires courage beyond bluster, involving compassionate resilience, and an authenticity that is borne of emotional maturity and profound wisdom. As leader-managers, we are in the "hope creation" business. And growth cannot happen in an environment of fear and insecurity.[1]

Research with executives and teams has shown us that senior managers are being asked to step up to a *new level of leadership and management thinking* in terms of managing both self and others. Some are having difficulty adapting to the challenge of this radical shift.[2] Stepping into a next level of leadership and management requires not only a transformation in your thinking and behaviour, but also significant mental and emotional agility. In these times, leader-managers need to develop new competences and are required to demonstrate stability and resilience with their own teams.

We are working with becoming a leader-manager – mastering both leadership and management skills to "achieve results through others" (the classic definition of management). We need to talk about both leadership and management if you are to be successful in inspiring, motivating, upskilling, and stimulating the highest potential and performance from your team.

Leader-managers need agility, the ability to learn, and the ways and means to manage conflict. At the same time, they need to develop resilience, emotional intelligence and empathy among their direct reports and team members. They need to be functionally savvy, with an ability to learn fast and go deep with their people to help them discover who they are and how they can achieve their potential.

So where should we start? The process always begins with you – and as we go through this book we will help you to think about what knowledge, skills and experience you already have and what you need as both a manager and a leader of people, teams and processes. Please answer the questions below before you start working your way through this book. Enjoy your journey!

1. *Purpose* – what is your purpose as a leader-manager, and what are you doing that feels meaningful?

2. *Concerns* – what are you worried or concerned about both at home and in the workplace in terms of yourself, your team and the organisation?

3. *Self-care* – what are you doing to manage the stresses and strains of your job as a leader-manager, particularly in the light of our new hybrid way or working? And what new habits are you building?

4. *Support* – what support, resources and assistance do you need, and what (if anything) is stopping you from acquiring them?

5. *Personal and professional development* – what are your aims for your future as a leader-manager, and what are you currently doing to develop yourself?

Part One – Making the change to becoming a leader-manager

Chapter 1

Challenges to leading and managing in a hybrid environment

This chapter is adapted from a presentation to the Knowledge Resources Conference in Johannesburg in June 2021, and an article by the authors.[3]

Introduction

By nature, humans are adaptable – and that showed up strongly in 2020–2021 during the global COVID-19 pandemic and the resulting lockdowns, forcing us to work from home instead of in our workplaces, and to educate our children from home both with and without teachers – and managing to juggle everything simply to survive and prosper. This has brought with it anxiety and stress, plus (paradoxically) an extraordinary creativity to manage a reality that no one thought would have ever existed. How have we managed, when everything has come home to roost in one place – that is, our own homes? Trying to meet deadlines while having to deal with myriad domestic issues took a heavy toll on many employees and executives. Such personal experiences, however, should open a door for leader-managers to be more insightful about the life and pressures of team members outside of the "office bubble". The sensitivity of seeing others "in the round", not merely as office functionaries, but as individuals with their unique concerns and challenges will enhance understanding and trust, leading to better results.

Agility and adaptability

We have managed because we have had to become more *agile* – developing a range of *intelligences* that we had never tested before the onset of the global pandemic in early 2020. Agility is a core intelligence needed by leaders, and at the same time by coaches and mentors, whose job is to help those leader-managers to survive, cope and thrive to become the best they can be. The last few years have shown us that innovative leadership solutions do not occur in a vacuum. They are the result of the efforts of highly adaptable leader-managers who have become committed to solving difficult and sometimes seemingly intractable problems in an ever-shifting and unpredictable context. Joiner and Josephs[4] define leadership agility as the "master competency" needed for sustained success. Joiner defines it as the ability to lead effectively when rapid change and uncertainty are the norm and where success requires a consideration of multiple views and priorities.[5] (See Chapter 4 for the difference between leadership and management, and Chapter 13 on next-level leadership to identify how you can adopt greater agility.)

What do we mean by a hybrid work environment?

The hybrid workplace is a business model combining remote work with office work. Similarly, to how schools offer a hybrid learning approach, a hybrid work environment blends in-office work with remote work.

What we saw in hard lockdown was a complete shift to working from home rather than the office, which created enormous changes in how organisations worked and how managers went about managing their employees and teams. For two years we saw a dynamic shift in those who were keen to get back to work and those who were happy to work from home by preference. Many clients we have spoken to have indicated the need to get back to the office in some shape or form. The novelty of working from home full-time has begun to recede, because organisations have created a situation where some people were working up to 16 hours a day. This had become an overcompensation due to working from home only which had created some emotional burnout, along with emotional and psychological wellness issues.

However, hybrid work structures have a different kind of advantage from working solely from home or the workplace. The reality is that hybrid work structures may be here to stay. Knowledge Resources conducted a poll among 100 Human Resources executives across various industries. 58% indicted that they will provide a hybrid work environment within six months, up from 54% at the moment. Although it is more complex to manage, organisations are beginning to find answers to it. There is a plethora of online collaboration tools available to help, and more are coming onto the market daily.

Challenges in a hybrid working environment to be aware of

1. The environment – anxiety, stress, and uncertainty in an unknown world with less and less certainty. We know how we got here – but where do we go from here?

2. Leader-manager adaptability. What is most needed is often missing, which is the adaptability to work well online, facilitating virtual meetings, bringing in all the voices and the faces in an online meeting, and working inclusively to manage isolation for those working from home, or in a hybrid environment of home and physical workspace. This means communication has become the most critical skill for leader-managers.

3. Facilitating virtual meetings. From the beginning of the pandemic not all voices have been heard or brought into meetings. Working from home has meant internet connection and technological problems. Often people keep their video cameras off so they cannot be seen; it is not always known if they are even

present. Not only is there a lack of equality when all voices and ideas are not heard, but conflict and tension erupts more often than in physical face-to-face meetings.

4. Trust and conflict issues. In a hybrid environment we have noticed a loss of trust and confidence in themselves for many individuals, deprived of normal support, appreciation and acknowledgement of colleagues that happens in the physical working environment. This leads to isolation and can result in a loss of trust in others. People in a stressful or anxious state do not feel in control of themselves. If the facilitator of the meeting is not skilled in managing tensions, conflict can easily flare into something more serious. This means loss of collaboration and often leads to the lack of resolving inaccurate assumptions about others as well as emergent conflict. In online meetings, tensions and conflict not dealt with begin to fester.

5. Execution of tasks and taking of accountability is impaired, leading to a bottom-line impact on the business. If collaboration, solving problems and making decisions together is missing – individuals begin to lose motivation, feel even greater isolation and eventually, if they are not working up to the level of performance required, the bottom line of the business and unhappy customers may become a problem. Leaders frequently feel a lack of control over execution of tasks when everyone in the business is working online – and may lose trust in those they manage.

6. Lack of developing self and others. As a result of the various lockdowns experienced around the world, the loss of continued professional development of individuals within the business has, in some instances, seriously impacted the growth of the business. This professional development is key for any leader who needs not only to coach and mentor their direct reports, but is also one of the primary areas for a coach/mentor to work with their client. A loss of professional development may seriously impact individual self-confidence and may impact their ability to perform effectively.

How to resolve these challenges

Create a thinking and feeling environment that embodies safety and sharing

Create an environment where people can think out loud and share their challenges and find common ground with their team members. Create diversity and inclusiveness – ensuring that everyone's voice is brought into the team and work with a virtual system that allows everyone's face to be seen, whether they are at home or in the office. Diverse voices bring more creative and innovative solutions and ensure isolation is managed within teams. Have people work with a peer on a regular basis, and create smaller committees to bring new ideas into meetings.

As a leader-manager, coach your team through the stresses and strains of working from home, offer counselling where needed and ensure that communication is prioritised within your team and between individual members of your team, and within the organisation as a whole. Use this time to work with other leaders regionally and globally, taking courses, interacting with other leader-managers who wish to work together to share their challenges and stresses. It means enhancing your own skills and building a supportive network. (See Chapter 6 on managing stress, and Chapters 11 and 12 on communication skills.)

Develop an emotionally intelligent leadership style – building trust in the team

Daniel Goleman's[6] emotional intelligence research claims that leaders today use six styles of leadership. Each is the result of different components of emotional intelligence. Be careful not to default to a *laissez-faire* style or autocratic mode of leadership which decreases trust between team members. And know that there is no right or wrong style of leadership (see Chapters 2, 3 and 4 on management and leadership). Goleman's six original styles were researched and renamed by Korn Ferry in 2006:[7]

- *Directive* – Do what I tell you. This style relies on directives rather than direction, and demands immediate compliance with little dialogue.

- *Visionary* – Where are we going and why? This style mobilises people towards a vision. The primary objective is to provide long-term direction and vision for employees.

- *Affiliative* – Leadership through relationship. Creates harmony and builds emotional bonds with the primary objective to create harmony and manage conflict.

- *Participative* – Let us decide together. This style forges consensus through participation to build commitment among employees and to generate new ideas.

- *Pace-setting* – Run fast and keep up. This style sets high standards for performance to accomplish tasks to high standards of excellence.

- *Coaching* – This style emphasises long-term development of people, developing them for the future.[8]

Facilitating virtual meetings

The ability to see others in online meetings is crucial for safety and collaboration and trust. And it is best to choose *either* an online platform, or choose instead to be all together physically. Hybrid virtual calls with some on an online platform and others physically together is not an effective hybrid. It is an unequal experience for all in the meeting. It needs to either be all online or all face-to-face. There is a way to lead hybrid meetings successfully – but only if working with inclusivity as a methodology such as the Thinking Environment® or Ubuntu. The new hybrid workplace means being able to manage change becomes a key competence. (See Chapter 7 on creating a thinking environment and transforming meetings).

Building trust, letting go of control, and managing difficult people and situations

To build trust it is important to be open to others and create openness in the team. This means involving people in thinking and decisions, and creating shared meaning. This moves people away from isolation and creates confidence in self and others. For the leader this requires a willingness to let go of control and to develop the skills and competence of others. This also speaks to leadership agility. Another aspect of building trust is to learn how to manage difficult people and situations as they can cause stress for everyone involved – including the entire team. One of the first steps is to understand how you react when facing difficult people or situations – and once you understand yourself you can begin to manage others who are struggling to deal with difficulties as they arise. If you are not comfortable managing conflict, perhaps work with your coach or take a course in conflict mediation.

It is critical for any leader-manager to learn how to handle difficult situations or behaviour and to manage conflict when it arises. This is regularly a core fear of many managers – having to deal with any kind of conflict. Conflict is a signal that something new is trying to happen. When handled skilfully it is the transition to constructive change. But toxic conflict can paralyse a team, increase job turnover and absenteeism, and reduce productivity.

It is vitally important as a leader-manager to be able to manage conflict, and it is a skill that you need to develop to manage your teams effectively. The place to start is with your own self-awareness. Check out Chapter 11 on managing difficult people and situations.

Reflection and learning from experience

As a leader-manager it is your role to mentor or coach your direct reports and individual team members. (See Chapters 8, 9 and 10 for specific tips on motivating, coaching and delegating to empower those who work for you.)

The focus of a coaching conversation is to help your direct reports to work towards achieving their desired outcomes. It is in this process of reflection – where you as a manager help your team members to reflect on and learn from their experiences. There is great potential for learning and emerging action. If you, yourself, choose to work with a coach, you can also explore what is holding you back or preventing you from achieving your goals. Leader-managers need to understand how they learn, beginning to cultivate self-awareness through reflection on their own experience, values and intrinsic drivers. Understanding how others experience them, their impact on others and their environment – is an indication of how successful they will be in achieving future goals for themselves and the organisation.

Developing self and motivating others

Once you understand yourself, you can begin to try to understand those you lead and manage. This means you need to understand your people at a deeper level – what are their drivers, and how can you tap into those? Most organisations throw external or extrinsic motivators at people, without understanding people's internal, or intrinsic motivators. External motivators tends to be bonuses, share schemes, promotion, salary increases, or a company car. However, it is crucial to understand which extrinsic motivator will tap in to that individual's intrinsic motivators. Understanding motivation in all of its component parts will help you to deepen your awareness of yourself and to manage others more effectively. (See Chapter 5 on developing emotional intelligence and self-awareness, and in Chapter 9 try out a useful coaching model, GROW, to work with your direct reports.)

Coaching and mentoring

Coaching may share some ancient roots with the discipline of "mentoring". The word "mentor" is often attributed to Homer's *Odyssey*, wherein Mentor is referred to as an advisor to Odysseus' son, Telemachus. In 1699 *Les Aventures de Telemaque* (*The Adventures of Telemachus*) was published by François de Salignac de la Mothe-Fenelon (1651–1715), a French writer and educator. It has been argued that in Homer's original work, Mentor acted as more of a caretaker than a "mentor", and Fenelon reinterpreted this to idealise his own role as tutor to the Dauphin.[9] In so doing, Fenelon created the modern-day mentor who embodies the attributes of teacher, guide and counsellor – a definition which has entered contemporary organisational jargon.

Whatever its origins, mentoring takes place in conversations with clients, as does coaching – but while the coach uses question frameworks and coaching models to help the client work out solutions to specific issues, the mentor simply acts as an adviser, directly sharing their experience, expertise, advice and wisdom with the mentee. Not surprisingly, there is currently a great debate among experienced business coaches as to whether being "directive" and "giving advice" is a mentoring rather than a coaching activity, possibly encouraging the client to be too reliant on the coach.

What we need to succeed

Mental and emotional resilience

Leadership agility is the ability of a leader to sense and respond to changes in the business environment with actions that are focused, fast and flexible. It is about a leader's ability to prepare all employees for a volatile and uncertain world. This requires mental and emotional resilience for every individual tasked with the responsibility of leadership – and for the coaches and mentors whose role it is to enable their clients to shift more fluidly from one circumstance to the next.

Resilient people are able to use difficult situations as a motivator to try harder. This requires being able to absorb great pressure and build the necessary courage and resilience. Some individuals seem to flourish and take stress in their stride, while the same situation can cause mental and physical anxiety in others.[10]

That's why resilience – maintaining equilibrium under pressure – is one of the most important skills to master for leader-managers and coaches at all levels. The question isn't how you can avoid difficulty and stress. The question is, "How can you face it?" We can all benefit from improving our own levels of resilience – making us better able to face crises, recover, and adapt.

Research suggests that as managers advance from one development stage to another, *they develop a distinct set of mental and emotional capacities* that enable them to respond more effectively to change and complexity. That is, *their level of leadership agility increases.*[11]

Emotional self-awareness is critical

Our initial reaction to unforeseen change is generally a mix of fear and overreaction. No one *wants* to fail. If we can learn to understand our own unique fears, and not project them onto others, we will discover that team members who are fully engaged are far more creative and productive than those who are anxious and insecure.

Self-awareness means having a deep understanding of one's emotions, strengths, weaknesses, needs, and drives. People with strong self-awareness are neither overly critical nor unrealistically hopeful. Rather, they are honest – with themselves and with others. People who have a high degree of self-awareness recognise how their feelings affect them, other people, and their job performance. A lack of self-awareness is *the* single biggest factor in leadership derailment. Self-awareness extends to a person's understanding of their values and goals, and someone who is highly self-aware knows where they are headed and why.[12]

Learning agility

The relatively new construct, *learning agility*, has increasingly been recognised as essential for long-term leadership success. Learning agility is the willingness and ability to learn from experience and then apply those lessons to succeed in new situations. Leaders who possess or develop learning agility constantly seek new challenges, solicit direct feedback, self-reflect, and get jobs done resourcefully.

Conclusion

As leader-managers embrace a hybrid model of working, three competences (*mental and emotional resilience, emotional self-awareness,* and *learning agility*) are the keys to leadership and organisational success.

Chapter 2

Becoming a leader-manager

Becoming a leader-manager

Today, managers need to be able to lead people, and leaders need the skills and competences to manage them. Management is a profession, whereas leadership is a way of being. Many think being a leader is more exotic-sounding than being a manager, and yet executives and managers are often promoted into leadership positions due to technical expertise without having mastered how to manage people. We need both – leaders need to manage, and managers need to lead.

We are actually working at becoming leader-managers – mastering both leadership and management skills in order to achieve results through others (the classic definition of a manager). We need to talk about both leadership and management if you are to be successful in inspiring, motivating, upskilling, and getting the highest potential and performance from your team. Leader-managers need agility, the ability to learn and the skill to manage individual and team conflict – at the same time as developing resilience, emotional intelligence and empathy among their direct reports or team members.

Today a new model of leadership is beginning to be emphasised globally, as are leadership attributes such as determination and drive, self-confidence, integrity and sociability, core self-evaluation, and emotional intelligence. According to former US Senator Barbara Mikulski, leadership involves "creating a state of mind in others".[13] Leaders are therefore "individuals who significantly influence the thoughts, behaviours, and/or feelings of others".[14]

Moreover, according to Bolman and Deal[15] true leadership also includes a spiritual dimension. Two leadership images dominate: one of the heroic champion with extraordinary stature and vision, the other of the policy wonk, the skills analyst who solves pressing problems with information, programmes and policies. Both images miss the essence of leadership. Both emphasise the hands and heads of leaders, neglecting deeper and more enduring elements of courage, heart, spirit, and hope.

Research shows that successful management of our increasingly diverse workforce is one of the most important global challenges faced by all managers – at a time when we face dizzying challenges from unimaginable advances in digital technology and artificial intelligence, as well as the social and economic disruption of a global pandemic. It is important not only that managers comprehend the dynamics of diversity and culture, but that they also grasp the dramatic transformation of society and organisations driven by the "Fourth Industrial Revolution" and by the COVID-19 pandemic, which has seriously impacted how organisations will continue to work in the future.[16]

This is also the time when people most need to work together and develop a globally shared view of how technology is shaping our lives. As leaders, we need to move away from traditional linear thinking and rise above daily crises, to think strategically about how to innovate and manage disruption. As always, it comes down to people and values. We need to put people first and empower them if we want to avoid becoming dehumanised. While continuing to create and innovate, we need to maintain our compassion, empathy and stewardship, helping to forge a new collective sense of moral consciousness. This is where your role as a leader-manager will be critical.[17]

Activity: Thinking of yourself as a leader-manager

1. What functions do you fulfil as a manager? What competences do you require to step into these management functions?

2. What roles do you fulfil as a leader? What competences do you need to step into these leadership roles?

The history of management

Management is considered a profession because it consists of special knowledge, has formal training methods, fees, a code of conduct, and several representative organisations. Peter Drucker is considered the father of modern management. His basic principle is that if organisations set challenging but attainable objectives, their employees will be motivated and empowered. He believed in the growth of business and the development of people rather than punishing them. He popularised a form of appraisal, the technique of setting targets or goal performance, and suggested a quantifiable measure of performance.

The practice of modern management

The practice of modern management has evolved from the sixteenth-century study of low efficiency and failure by certain types of enterprise. According to research conducted by Sir Thomas More (1478–1535), management consists of the integration of corporate policy and *organising, planning, controlling, and directing the resources* of an organisation to achieve organisational objectives. Most managers have tasks which call for the manager to do something which is not strictly *managing* but *doing*. Although there is nothing unusual about this aspect of a manager's role, it is distinct from *managing* the following four task areas:

- *Planning* – forecasting, budgeting, scheduling, setting objectives, policy making, organisational procedures, standards, development for change.

- *Directing* – staffing, talent development, transformation and training, motivating, co-ordinating, delegating, counselling and supervising.

- *Controlling* – evaluating, measuring and correcting.

- *Communicating* – writing, speaking, listening, guiding and inspiring.

Management theory

It is useful for us to have an understanding of the theoretical underpinnings of management. Six leading theories were advanced after the industrial revolution: Frederick Taylors' Scientific Management; Henri Fayol's Administrative Management Theory and his 14 Principles of Management; Max Weber's Bureaucratic Management Theory; Elton Mayo's Human Relations Management Theory; the General Systems Theory of Ludwig von Bertalanffy; and Douglas McGregor's Management Theories X and Y.[18] As a result of the industrial revolution, organisations were able to grow far bigger, with thousands of employees, which was a turning point in the development of management theory. However, we also need to consider the importance of Organisational Development Theory and the impact of multi-generational trends in the workplace today.

Frederick Taylor's Scientific Management

One of the earliest advocates of management theory was Frederick Winslow Taylor, a mechanical engineer. Taylor suggested that "scientific management" may be summarised as:

- Using a scientific method to study work and determine the most efficient way to perform specific tasks.

- Harmony versus discord.

- Co-operation, not individualism.

- Maximum output, in place of restricted output.

- "The development of each man to his greatest efficiency and prosperity".[19]

Taylor's original influence was due to his scientific approach to organisational management. To increase physical effectiveness, Taylor considered the worker a part of the production process on a level equal to the tools they used, but without acknowledging the worker's ability to reason and act individually. One of the most frequent criticisms of Taylor's theory is that it lacked appreciation of the value of the human being in the workplace; it does not consider the need for individual motivation or finding meaning and purpose in their role.[20] Consequently, Taylorism has been largely discredited, because human beings are neither robots nor machines. They have emotional, psychological and motivational needs that are to be understood and managed in order to get the best performance from people, and to help people find satisfaction, meaning and purpose in their work.

Fayol's Principles of Management

Henri Fayol was the creator of Administrative Management Theory. He started his career at age 19 with a French mining company and rose through the ranks to become the company's director, managing over 1 000 people. He defined six primary functions of management and 14 principles of management, with a primary focus on administration, based on his experience as a director. He argued that many managers did not interact well with their employees. In this, he agreed with Taylor. But Fayol's principles focused less on science, and instead looked at how to create an efficient company structure. Fayol also believed that all employees should have only one direct manager – something that has been overturned by current matrix management structures in organisations.[21]

Management researchers over the years have indicated that Fayol's 14 principles of management have developed into "present-day management and administration, especially after 1949 when his book was translated from French to English, as *General and Industrial Administration*".[22]

Max Weber: Bureaucratic Management Theory

In one of the earliest examples of evolution in the history of management, the German sociologist Max Weber built on Taylor's theory, arguing for similar principles. Weber believed that all managers must build chains of command, and advocated standardisation. But they differed in one key area – Weber realised that Taylor's scientific theory did not account for emotions. He argued that the rise of technology could lead to an inhuman workplace culture, and differed from many management theorists because of this more negative focus. Weber maintained that bureaucracy was the most efficient and rational model on which private businesses and public offices could operate. His theory of management, called the Bureaucratic

Management Theory, stressed strict rules and a firm distribution of power. Weber also stressed the importance of hiring the ideal candidate for a job.[23]

Weber argued that too much change can affect morale, thereby touching on an important aspect of modern business. Managers need to hire for "fitness of purpose" and should search for employees with the correct skills. Managers cannot, however, simply hire for skill. An employee needs to be aligned with an organisation's culture – and have either similar values, or a deep understanding of company values.[24] What Weber's theory does not take into consideration is that individuals are hired to do a job that they can probably perform adequately up to 50 per cent. However, they should be expected to grow and develop into their new role so that they bring their own ideas to the role, and introduce a fresh way of working for the organisation.

Case study: Personal value conflict

It is especially important to note that if an employee has values which conflict with those of the organisation, it will be very difficult for that employee to stay motivated. One client with whom I worked was the editor of a journal for the international tobacco industry, and her job included translating and publishing new worldwide tobacco legislation. One day she decided to quit smoking, and decided that her top personal value was "health". All her colleagues and friends said she would become incredibly stressed if she continued to work for the journal – with which she disagreed, at first. After a few months, however, she rang me to say, "Help! I am stressed." Her values were no longer aligned with those of the organisation, and she decided to find a new job. She could not in all conscience continue to do her job with personal values in conflict with those of the company.

Activity: Aligning values and motivation

1. When was there a time that your values and those of the organisation were in sync? How did that impact your motivation and performance?

2. When was there a time when your values and those of the organisation were not aligned? How did that influence your self-confidence, self-esteem, and motivation to do your job?

Elton Mayo: Human Relations Management Theory

Historically, managers have believed that people worked for money, and that money influenced performance. But when Elton Mayo studied employees at Chicago's

Western Electric Hawthorne Works, his emphasis was on workplace conditions, and how those conditions impacted productivity. In his study, one of the key motivators for workers was the importance of relationships. People seemed to be more productive in teams, and this theory became known as the "The Hawthorne Effect".[25]

Today's management theorists focus on relationships and teamwork – with the emphasis on putting the right people in the right teams to increase productivity. This led to the Human Relations Management Theory and further studies into the creation of high-performing teams. Taking the human factor into account became increasingly important in understanding how to manage people and performance.

Ludwig von Bertalanffy: Systems Theory

In recent years, "systems thinking" has become an increasingly useful and popular approach to understand how organisations, businesses and groups of people behave, and how change comes about within those structures. "Systems thinking" teaches us about the interconnectedness of people, professions, disciplines and other "structures" within a team, organisation, business, or family. Note that "the components and relations that make a particular unity comprise a system's structure".[26]

Family system therapies developed to explain individual behaviour "arising from the behaviour of the family system or of the immediate family plus other relevant people and institutions".[27] Systems theory, although originally developed to work with the nuclear family, was eventually seen to be particularly relevant to organisations, teams, other work groups, and communities (e.g. social, cultural and religious groups). This is because "human systems" consider the various components of human nature, i.e. thinking, feelings, attitudes and thinking patterns, and the behaviours that impact on performance within the working system.

The work of biologist Ludwig von Bertalanffy influenced management theory during the 1940s by introducing the concept of systems thinking. "Systems thinking" has its roots in engineering theories, and looks at the whole rather than component parts of the whole. All systems are governed by the principle that the whole is greater than the sum of its parts, suggested by Jan Smuts.[28] It follows that no system can be adequately understood if it is broken down into its component parts, and that no element in the system can be understood in isolation as those elements never function independently.

The concepts of organisation and wholeness are crucial to understanding how systems operate. All the components of a system have an organised, consistent relationship to one another. These components interact in a predictable, organised fashion with one another, and are interdependent on one another. If one division within an organisation does not play its part, or even if one person within a team does not fulfil their role in terms of performance, the organisation can suffer. Outside influences can affect how a system operates, which can ultimately produce toxicity. This highlights the issue of an individual's levels of motivation and how that can impact the organisational system.

Douglas McGregor's Management Theories X and Y

Theories X and Y were developed by Douglas McGregor at the MIT Sloan School of Management to describe employee motivation at work. McGregor's book, *The Human Side of Enterprise* (1960),[29] had a profound influence on the field of management. His two theories described opposing models of motivation, and how management viewed human behaviour at work. Based upon Maslow's Hierarchy of Needs, McGregor grouped the hierarchy into lower-order needs (Theory X) and higher-order needs (Theory Y), suggesting that management could use either set of needs to motivate employees, although better results would be gained through the use of Theory Y.[30]

Theory X is an authoritarian management style which assumes that workers inherently dislike work and will avoid it if they can. The Theory X manager believes that workers need to be closely supervised with comprehensive systems of control put in place. This includes a hierarchical structure with control at each level. According to this theory, employees will not show ambition without an incentive programme, and will try to avoid responsibility if they can. Because the Theory X manager may rely on threat and coercion, this can lead to mistrust, highly restrictive supervision, and a retributive atmosphere.[31]

Theory Y is a participative management style which assumes that workers are ambitious, self-motivated, enjoy their work, and can exercise self-control. A Theory Y manager believes that, given the right conditions, most people will want to do well at work, and that the satisfaction of doing a good job is strongly motivational. Many people interpret Theory Y as a positive set of beliefs about workers. McGregor thought that Theory Y managers are more likely than Theory X managers to develop an environment of trust with employees, which is required if employees are to grow and develop.[32]

Organisational Development Theory

Organisational Development is the study of change and performance to make organisations successful. It emerged from human relations studies during the 1930s, when psychologists realised that organisational structures, processes, and culture influenced the behaviour and motivation of people. Organisational development's primary focus is on the relationships between individuals and teams, developing collaboration, co-operation, and support between them so that they work together in harmony for the success of the organisation.

Today Organisational Development focuses on an alignment of organisational learning, knowledge, and talent management to help with the transformation of organisational values, culture, and people development. Key Organisational Development concepts are organisational climate, culture and strategy.

Understanding multi-generational trends

To understand your workforce today it is important to understand that there are now five generations working together, with each group requiring a different set of motivations as well as training and development. The six generations in the workplace are:

- Traditionalists – born 1925 to 1945;

- Baby Boomers – born 1946 to 1964;

- Generation X – born 1965 to 1980;

- Millennials – born 1981 to 2000;

- Generation Z – born 2001 to 2020; and

- Generation C – continually connected digital consumers who create and consume content.[33, 34]

The "Working Better Together Report" published by Peakon in *Inc* magazine analysed how generational groups were engaging in the workplace today.[35] Engagement is how committed an individual is to the organisation which currently employs them. The highest level of engagement is in the Baby Boomer generation, whereas Generation Z and Millennials decline steeply over the number of years that they stay in the organisation. Baby Boomers maintain higher loyalty and stay longer in their positions the closer they are to retirement, whereas Generation Z and Millennials tend to look for new work after three years.[36] Generation C has no particular age group, its members being bound together by their values, interest, personality traits, attitudes and life styles. They look for personalised service, individual attention and instant gratification. Businesses and institutions ignore them at high risk.[37] There are a number of factors that you as a leader-manager need to be aware of in managing these different generations.

Activity: Generational worldviews

1. What are the values, beliefs and worldviews of each generation? And how do these differ from those of the organisation?

2. What would be the best way to motivate and manage each of these generations differently? Remember, they are different age groups with differing work experience, and particularly social, familial and political history which has shaped their worldviews and expectations of life and career.

3. What do the generational trends mean to your organisation in terms of recruitment, introductory orientation into the company, managing talent, retention, and succession planning?

Traditionalists were formed by the Great Depression of the 1930s, the Second World War, radio and cinema. Baby Boomers are heavily influenced by the Vietnam War, apartheid in South Africa, and the Civil Rights Movement and Watergate in the USA. Generation X is shaped by the HIV/AIDS epidemic, the fall of the Berlin Wall, and the dotcom boom. Millennials have been influenced by the fall of apartheid in South Africa, the high school massacre in Columbine, Colorado, the 9/11 terror attacks, and in particular the internet and social media. Generation Z are shaped by life after the advent of equal voting rights in South Africa, 9/11, the great recessions of the last ten to 15 years, and access to technology from a very young age.[38]

Traditionalists tend to be dependable, straightforward, tactful and loyal, where Baby Boomers are optimistic, competitive, workaholics, and team-oriented. Offer traditionalists satisfying work and opportunities to contribute to the workplace, but emphasise their stability in the organisation. Baby Boomers need specific goals with deadlines. They also need to be put into mentorship roles and be offered coaching-style feedback from their line manager.[39]

Generation X individuals need immediate feedback, and want very flexible work arrangements, insisting on having work-life balance with extensive opportunities for personal development. Millennials want their employers to get to know them personally. They want to be managed by results, and insist on a flexible schedule with immediate feedback for their tasks. Generation X employees are flexible, informal, sceptical and independent, whereas Millennials are competitive, civic-minded, open-minded and achievement-oriented. Generation Z individuals are more global, entrepreneurial, progressive, and less focused.[40] Generation C is more about mind-set and lifestyle, and includes members from every age group. They are technologically well-connected, and have a strong sense of entitlement.[41]

Activity: Finding your deeper purpose

1. What is your purpose as a leader-manager? Try to write it in one or two sentences.

2. Why is this important to you? What do you value about this? What else makes this so rewarding for you?

3. What do your direct reports, staff and customers find most valuable about your work? What is the lasting value that you want to create? How do you actually deliver that value? What do you do that creates lasting value?

4. What do your customers most care about that your organisation delivers? What would make them refer one of their friends or colleagues to your company?

5. How does this work fit into your own life? How does it relate to your other more personal values? If it does not fit, how might you adapt your purpose into your broader life?

Source: Peterson and Goldsmith.[42]

Conclusion

It is useful to understand the background and development of management theory, as it is helpful for you to identify what theories and popular literature have most influenced you, and to understand how your thinking has developed in your role as a manager. Every style and theory of management is dependent on its time in history and prevailing societal trends. However, it is equally important that you continually develop your skills and competence as a manager as you go through your career, and understand your purpose in leading and managing people. Trends change in leadership and management, and new research is constantly emerging that helps you not only to understand yourself but also those whom you lead, manage, and develop.

Chapter 3

What is your managerial style?

Blake and Mouton's Managerial Grid

Although no one management style is best for all situations, it is important to understand what your approach is so that you can develop the skills you may need in managing both people and tasks. Although you may compromise between a concern for results versus a concern for people, that may not result in the best performance. It is important to meet both the needs of people in the workplace, as well as focusing on the results required if you want to motivate for excellence. Equally, a compromise between the two approaches may only result in average team performance.

In this section, we look at the original and the revised Blake and Mouton Managerial Grid, a popular framework for thinking about a leader's "task versus person" orientation. The Managerial Grid plots a manager's or leader's degree of task-centredness versus their person-centredness, and identifies five different combinations of leadership or management styles. The model is based on behavioural theory, was developed by Robert Blake and Jane Mouton,[43] and suggests five different leadership styles, based on a leader's concern for people and concern for goal achievement – i.e. people-orientation versus task-orientation.

The grid focuses on concern for results on one axis, and concern for people on the other axis (see Figure 1). Each concern is measured on a continuous scale of 1 to 9 to denote an uninterrupted sequence. As Miner[44] points out, "task-oriented leadership is job-centred, with goal emphasis. People-oriented leadership is relationship-oriented and supportive." The two concerns interact on the Managerial Grid to create the five styles of management, as follows:

- 1/1 the *Impoverished Manager* (neither committed to mastering the work environment nor to being appreciated by the people);

- 1/9 the *Social Manager* (placing high value on personal relationships);

- 5/5 the *Organisational Manager* (aiming for security through compromise and being a member of the team);

- 9/1 the *Authoritative Manager* (having maximum concern for getting the job done, motivated by achievement through control of people); and

- 9/9 the *Team Manager* (involved, participative and placing high value on creativity and new ideas).[45, 46]

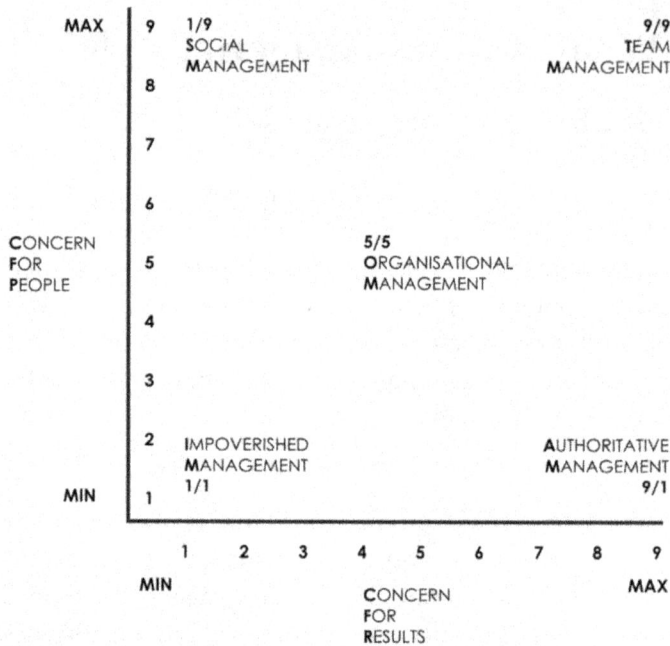

Figure 1: Blake and Mouton's Managerial Grid

Source: Blake and Mouton.[47]

While the individual numbers do not represent any precisely measurable degree of concern, they can be taken to signify recognisable extremes of style, and some of the intermediate degrees between.

Styles of management

Five management styles are shown on the Managerial Grid diagram in Figure 1: 9/1, 1/9, 1/1, 5/5 and 9/9.

9/1 – The Authoritative Manager

These managers have maximum concern for getting the job done, and are motivated by achievement through the mastery and domination of the people involved. Once they adopt an approach they are likely to cling to it and forge ahead. They may not always be right, but they seldom suffer from self-doubt. Their style may achieve high productivity in the short term, but in the long run the side effects have been shown to actually lower production.

1/9 – The Social Manager

Placing high value on personal relationships, these managers feel secure surrounded by those who give support and appreciation. They therefore rarely criticise, accepting the ideas of others in preference to pushing their own views. When conflict occurs, they try to soothe bad feelings; and when others disagree with them, they regard such attitudes as a personal repudiation. Productivity is unlikely to be high in either the short or long term.

1/1 – The Impoverished Manager

These managers are committed neither to mastering the work environment nor to being loved or appreciated by the people at work. Their motivation is to survive through retreat and inaction – but always within the system. They behave in such a way as to avoid being conspicuous or even noticed. Productivity will sink to the lowest tolerable level, and if instructed to increase it, they will plan to do so by employing more people or equipment.

5/5 – The Organisational Manager

These managers aim for security through compromise and being the member of a team. They seek solutions which please the majority and appease the minority. As a loyal corporate executive, they may appear reliable and quite competent in bureaucratic situations where they can follow tradition, past practices or the judgement of others. But where such guidelines are not available, they may lack the confidence to take risks or the initiative to achieve or inspire their staff.

9/9 – The Team Manager

Involvement, participation, and commitment form the basis of teamwork. The Team Manager seeks to encourage these aims from all those concerned. Placing high value on sound and creative decisions, they will look for new ideas, opinions and attitudes which are different from their own.

Activity: What is your style as a manager?

Look at the Managerial Grid diagram in Figure 1. Where do you think you fall in the interaction of the two concerns, i.e. concern for results versus concern for people? Please explain why you think so.

Dominant styles

Which managerial style becomes dominant for a particular manager will be decided by one or more of several sets of conditions:

- *Personality* – The Manager's dominant style may to an important degree result from their personality characteristics, and may be based on values they hold regarding the way to treat people or how to obtain results.

- *Experience* – They may have based their style on that of an individual whom they admire, or otherwise have developed a style which they find works for them. They may even be unaware of the other methods of management available to them.

- *Environment* – Managerial behaviour is often determined by the culture of the organisation in which they are employed, or may be dictated by a special set of circumstances.

Desired styles

Blake and Mouton[48] recommend the following desired styles:

- *Team Manager* – 9/9.
- *Authoritative Manager* – 9/1 (Backup style).
- *Social Manager* – 1/9 (Backup Style).

Interestingly, they select the authoritative leader as the second style. The first is the Team Manager, to encourage harmony and integration of task and people, with the Authoritative Manager as second to ensure the goal is achieved if the people side is not entirely well-managed. The Social Manager has a good team of people committed to the manager, but without focusing equally on the task involved, the job may not get done.

Average styles

- *Team Manager* – 9/9.
- *Social Manager* – 1/9.
- *Authoritative Manager* – 9/1.

Backup styles

When a manager finds it difficult or impossible to apply their dominant style, a backup style may take over from their normal or natural approach. They adopt this backup when under pressure, tension, strain or frustration, or at times when conflict cannot be resolved in their characteristic manner.

Any style can be employed as backup to any dominant style, as for example:

- a natural 9/1 manager who meets continued resistance from subordinates may shift to a 9/9 teamwork basis for co-operative problem solving;

- a 9/9 manager may switch to a 9/1 style when a crisis arises;

- the people-oriented l/9 approach may change to a stubborn and demanding 9/1 style when outside pressures become uncomfortable; or

- a manager with any of the dominant styles may decide to withdraw into a l/1 attitude when all other options appear to have failed.

Façade styles

All dominant and backup styles are authentic. But some management behaviour is less than honest, and there can be many inducements for a manager to adopt a façade. It may be that they pretend to adopt the style which they feel is expected of them by their company or their superiors. Or they may assume a style to impress their staff. A façade is sometimes adopted to cover a personality defect which would prove a disadvantage in the job. In fact, the façade style – whether adopted consciously or not – is always a cover to hide the manager's true assumptions about leading and managing people.

Blake and Mouton's revised Managerial Grid

Today the environment and context for leadership are important, and times have changed in recent years in terms of expectations of leader-managers. In the revised managerial grid, to keep up to date, Blake and Mouton have revised and renamed the five leadership styles. The Team Management style is now more akin to a *Transformational Leadership* style. Use the grid to identify where you fall in terms of your dominant style, but do not "box yourself in". Think about the variety of styles you use and the dominant style you would prefer to develop.

- 9/9 – *Team Management* has high concern for both people and results. This is seen to be the most effective style of management. The team leader is dedicated and passionate about their work and their team, clearly motivated to inspire people to stretch themselves and perform to the best of their ability. This type of manager takes the time to empower their team and involve them in the thinking and decision making around performance.

- 9/1 – *Produce-or-Perish Management* has high concern for results and low concern for people, and assumes that people are not motivated to do a good job. This is the more authoritarian manager who waves the stick rather than the carrot. Punishment, strict rules and procedures can create performance at first, but the result is usually low team morale and low motivation. High performers will not last in this team.

- 5/5 – *Middle of the Road Management* has moderate concern for people and results. Trying to balance results and people often ends up with a *status quo* that goes through continuous compromise, but fails to either inspire high performance or to meet the needs of people effectively.

- 1/9 – *Country Club Management* has high concern for people and low concern for results, assuming that people will work harder if they are happy and satisfied with their work and role. This style of management is very accommodating, and is particularly concerned with the feelings of staff and understanding their needs.

- 1/1 – *Impoverished Management* has low concern for both results and people. This is the most ineffective manager, with little interest in creating a motivating team environment. Primarily an indifferent manager, this is the least effective style of management to create either motivated people or high performance. As a result, there is often conflict and unhappiness within the team.

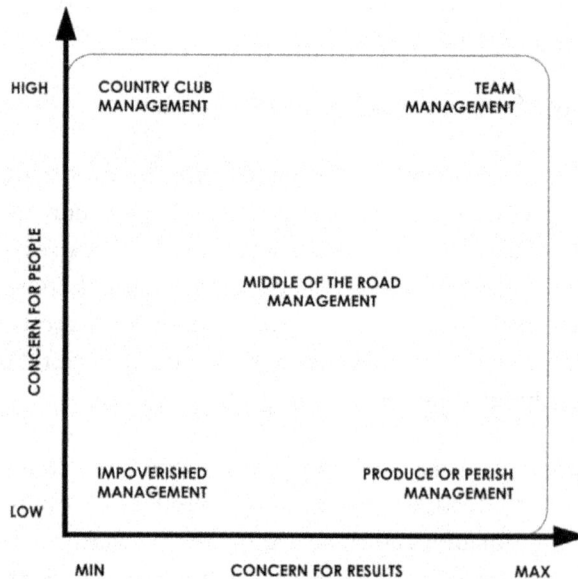

Figure 2: Blake and Mouton's revised Managerial Grid
Source: Blake and McCanse.[49]

After 1987 with the loss of Mouton, Blake and his colleagues added two more management styles, Paternalistic and Opportunistic.

- *Paternalistic Management*: A Paternalistic Manager will move between the Country Club and Produce-or-Perish styles. Although the Paternalistic Manager can be supportive and encouraging, they will also guard their own position – and Paternalistic Managers do not welcome being questioned about how they think.

- *Opportunistic Management.* Although this doesn't appear on the grid, this style can pop up anyplace on the grid. Placing their own needs first, Opportunistic Managers move around the grid to adopt the style which most benefits them for the situation at hand. They are known to manipulate and take advantage of others to get what they want.[50]

In the following Activity we will help you to determine which of the Blake and Mouton styles are your preferred styles of management.

Activity: Determine your management style in decision making (part 1)

1. Consider the management decisions you have reached in your role as an individual leader-manager or as a member of a work team within an organisation. Review the significant details of your process of thinking in making those decisions.

2. Table 1 is divided into the following areas or topics of decision making: *Planning, Control, Achieving results, Conflict,* and *Communication.* Each area of decision making contains five statements. Within each area, rank the five statements in descending order of applicability from 1 (most applicable within this area) to 5 (least applicable within this area). If you are completing this Activity as an individual leader-manager, record your rankings in Column A of Table 1. If you are completing this Activity with a team, also record the team's rankings in Column B of Table 1.

3. Using the rankings you have recorded in Table 1, complete Table 2 by listing the five statements within each area by letter in descending order of applicability from 1 (most applicable within this area) to 5 (least applicable within this area), in Column A for an individual leader-manager and in Column B for a team. Once you have listed both your individual and the team results you can then compare your results and the team's results against the recommendations of Blake and Mouton in Column C of Table 2.

Source: Adapted from Spearhead Training Group.[51]

Table 1: Statement rankings for Activity: Determine your management style

Statements to be ranked within each area of decision making (1 = most applicable within this area, 5 = least applicable within this area)	**A** *Indiv.*	**B** *Team*
Planning:		
(a) Plans are based on past performance and acknowledge the need for change constantly.		
(b) Plans must stem from top management. Criticisms from junior staff should be discouraged, as they cannot appreciate all the aspects involved.		
(c) Plans should be devised so as to minimise friction between people and keep work moving smoothly.		
(d) Complex plans do not work. It is best to tackle one thing at a time as it arises.		
(e) Plans should be produced jointly by all involved.		
Control:		
(a) Control is achieved through the understanding and agreement of those involved.		
(b) A detailed reporting system keeps management informed so that they can issue corrective instructions in good time.		
(c) People should work on their own. Control should be imposed only when a crisis arises.		
(d) Actions should be guided by suggestion and praise. Criticism is destructive.		
(e) Strengths and weaknesses should be analysed by the boss and thus prevent people from going too far astray.		
Achieving results:		
(a) Results should be obtained because people are committed to them, not because they get pushed.		
(b) Pressure to achieve results must be balanced against concern for how far people will co-operate.		
(c) If you treat people well you will get better performance than by demanding results.		
(d) Results should be sought on a no-nonsense basis.		
(e) Simple minimum results should be accepted – performance over that should be special.		

Conflict:		
(a) Disagreement is kept low when people avoid expressions that introduce controversy.		
(b) People should step in to soothe feelings and bring parties together.		
(c) Negotiation should take place towards compromise. People should back off as necessary once they have pushed a point far enough.		
(d) Any conflict should be brought into the open, and the reasons for it should be examined so that the causes can be resolved.		
(e) Conflict is bound to occur. Senior Management should step in early to decide between viewpoints and end the problem.		
Communication:		
(a) People should participate in depth by discussing things as they happen.		
(b) Communication through routing channels is never good enough. Much information is supplied by informal sources.		
(c) Informal sources are an important factor in communication. A good grapevine is essential.		
(d) People should never be told more than is strictly necessary for their job.		
(e) Communication should come clearly from the top. With proper control, little extra information is needed from below.		

Source: Adapted from Spearhead Training Group.[52]

Table 2: Statement orderings for Activity: Determine your management style

Rankings	**A** *Individual*	**B** *Team*	**C** *Blake and Mouton*
Planning:			
1.			(e)
2.			(b)
3.			(a)
4.			(c)
5.			(d)

Control:			
1.			(a)
2.			(b)
3.			(e)
4.			(d)
5.			(c)
Achieving results:			
1.			(a)
2.			(d)
3.			(b)
4.			(c)
5.			(e)
Conflict:			
1.			(d)
2.			(e)
3.			(c)
4.			(b)
5.			(a)
Communication:			
1.			(a)
2.			(e)
3.			(b)
4.			(c)
5.			(d)

Source: Adapted from Spearhead Training Group.[53]

Activity: Determine your management style in decision making (part 2)

4.   Copy your ordered list of statement letters for each of the management decision making areas (Planning, Control, Achieving results, Conflict, and Communication) from Column A of Table 2 to the corresponding areas of the "Individual results" section in Table 3.

5. Copy your ordered list of statement letters for each of the management decision making areas (Planning, Control, Achieving results, Conflict, and Communication) from Column B of Table 2 to the corresponding areas of the "Team results" section in Table 3.

6. In the "Individual results" section of Table 3, find the following statement letters and circle them: letter (e) under Planning, letter (a) under Control, letter (a) under Achieving, letter (d) under conflict, and letter (a) under Communication. Join the five circled letters with lines, and next to letter (e) in the left-hand margin, label the resulting segmented line "9/9". This segmented line represents the Blake and Mouton management style *Team Management*.

7. Similarly to Step 6 above, in the "Individual results" section of Table 3, find each of the following sets of statement letters in turn under the relevant decision making areas, circle the five letters within each set in turn, and link the circles within each set with lines:

	Planning:	Control:	Achieving:	Conflict:	Communica-tion:	line label:
set 2:	(b)	(b)	(d)	(e)	(e)	9/1
set 3:	(a)	(e)	(b)	(c)	(b)	5/5
set 4:	(c)	(d)	(c)	(b)	(c)	1/9
set 5:	(d)	(c)	(e)	(a)	(d)	1/1

The four segmented lines you have added represent the Blake and Mouton management styles *Produce-or-Perish Management*, *Middle of the Road Management*, *Country Club Management*, and *Impoverished Management* respectively.

8. Repeat Steps 6 and 7 above for the "Team results" section of Table 3.

9. By identifying which of the labelled lines touches row 1 under each management decision making area, you will be able to determine the dominant management style applied within that area by yourself and your team. Similarly, by identifying which of the labelled lines touches row 2 under each decision making area, you will be able to determine your backup management style within that area – and so on for row 3 (second backup management style), and rows 4 and 5 (least dominant management styles).

10. By comparing your results to the recommendations of Blake and Mouton listed in Table 3, you can ascertain where you and your team may need to work on your management styles. Blake and Mouton recommend a 9/9 style for all five decision making areas, with 9/1 as a backup style, and 5/5 as the second backup style.

Source: Adapted from Spearhead Training Group.[54]

Table 3: Results sheet for Activity: Determine your management style

Individual results:				
Planning	**Control**	**Achieving**	**Conflict**	**Communication**
1.	1.	1.	1.	1.
2.	2.	2.	2.	2.
3.	3.	3.	3.	3.
4.	4.	4.	4.	4.
5.	5.	5.	5.	5.
Team results:				
Planning	**Control**	**Achieving**	**Conflict**	**Communication**
1.	1.	1.	1.	1.
2.	2.	2.	2.	2.
3.	3.	3.	3.	3.
4.	4.	4.	4.	4.
5.	5.	5.	5.	5.
Blake and Mouton recommendations:				
Planning	**Control**	**Achieving**	**Conflict**	**Communication**
1. (e)	1. (a)	1. (a)	1. (d)	1. (a)
2. (b)	2. (b)	2. (d)	2. (e)	2. (e)
3. (a)	3. (e)	3. (b)	3. (c)	3. (b)
4. (c)	4. (d)	4. (c)	4. (b)	4. (c)
5. (d)	5. (c)	5. (e)	5. (a)	5. (d)

Source: Adapted from Spearhead Training Group.[55]

Conclusion

Once you understand the different styles of management, including your style of decision making, you can begin to think about what is working and not working in how you and your team manage thinking, planning and decision making. What is critical for you as a manager is to be a role model in terms of your style of management, and to understand at a deep level what your default styles of management are when times are tough and difficult situations arise – both in terms of the business and people. Knowing yourself is the first step in becoming a better manager, and understanding what motivates both you and your team, as we will see in subsequent chapters.

Chapter 4

How does leadership differ from management?

Management competences

Having identified your style of management, let us think about what knowledge, skill and experience you already have as both a manager of people, teams and processes, and what is actually required of you as a leader.

A skill is "the output of combined knowledge, experience, personality, belief systems and the ability to cope with certain triggers and or stimuli that a person is exposed to".[56] For example, the ability to brief and delegate a task or project to a member of your team. A competence is "an effective behaviour under specific, required and challenging conditions, which reduces risk. It is conducted unconsciously and at speed. A competency requires ability at 100 per cent. A skill does not".[57] An example of a competence would be communication skills which can be broken down into a number of skills, such as influencing others, speaking to a large audience on a specific subject, or giving a one-to-one performance review.

Activity: Your management competence profile

Rate yourself on a scale of 1 to 10 as to your current capacity in each of the following management competences. Identify the areas in which you need most to develop, and where further training and development is required. One is low, ten is high.

Competence	Score	Competence	Score
1. Action-oriented.		35. Managing and measuring.	
2. Dealing with ambiguity.		36. Motivating others.	
3. Approachability.		37. Negotiating.	
4. Boss relationships.		38. Organisational ability.	
5. Business acumen.		39. Organising.	
6. Career ambition.		40. Dealing with paradox.	
7. Caring about direct reports.		41. Patience.	
8. Comfort with higher authority.		42. Peer relationships.	
9. Command skills.		43. Perseverance.	
10. Compassion.		44. Personal disclosure.	
11. Composure.		45. Personal learning.	

---

12. Conflict management.	46. Perspective.
13. Confronting direct reports.	47. Planning.
14. Creativity.	48. Political savvy.
15. Customer focus.	49. Presentation ability.
16. Decision making ability.	50. Setting priorities.
17. Decision quality.	51. Problem solving.
18. Delegation.	52. Process management.
19. Developing direct reports.	53. Drive for results.
20. Directing others.	54. Self-development.
21. Managing diversity.	55. Self-knowledge.
22. Ethics and values.	56. Sizing people up.
23. Fairness to direct reports.	57. Standing alone.
24. Functional and technical skills.	58. Strategic ability.
25. Recruitment and staffing.	59. Managing through systems.
26. Humour.	60. Building effective teams.
27. Informing.	61. Technical learning.
28. Innovation management.	62. Time management.
29. Integrity and trust.	63. TQM, re-engineering.
30. Intellectual focus.	64. Understanding others.
31. Interpersonal savvy.	65. Managing vision and purpose.
32. Learning on the fly.	66. Work/life balance.
33. Listening.	67. Written communication.
34. Management courage.	68. Emotional intelligence.

Source: Terrapinn Training.[58]

Activity: Competence application

Choose 10 competences to work on from the list in the Activity: Your management competence profile above that most apply to your line of work. List the behaviours that you think would best describe these competences, and finally rank the top ten behaviours in order of importance for your own development as a manager. Work with these as you go through the next six months, and evaluate them again at that time to identify your progress.

Time and self-management

It takes time to develop our levels of competence, and time is just what a leader-manager most lacks. But it is critical to be consistently learning on the job, and finding time for professional management and leadership development programmes as well. Here are some tips to think about how to manage time and yourself.

It is a misnomer to think that we can achieve work/life balance, as we work two-thirds of our day and have one-third left to ourselves and our personal lives. There are, however, some priorities that can be set. You cannot manage the clock as it just ticks on – but you can manage yourself. If you manage yourself and your time well, it means:

- improved communication;

- handling people effectively; and

- developing a new approach to your work.

How to prioritise time and boundaries to manage yourself

- Set goals.

- List your priorities.

- Keep a daily "to do" list – write things down!

- Ask yourself: What's the best use of my time right now?

- Do it now!

- Sort paperwork and emails into A's, B's and C's. Sort B's into A's and C's. Do A's, not C's – in effect, concentrate on the 20 per cent of the activities which represent 80 per cent of the true potential value to you. Handle each piece of paper and email once after sorting. Sort reading from emails into a separate folder.

- Use the "Swiss cheese technique" to reduce the A's in your paperwork and email. The Swiss cheese technique is a great tool which eliminates procrastination, because you work in ten-minute segments rather than working with large chunks of time. You use this technique to punch holes (like Swiss cheese) in large tasks or complex projects.

- Learn to say "No" more often.

- Get your name off all unnecessary mailing lists.

- Sort emails only two or three times a day.

- Read books like newspapers, i.e. read the headlines and skim the text.

- Most importantly, leave white space daily in your diary to be able to manage the unexpected and to build in time to think.

Activity: Your leader-manager strategies

List as many strategies as you can for yourself as a leader-manager. This will be a combination of what is required of you as both leader and manager. Think about what people have said to you in the past about how you show up as both a leader and manager. Use this list of possible leader-manager strategies for suggestions:

- Motivate, inspire and inform through consistent communication.

- Set objectives (clearly stated, measurable, challenging, achievable) and hold people accountable.

- Be a role model and set an example (be committed, honest, self-disciplined, courageous, loyal and be willing to be vulnerable).

- Develop personal and professional relationships with your team – take time to get to understand their values, thinking, feelings and behaviour.

- Empower your employees on an on-going basis through inclusion, motivation and delegation.

- Delegate at least 10 per cent of your job to develop your team members.

- Lead by involving the team in mission and objective setting.

- Let go of micromanaging your team members.

The Management Wheel – measuring time in your activities

The Management Wheel in Figure 3 is a pictorial view of the process of managing any project. It should be read as a clock starting at the noon position and reading clockwise. The ability to communicate lies behind the management process. The pie chart shows the segments as equal spacing, which in practice they are not:

- What proportion of your time would you say you spend in each activity?

- Are there any other activities in which you are already involved that do not fit into any of the categories depicted in the wheel?

- What do you need to change to use your time more effectively?

- Where should most of your time be spent?

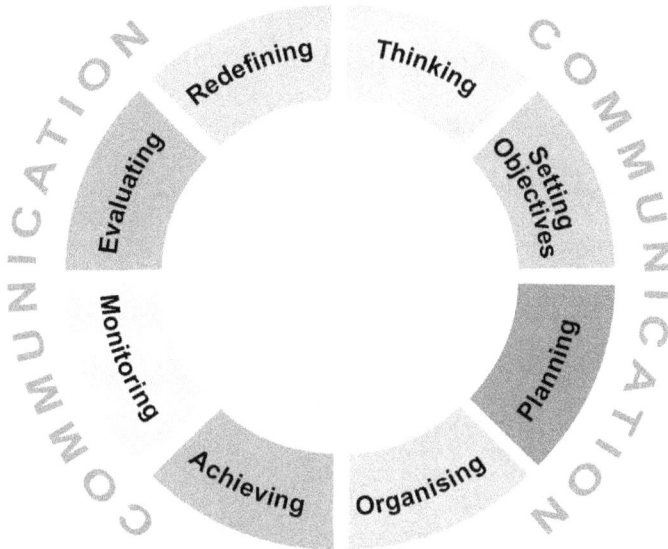

Figure 3: The Management Wheel

Source: Spearhead Training Group.[59]

How is leadership different from management?

Chapter 2 mentioned management theories which are the basis of modern management – and are part of the post-industrial history of management. And since executive performance leads the company's results, the same applies to an organisation as a whole – its performance is shaped by the quality of thinking by its management.

A manager may have excellent skills in organising work, creating policies and procedures, following disciplines and delivering services. But if others don't willingly follow their lead, they are not a leader. Key differences between leadership and management include the following:

- Leaders are not always managers or supervisors, formally appointed by others. Managers are invariably appointed from above, while leaders are often appointed from below by their followers.

- Leaders don't need to have responsibility for a team.

- Sometimes people are recognised as having leadership characteristics or qualities by others, who then simply choose to follow what the person says or does.

- Being a manager does not make you a leader.

The dimensions of leadership

The dimensions of leadership (see Figure 4) are equally:

- achieving the task;

- building and maintaining the team; and

- developing individuals within the team.

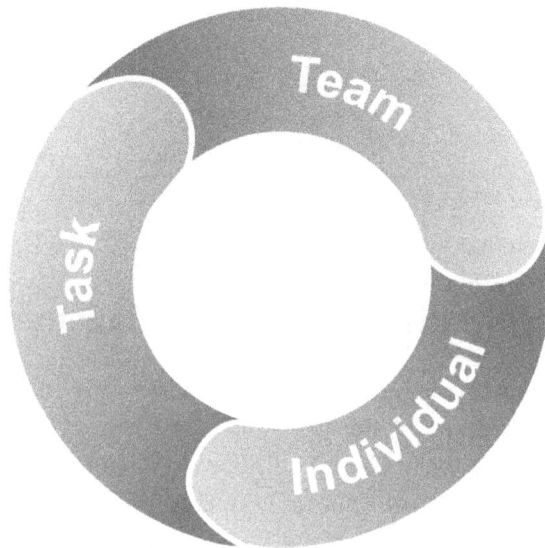

Figure 4: The dimensions of leadership

Source: Adair.[60]

Different to leadership, management is a profession. Management is about purpose, structure, disciplines, processes, delivery, and the mechanics of an organisation. Managers get their authority and power from being appointed to a position by more senior managers. Leaders, in contrast, must offer their followers a cause, a direction or objective that is interesting, attractive, or satisfying enough for others to wish to follow. Is a leader created, or is leadership defined by giving someone a job title? (See in Chapter 13: Understanding next-level leadership, "Are great leaders born or made?") In most instances, in fact, we find that leaders are defined by what their qualities are, by the skills they have learned and the actions they take. Others recognise these attributes and choose to willingly follow them.[61]

Seven decades of leadership development

We have had seven decades of leadership development and over 500 definitions of leadership. Bennis and Nanus[62] complained that "Decades of academic development have given us more than 500 definitions of leadership. Literally thousands of empirical investigations in leadership have been conducted in the last 75 years alone, but no clear and unequivocal understanding exists as to what distinguishes leaders from non-leaders, and perhaps more importantly what distinguishes effective from ineffective leaders, and effective organisations from non-effective organisations."

Studies of leadership have produced a variety of theories: trait theory, behavioural theories, contingency theories, functional leadership theories, situational theories, attitude pattern approach, transactional and transformation theories, relationship theories, distributed leadership, and ethical and values-based theories. A new definition of leadership is beginning to emerge globally, as are key leadership attributes such as determination and drive, self-confidence, integrity and sociability, core self-evaluation, and emotional intelligence.[63]

Gender differences in leadership styles are a contemporary hot topic. The issues of diversity, culture and gender help us to understand the developmental needs of leaders due to individual perspectives, culture, gender, ethnicity and experiences of isolation. Research also reveals that *mindfulness* is beneficial to the best leaders; mindfulness helps to improve personal and professional effectiveness and overall organisational productivity.[64]

So far, we can assume that:

- A leader is someone who influences others to follow a given direction, and someone whose direction and approach other people are willing to follow. Leaders get their authority and power from being able to influence and persuade others to follow them.

- Leadership has been described as a "process of social influence in which one person can enlist the aid and support of others in the accomplishment of a common goal".[65] Therefore, leadership is about vision, direction, influence, communication and the aspirations of people.

Good leaders today are striving to be highly productive, visionary, creative and innovative, authentic, and balanced. Leadership development programmes can help to develop many skills – such as public speaking, strategic thinking and problem solving, giving feedback, leading change and building teams – but cannot tell leaders when to use those skills. And there are some qualities of terrific leaders that cannot be developed by merely learning about their value or the right times to develop them. For example, authentic leadership is something that others recognise and acknowledge.

Emergence of a new definition of leadership

New definitions of leaders and leadership are continuing to emerge globally:[66]

- Human-Based Leaders™ embrace people, recognise their talents, fundamentally desire to see others succeed in their own right, and earn the loyalty and respect of those working with them. People pay attention to what they say, trust in the safe environment they create to share their thoughts and critiques, and choose to engage more fully. They know these leaders have their backs.[67]

- Visionary leaders articulate a purpose that rings true for themselves and attune it to values shared by the people they lead. And because they genuinely believe in that vision, they can guide people toward it with a firm hand. When it comes time to change direction, self-confidence and being a change catalyst smoothes the transition.[68]

- Effective leadership involves simple governing principles such as guiding visions, sincere values, and organisational beliefs – the few self-referential ideas individuals can use to shape their own behaviour. The leader's task is first to embody these principles, and then to help the organisation attain the standard it has declared for itself.[69]

- True leadership stems from individuality that is honestly and sometimes imperfectly expressed.[70]

- Leaders should strive for authenticity over perfection.[71]

- Leaders who work with a panoramic view of success do not operate with total selflessness, but they do define their own success within the context of the bigger picture. If "we" don't succeed, "I" won't succeed.[72]

- Successful leadership is a lifelong task of constant self-examination. When you are in touch with your own vision, values, perspectives, and roles, you will find a rewarding leadership path.[73]

- Resonant leaders help blend financial, human, intellectual, environmental, and social capital into a potent recipe for effective performance in organisations. In addition to being great to work with, they get results. To be great, a leader needs to understand the market, the technology, the people, and a multitude of other factors affecting the organisation.[74]

- Great leadership works through the emotions, whether it's creating strategy or mobilising teams to action, and the success of leaders depends on how they do this. If leaders fail in this primary task of driving emotions in the right direction, nothing they do will work as well as it should. The leader acts as the group's emotional guide.[75]

- Leadership is a process of social influence in which one person can enlist the aid and support of others in the accomplishment of a common goal.[76]

Activity: The personal qualities and behaviours of a leader-manager

1. Complete a list of the qualities and behaviours you feel are necessary to be an effective "leader-manager" in the business context. Use these options as suggestions:

   Qualities of a leader-manager: knowledge of business or industry; visionary; risk-taker; positive attitude; confidence; leads by example; mental agility; thinks on their feet; decisive; decision-maker; self-confidence; good overall appearance; good communicator; motivator; loyal to team; approachable; effective listener; empathetic; tough but fair.

   Behaviours of a leader-manager: authoritative; decisive; consistent; sense of humour; open-minded; listens before making assumptions or judgments; willing to be influenced by others' points of view; inspires; motivates; enthusiastic and encouraging; delegates; good delegator; coach; mentor; supportive of staff; builds trust in the team.

2. Put your list in order of personal significance.

The six intelligences of leadership

According to Eichinger and Lombardo[77] there appear to be six major building blocks or intelligences fundamental to managerial and executive success:

- IQ – Intelligence Quotient – how bright you are.

- TQ – Technical or Operational Quotient – how able you are to get things done.

- MQ – Motivational Quotient – how driven you are to achieve and grow.

- XQ – eXperience Quotient – how many of the requisite kinds of experiences you have had.

- PQ – People Quotient – how well you handle yourself and work with others (sometimes referred to as EQ).

- LQ – Learning Quotient – how deftly you adopt new skills, behaviours and beliefs.

Factors of derailment

Often successful and seemingly soaring leaders have everything going for them and then suddenly they fail. What has happened? Eichinger and Lombardo[78] note that "people are promoted for technical/operational (TQ) and intellectual (IQ) reasons, but fail for emotional ones (PQ)", a suggestion they attribute to Daniel Goleman.[79]

As Eichinger and Lombardo[80] point out, Zenger and Folkman[81] identified five fatal flaws that lead to failure as a leader:

- inability to learn from mistakes (LQ);

- lack of core interpersonal skills (PQ);

- lack of openness to new or different ideas (LQ);

- lack of accountability (TQ); and

- lack of initiative (MQ).

Eichinger and Lombardo[82] explain that four out of the six intelligences (TQ, XQ, PQ and LQ) account for most failures at the top. All six intelligences are observable and can be measured, and five of them (except for IQ, which they suggest is largely innate) can be developed. Their recommendations to develop mastery as leaders include putting more emphasis on LQ, XQ and PQ, integrating these values into organisational culture, and aligning recognition and reward systems. Also, it is important to assess LQ much earlier in people's organisational tenure, to focus on aspects of PQ that doom or enhance careers, and to ensure a variety of experiences for leaders giving opportunities to gain breadth as well as depth of skill.[83]

Activity: Rate your intelligences

When studying Learning Quotient (LQ) in 10 companies, it was found that those with higher LQ did five things particularly well:

1. They dealt well with complexity and ambiguity and made fresh connections to solve difficult problems.

2. They knew themselves well and handled tough situations deftly (PQ).

3. They liked to experiment and deftly handled the personal consequences of introducing new and different ways of doing things.

4. They motivated teams and used personal drive and presence to deliver results, even in first-time situations.

5. They were creative, childlike in their curiosity and imagination. They proactively seized opportunities and adapted well to new situations. Business is no different from Darwin's biological world: the adaptive are the fittest to survive.

Rate yourself on your ability to do well in these five dimensions (1 is low, 5 is high). Ask someone who knows you well to also give you feedback and have them explain why they rate you at that level. Look at how you can develop the areas in which you rated yourself to be less proficient, and work with your manager or coach to improve.

Source: Eichinger and Lombardo.[84]

Activity: Stepping into becoming – how do you be you?

Think about how you "do you" – and how people experience you. And think about your own story – where you have come from, and from where you have travelled to arrive at the point where you are now. Think about these two questions seriously to understand where you are heading as a leader-manager. Build these answers into your development plan.

1. What are you doing to develop a deep understanding of yourself – as well as understanding how others experience you – and how would you articulate who you are right now, as a leader, as a manager, as a human being?

2. Who do you want to step into becoming in your life in this world – and how will that create a shift in you and in those you are managing and coaching in your team?

Conclusion

As organisations struggle more than ever to find and develop qualified and effective managers and leaders, your skills and competence as a leader-manager are very much in demand in terms of managing and developing your staff, your teams and your organisation. Every one of your team members brings their own stories and their own powerful dynamic into your team. Have you made time in your breakaways to hear their individual and personal stories – as well as their professional hurdles and successes? Your job as a leader-manager is to manage your people through their personal and professional difficulties, and to help them step into their potential.

There is a growing recognition that the development of leader-managers is complex, and includes interactions between the leader-manager and their social and organisational environments. You will need to help your team members acquire a certain level of self-awareness so that they are conscious of how they impact others. In addition, you will need to be aware of how you are influencing and impacting the team and the organisation. You will also be responsible for motivating and inspiring your direct reports as they grow into and out of their jobs, increasing their skills and competence under your watchful eye.

In Part Two we look at developing greater self-awareness of your own needs and growth requirements, as well as becoming conscious of how people experience you as a leader-manager. We will also look at the role that emotional maturity plays in managing people, and the emotional intelligence you need to be a leader-manager.

Part Two – Managing self and others

Chapter 5

Managing self: Emotionally intelligent leadership styles and mindfulness

Emotional intelligence

Managing self begins with developing greater emotional intelligence, which is the journey to personal mastery. In the last decade emotional intelligence has become one of the most researched attributes of effective leaders, and researchers have offered evidence indicating that emotional intelligence contributes to leadership outcomes beyond the effects of cognitive abilities or personality.

Goleman defines emotional intelligence as the capacity for recognising our own feelings and those of others, for motivating ourselves, and for managing emotions in ourselves and in our relationships. It includes five basic emotional and social capabilities: self-awareness, self-regulation, motivation, empathy and social skills.[85] Emotional intelligence traits associated with leaders with high EQ indicate that they:

- are intrinsically more self-aware;
- understand their mental processes;
- know how to direct themselves;
- are more in touch with what they are deeply passionate about;
- naturally care more for others and receive more compassion in return;
- are more socially in tune (e.g. engage with social media);
- know that leadership is more about soft skills; and
- understand that what drives the bottom line is valuable, yet the leader who gets others to perform at their best ultimately creates winning organisations.[86]

Understanding the importance of EQ

The EQ Model developed by Daniel Goleman[87] usually starts with addressing questions about *self-awareness* and *self-management* (see Figure 5). It moves on to develop *relationship awareness* and *relationship management* at a systemic level (i.e. teams working with teams, or the organisation working with the wider community).[88]

All four emotional intelligence competences are worth talking about and bringing into your conversations with your managers or your team of direct reports, as discussed in the following outline. It is your responsibility to bring up issues, concerns, achievements, successes, failures and developmental progress, as well as motivating, managing and disciplining others to manage their own interpersonal challenges. For example, what is their ability to give feedback, speak in public, understand where they lack confidence, and identify what progress they have made towards achieving specific overarching goals to develop themselves and the business?

Self-awareness

The first emotional intelligence competence is *self-awareness*. *Self-awareness is about knowing yourself, understanding your own resistance to situations, and having a deep understanding of your purpose.* How aware are you of your own blind spots in terms of how you think, what you feel and how you behave? What have you noticed about yourself in relation to your own thinking and feeling in easy or difficult situations? To which type of behaviour do you default when you are not thinking? And how aware are you of what you say and do, as you engage with others? In other words, what do you sound like, and in what ways do you engage with others?[89]

Self-management

The second competence is *self-management*. *Self-management is how you engage with others, your interpersonal behaviour, communication and management skills.* How are people experiencing you as you engage with them? How are you engaging with others in talking, managing, negotiating, dealing with conflict and giving feedback – and how are you engaging with others on a good day, as well as on a bad day? Which behaviours bring success, and which behaviours sabotage your success? This will apply to every interaction you have on a daily basis. To whom do you show favouritism, who do you exclude from conversations or meetings, and with whom do you never engage? And with which individuals are you not engaging – who are critically important to the success of yourself, your team and your organisation – through networking and creating visibility through public speaking or the attendance of professional social or business events?[90]

Relationship awareness

The third competence is *relationship awareness*. *Relationship awareness is understanding the institutional culture (values, beliefs, feelings), the working environment, and the politics within your organisation.* What is the culture, what are the values and beliefs which underpin how the organisation operates, and what are the diverse relationships which operate concurrently within the organisation? What are the "unspokens" in the working environment? They relate to values, culture and diversity issues that lie below the surface, and which might not be openly spoken about. How are you contributing to the values and culture in the way you speak, behave and engage with superiors, peers, direct reports, customers and the wider stakeholder community within which you work? How are you actually living the values of the organisation? And what issues exist within your team that need to be addressed, and spoken about openly to ensure a more transparent and collaborative culture? What is needed from you to make this happen?[91]

Relationship management

The fourth competence is *relationship management. Relationship management is about team behaviour and people management, conflict management and the integration of the systems within the organisation or those linking you to the wider community.* These relate to the interaction of all the systems within the organisation. What is your responsibility in ensuring that different divisions engage positively with each other, and what influence do you have on the organisation to make a positive contribution to your customers, stakeholders and the community at large? How does your behaviour influence your team, and how does the team influence the organisation? What is working, and what needs to change? This might be something as core to the success of the business as to the way you facilitate meetings across all units or divisions, or how your customer call centres manage their interactions with customers. What influence do you have – and how aware of it are you?[92]

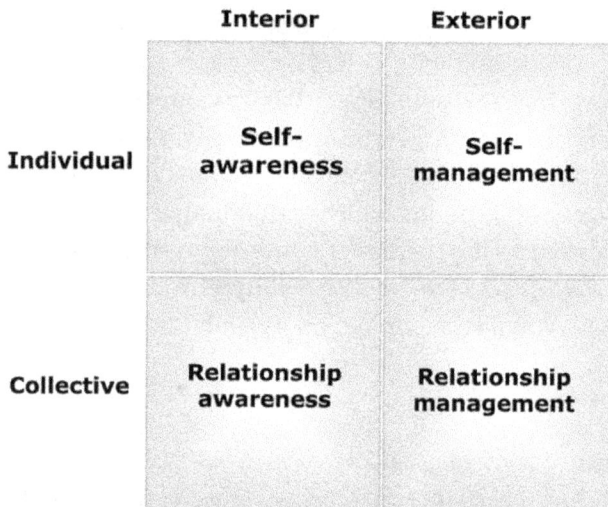

	Interior	Exterior
Individual	Self-awareness	Self-management
Collective	Relationship awareness	Relationship management

Figure 5: A four-quadrant adaptation of the EQ Model

Source: Adapted from Goleman and Wilber.[93, 94]

Table 4: Emotional intelligence competences and associated skill development areas

Self-awareness ➜	Self-management ➜	Relationship awareness ➜ (Team or system awareness)	Relationship management ➜ (Team or system management)
Knowing self.	Interpersonal behaviour.	Organisational culture (values, beliefs, feelings).	Team behaviour; client management.
Resistances.	Communication skills.	Environment.	Conflict management.
Purpose.	Management skills.	Politics.	Systems integration.

Source: Stout-Rostron[95]

EQ Model case study

In the case of one executive, with whom I worked for two years, we focused during our first year on his growing self-awareness. Through our work together he began to think about his own limiting messages that derailed him at important moments in meetings, or stopped him from stepping into situations that would create more professional visibility for himself. We began to transform those limiting personal messages into more liberating ways of looking at his substantial contribution to the organisation (self-awareness).

At the same time, we explored how he communicated with his direct reports, one-on-one, and in the team; as well as how he actually *spoke* to them and with them (self-management). Insights were gained about his tendency to speak too fast, mumble and keep his teeth clenched together as if getting every word out was difficult. It meant that clarity was limited in his communications with his team, and similarly with superiors, colleagues and other important stakeholders in this complex international organisation. As his communication skills improved, I asked him to work with an actress on his voice, body and speech to improve how he put his presentations together, how he engaged with both large and small audiences, and how he incorporated stories to create a more dynamic presence (self-management).

We also began to think about the values of his particular division, and where those values were and were not in alignment with the organisation overall (relationship awareness). We began to identify the culture of *encouragement* and *learning* that became more present within his division; this was in tandem with his growing self-awareness and different ways of engaging with others. The changes in his behaviour were subtle, but an awareness of more openness in the culture began to be acknowledged (relationship awareness).

As we continued our work together, dealing with the various constraints in the system that he had to contend with, and the resistances he felt towards the matrix system within which he was working, we identified the systemic issues and dynamics that created anxiety in his ability to move his division forward (relationship management). We began to look at the dynamics between the international head office and the regional head office, and both offices' relationship with him as the leader of his division (relationship management). As we began to work with his resistance to the system and its detailed rules and complexity, he began to be more aware of the trust put into him and his division for the projects and disciplined work successfully completed in the last two years. This client was ultimately ready to transition into a new role, having greater awareness of how he thought, felt and behaved, as well as how he engaged with others and how they experienced him in the workplace. He developed a much greater awareness of his own power and reputation, and an understanding of his impact and influence on the culture and system overall.[96]

Core self-evaluation

Although emotional intelligence has become a very popular concept among consultants and coaches in the business world, it has been argued that intelligence may apply not to emotions but rather to the "willingness and ability to introspect".[97] Some researchers see emotional intelligence as a fad to avoid. Recent research has begun to focus on a trait pattern called core self-evaluation "which combines four personality and motivational attributes – self-esteem, locus of control, generalised self-efficacy, (e.g. self-confidence) and emotional stability".[98]

However, another view is that emotional intelligence "helps leaders understand and identify with followers, which also assists in evoking self-confidence, optimism and other positive emotions and beliefs in followers".[99]

Self-confidence and performance

Self-confidence is considered one of the most influential motivators and regulators of behaviour in people's everyday lives. A growing body of evidence suggests that one's perception of ability or self-confidence is the main paradigm in striving for achievement. The major influence in acquiring expert performance is the confidence and motivation to persist in deliberate practice.[100]

Self-confidence is not motivation. It is a personal judgment about your ability to accomplish a goal. Motivation is composed of two factors: goal choice and self-regulation. Self-regulation consists of self-monitoring, self-evaluation, and self-reactions. This framework relates to motivational processes, including setting goals.[101]

Self-confidence seems to be a core attribute for leader-managers throughout the recent decades of research:

> Unless an individual has a considerable degree of self-confidence or faith in his own ability and the 'worthwhileness' of his own ideas he probably will never attempt leadership in any really significant capacity. The leader's ability to carry his programme to completion seems to depend very largely upon the maintenance of self-confidence.[102]

Self-confidence encompasses the traits of high self-esteem, assertiveness, emotional stability, and self-assurance. Individuals that are self-confident do not doubt themselves or their abilities and decisions; they also need to project this self-confidence onto others, building their trust and commitment.[103] In Chapters 11 and 12 we will spend time on developing the communication skills of managing difficult people and assertiveness to build your self-confidence and trust in yourself as a leader-manager.

Nelson Mandela – a leader with strong emotional intelligence

The one leader who stands out in recent history as embodying the strongest qualities of emotional intelligence is Nelson Mandela. In his autobiography, *Long Walk to Freedom*,[104] Mandela recalls attending the Councils of the Thembu King, the Regent of his rural area in the Eastern Cape of South Africa, as a very young man. This experience, in many ways, formulated Mandela's understanding of leadership and achieving consensus. Rather than give his views, the Regent would instead listen attentively to all his Councillors. Each person was allowed to speak fully and freely. In this way, the Regent could be sure that he was not hearing the advice his Councillors thought that he might like to hear, but instead was able to gain a clear idea of the whole variety of opinions on any matter. He saw his job as summing up the emerging consensus of the meeting.[105] But there was also a more subtle approach behind the leader not stating his views right from the start. It was the idea that the leader is like a shepherd. Mandela wrote, "I always remember the Regent's axiom: a leader, he said, is like a shepherd, who stays behind the flock, letting the most nimble go on ahead, whereupon the others follow, not realising that all along they are being directed from behind".[106]

One of the most common evaluations of Mandela is that he lacked bitterness. Even before his lengthy imprisonment, his own father was removed from a chieftainship by a white magistrate. His father had stood firm on a point of principle, which the white magistrate thought "impertinent".[107] So, from a very early age Mandela had cause for anger and resentment. Indeed, as a young man, he admits that he was often angry and intemperate. But as his leadership qualities grew, he understood that such emotions were detrimental to his own wellbeing and clouded his judgement. Perhaps one of the most extraordinary signs of his emotional intelligence and far-sighted vision, is that during his 27 years of imprisonment Mandela not only studied Afrikaans, but also read Afrikaans novels and poetry. The point was not simply to be able to speak the language of the people who had imprisoned him – he knew that one day he would have to negotiate with them. He wanted to read their literature to understand their culture and their way of thinking – to comprehend the people with whom he would be conducting the toughest possible negotiations.

In this sense, he gained an immeasurable advantage. He later often dealt with people whose emotions and fears he understood, while they – the ostensibly all-powerful – had very little understanding of his real feelings or way of thinking. The irony is that, in this case, the prisoner was streets ahead of his jailers. It took a rare form of emotional intelligence to put himself in a position of having the stronger hand when he was face-to-face with his opponents – although they may not have realised it.

The fact that Mandela had a very consensus-oriented style of leadership should not be confused with the fact that when he felt strongly about something, he was prepared to go out on a limb – even risking the distrust of his own colleagues. For example, during his last years in prison, he began to negotiate with the National Party, his jailers.[108] This was, at first, unknown to his own closest companions in jail. He knew this was risky, and that some of them would fear he had "sold out". Some of them did indeed feel he had given in when they first discovered he had been conducting negotiations. However, Mandela felt that not only was this important, but that it was the right time for him to go out in front as a leader, presenting his followers with a *fait accompli*. His success lay in his judgement of knowing when to consult, and when to go out ahead alone. This is a supreme test of emotional intelligence in leadership.

Shortly after his release from prison, he attended an event where one of those present was Wilhelm Verwoerd, grandson of the supreme apartheid ideologue and former Prime Minister, Hendrik Verwoerd. Embarrassed, young Wilhelm tried to avoid Mandela, but the ex-prisoner soon tracked him down. Whereupon Wilhelm began to apologise for the system of racial tyranny that had imprisoned Mandela and the part that his own grandfather had played. Mandela interrupted him to say that, with his surname, he had a voice which people would listen to. "So you have to think carefully", counselled Mandela, "what you do with that power".[109] This is a good example of intuitive leadership – putting someone at their ease and potentially winning over an unlikely ally to his own cause and vision.

When someone asked Mandela what it was like to be free after 27 years, Mandela said, "We are now free to become free".[110] There was no triumphalism, always moving towards the bigger goal, and no resting on his laurels. But it was a goal that had to include everyone – something that he achieved triumphantly.[111]

Leadership styles

Autocratic, democratic and **laissez-faire** *leadership*

A "leadership style" is the way in which a leader mobilises and motivates people, provides them with direction and guidance, and implements strategies and plans. Individual leadership styles are the products of the emotional intelligence, personal characteristics, philosophy, and experience of the leader. Invariably, however, different situations call for different leadership styles.

In 1939, Kurt Lewin led Ronald Lippitt and Ralph White in a research study which identified three different climates of leadership: authoritarian (autocratic); participative (democratic), and delegative (*laissez-faire*).[112] Although later research identified more specific types of leadership, this early study was very influential.

The autocratic leader dictates how the task will be done and tends to stay aloof from those performing the work.[113] All decision making power resides with the leader, and although the autocratic leader is not necessarily hostile, they are remote or detached from the workers. The major difference between autocratic and democratic leaders is that productivity drops off when the autocratic leader leaves, but tends not to drop off when the democratic leader departs.[114]

Democratic leaders offer guidance to group members, but they also participate in the group process, and input is allowed from everyone. Technical advice may be provided by the leader, and the group decides on the division of labour.[115] Democratic leaders are thus more participative and work with the collective in a more encouraging way, even if they have the final say over the decision making process. Group members feel engaged in the process, and are more motivated and creative.

Delegative (or *laissez-faire*) leaders offer little structure or guidance to group members, and leave decision making up to group members. The leader may not take part in the division of work, and rarely offers praise or criticism – in fact, the delegative leader tends to supply information only when asked.[116] Although this style can be effective in situations where group members are highly qualified in an area of expertise, it can also lead to poorly defined roles and a lack of motivation.

Activity: Leadership styles

For each of these three leadership styles, give an example of when you have recently used each one, and explain why.

- Autocratic.

- Democratic.

- *Laissez-faire.*

Emotionally intelligent leadership styles

Daniel Goleman's[117] emotional intelligence research claims that leaders today use six styles of leadership. Each is the result of different components of emotional intelligence. Below is a summary of the styles, their related competence, the organisational climate within which they work, and the type of phrase or question a leader is likely to use when working with each individual style.

Korn Ferry refer to leadership style as the pattern of behaviour an individual leader uses across their full range of leadership situations. Although there is no wrong or right style of leadership, the most effective style will depend on the task, the people, and the situation to be managed. The six original styles Goleman defined were coercive, authoritative, affiliative, democratic, pace-setting, and coaching. Korn Ferry has researched and renamed coercive, authoritative, and democratic as directive, visionary and participative:[118]

- *Directive – Do what I tell you.* Originally known as the "coercive" style. This style relies on directives rather than direction, and demands immediate compliance with little dialogue. (EQ competence: drive to achieve, initiative, self-control. Says "Do what I tell you." Used in a negative climate, crisis, or to kick-start a turnaround.)

- *Visionary – Where are we going and why?* Originally known as "authoritative", this style mobilises people towards a vision. The primary objective is to provide long-term direction and vision for employees. (EQ competence: self-confidence, empathy, change catalyst. Says "Come with me." Used when changes require a new vision, or when a clear direction is needed. Works when the climate is mostly positive.)

- *Affiliative – Leadership through relationship.* Creates harmony and builds emotional bonds with the primary objective to create harmony and manage conflict. (EQ competence: empathy, building relationships, communication. Says "People come first." Used in a positive climate, and heals rifts in a team or motivates people during stressful circumstances.)

- *Participative – Let us decide together.* Originally known as the "democratic" style. Forges consensus through participation to build commitment among employees and to generate new ideas. (EQ competence: collaboration, team leadership, communication. Asks "What do you think?" Used in a positive climate, and builds buy-in or consensus, or gets input from valuable employees.)

- *Pace-setting – Run fast and keep up.* Sets high standards for performance to accomplish tasks to high standards of excellence. (EQ competence: conscientiousness, drive to achieve, initiative. Says "Do as I do now." Used in a negative climate and gets quick results from a highly motivated and competent team.)

- *Coaching – Long-term development of people, developing them for the future.* (EQ competence: developing others, empathy, self-awareness. Suggests "Try this." Used in a positive climate, and helps an employee improve performance or develop long-term strengths).[119]

Activity: Leadership styles which work best for you

1. For each of these six leadership styles, give an example of when you have recently used it and why.

   - Directive.
   - Visionary.
   - Affiliative.
   - Participative.
   - Pace-setting.
   - Coaching.

2. List the one or two leadership styles which work best for you, and explain why.

3. List which leadership style(s) you would never use, and explain why.

Other styles of leadership worth understanding for the leader-manager are those that are engaging, narcissistic and toxic.[120]

Engaging leadership style

An engaging style of leadership is when a leader reaches out to their staff and is involved in their achievements and disappointments. Cohen[121] recommends the following "four key leadership practices for leading in tough times":

- make more informed personnel decisions;

- define roles and expectations;

- ensure continual skill development; and

- engage employees.

Engagement is seen here as the fourth key leadership practice, and Cohen[122] addresses the need for leaders to involve followers, particularly in difficult economic times:

> What all of these initiatives do for the organisation is engage both leaders and employees in understanding the existing conditions and how they can collectively assist in addressing them. Reaching out to employees during difficult times to better understand their concerns and interests by openly and honestly conveying the impact of the downturn on them and their organisations can provide a solid foundation for not only engaging them but retaining them when things do turn around.

Activity: Engagement leadership style

1. Write a story of how you use the engagement leadership style which will be a result of the above six styles that you have integrated.

2. Explain what is unique about the way you engage as a leader-manager with your own team, and with others in the organisation or to motivate, inspire and empower them.

3. Identify what you most need to develop in terms of expanding and improving your style of leading others.

Narcissistic leadership style

Narcissistic leadership is a leadership style in which the leader is interested only in themselves. The narcissistic leader's priority is themselves at the expense of their people or followers. They exhibit the characteristics of a narcissist, i.e. arrogance, dominance and hostility. Considered to be a common leadership style, narcissism may range from healthy to destructive behaviour. To critics, "destructive narcissistic leadership is driven by unyielding arrogance, self-absorption, and a personal egotistic need for power and admiration".[123]

Narcissistic leadership occurs when a leader's actions are principally motivated by their own egomaniacal needs and beliefs, superseding the needs and interests of the constituents and institutions they lead.[124] Egomaniacal needs and beliefs include many of the patterns pervasive in a narcissistic personality, i.e. a grandiose sense of self-importance, preoccupation with fantasies of unlimited success and power, excessive need for admiration, entitlement, lack of empathy, envy, inferiority, and hypersensitivity. However, narcissists also possess the charisma and grand vision that are vital to effective leadership.[125]

Toxic leadership style

It is important to understand the damage and destruction to people and the organisation that can be caused by a toxic style of leadership. Toxic leadership is related to an autocratic leadership style and not necessarily to a narcissistic style. Toxic leaders do not trust their followers, and need to feel that they are in control of others. This can have a destructive effect on the morale and self-confidence of individuals and teams with the organisation. "Toxic leadership is brought about by *lack of self-awareness*, *lack of self-control* and *confidence*, all of which are seeded by self-interest. ... Toxic leaders care all about themselves. They think only of their own feelings and disregard those of others".[126]

Toxic leadership prevents creativity, innovation, and the individual and independent expression of ideas: in a toxic leadership environment, people are rewarded for agreeing with the boss and punished for thinking differently. In a toxic leadership environment, "yes" people are rewarded and promoted to leadership roles, while people who more fully engage their critical thinking and questioning skills are shut out from decision making and positions of influence.[127]

The characteristics of a toxic leader are those of being: self-destructive, irritable, arrogant, incompetent, maladjusted and lacking in confidence.[128] They are capable of not just setting unrealistic objectives, but leading purely by power and control.

Activity: Self-reflection

1. Take a moment to reflect on when you have engaged in a narcissistic or toxic style of leadership. Give one or two examples.

2. Identify what it is you need to understand about yourself that triggers this kind of leadership, and how you can choose the leadership style that will work best for you, your team and your organisation.

Be honest with yourself – no one else is looking.

How are you and your team creating emotional and mental agility?

As a result of COVID-19, many of us have experienced working in new hybrid organisations – with part of the workforce working in place at work, and part of the workforce working remotely online with colleagues, customers and stakeholders. Leader-managers are being asked to step up to a different way of understanding themselves and their teams, which requires not only a transformation in thinking behaviour, but flexibility and adaptability mentally and emotionally. In these times, your team members need to develop new competences, and are required to demonstrate stability and resilience. But how are you doing?

Activity: Managing your meetings

What are some of the things we need to think about when managing our meetings and communications in remote settings?[129]

Working in a hybrid organisation

In Chapter 1 we looked at challenges to working in a hybrid environment. However, here are further questions that might be useful to think through. Take some time to reflect on them, and write down your reflections.

1. What positive impact is this new way of working having on you personally, and on your team?

2. What negative impact is this new way of working having on you personally, and on your team?

3. Working remotely requires a high level of trust and emotional maturity. What ideas do you have to help your team build emotional maturity, trust and collaboration in the way you work together remotely?

4. How can you continue to build sustainable relationships in this virtual environment? How can we preserve energy and our contact with others while we are working remotely? And what will be your contribution and commitment to that?

5. There is a generation of employees that have never had to self-manage, nor work remotely. How can we as managers provide the necessary guidance and support to these staff?

6. How can we help our team members to manage the constant change and uncertainty, and develop the ability to be able to pivot resiliently with this new way of working?

7. How can we help those we manage to develop more awareness and respect for the human being in each of us, and strengthen the emotional intelligence factors required in a new hybrid organisational way of working?

8. How do you encourage collaboration across departments and bridge the perceived "us and them" gap between your team and the rest of the organisation?

9. Think about a time when you faced a significant challenge. What did you do to deal with that challenge?

10. What are you doing that feels meaningful outside of the workplace (e.g. acts of kindness, volunteer work, taking on a hobby, or learning a new language)?

The key emotional issues with which you can assist your team members include:

- being present and conscious as team leaders;

- dealing with people's fears and uncertainties, and emotional trauma where it exists;

- helping people attain the clarity and certainty they need in these very uncertain times;

- giving people support and guidance, rather than suspicion, cynicism and criticism;

- being creative and innovative in building a remote team spirit;

- moving from blame to personal accountability and solution orientation;

- ensuring that physical distance does not have to mean emotional distancing; and

- making humour part of our coping mechanism.

Activity: Resilience practices

1. *Vulnerability* – Identify and describe the situations where you have been willing to show your team and direct reports that you are vulnerable, and where have you helped them to do the same to stretch themselves and to show up as an authentic leader-manager.

2. *Productive perseverance* – When have you found yourself able to focus and perform in difficult situations and with difficult people, and when not? Give examples.

3. *Connection* – Are you willing to hear the human stories in your team and with your customers, developing compassion, and then to also listen to your own inner voice? Give some examples of those stories and the impact on the team.

4. *Graviosity* – A useful term coined by my colleague, Michael Taylor, which means a combination of looking at a challenge and seeing the positivity and strength in resolving it.[130] When have you demonstrated graviosity, and why?

5. *Possibility* – Where are you now, and where can you and your team go that is new and yet mitigates risk?

Source: Taylor.[131]

States of being and mindfulness

Mindfulness is being taught and practised in a growing number of organisations worldwide in the effort to improve personal and professional effectiveness and overall organisational productivity. ... Additionally, research reveals that the best leaders have some method to manage the constant onslaught of inputs and stimuli to maintain their presence of mind and good health.[132]

Some of these "methods" are described as states of being, such as being relaxed, alert, curious, close-minded, open-minded, negative, positive or self-confident. These states of being are attained by having experiences, and discussing the experience of others who have attained them. This is all about learning from experience, which is an underlying premise of business coaching to help develop leader-managers.[133]

Jon Kabat-Zinn[134] says that mindfulness is "paying attention in a particular way: on purpose, in the present moment and non-judgmentally". Mindfulness is achieved by regulating one's attention – focusing attention on one's thoughts and emotions. Daniel Siegel[135] says that mindfulness is "good brain hygiene, as important to health as brushing one's teeth."

The benefits of mindfulness are that it:

- improves mental focus and reduces mind wandering;

- extends our attention span;

- discourages "black-and-white" thinking;

- assists in staying organised, managing time and setting priorities;

- lifts us from a constant, low level of panic and guilt;

- lowers wear and tear on our bodies;

- toughens immunity;

- improves mood and emotional stability;

- builds self-monitoring capacity; and

- offers neuro-protective effects and reduces cognitive decline associated with ageing.[136]

Being mindful requires working with attention, i.e. mastery of attention, clarity of attention, optimisation of attitude and emotional intelligence, and integration of these into every domain of daily life, work and relationships.[137] As we go into Chapter 7, I will refer to the potential of the Thinking Environment® to help leader-managers develop mindful practice and the ability to create a thinking environment with their teams.

Activity: Developing others mindfully

1. How are you helping your direct reports to think for themselves – individually and independently?

2. In what way do you interfere or intervene or direct their thinking processes?

3. What needs to shift in you to facilitate change or facilitate a shift in them?

Conclusion

The first step in managing self is increasing your emotional intelligence through greater self-awareness, self-management, relationship awareness, and relationship management. To be a great leader-manager does not mean following a formula or developing specific leadership competences and characteristics. It means digging deep down into who you are and how you do you, understanding the core skills of managing people, and developing a leadership style that is flexible and adaptable. And then becoming aware of those around you, and how they experience you – and beginning to develop an understanding of their traits and characteristics. It means being authentic and being willing to be vulnerable. There are elements of intuition, courage and the ability to react to the unexpected, developing resilience and flexibility. It requires breaking from our current mental models that may limit our thinking, creating a realistic future as we go forward in difficult times – and being driven by sustainable values such as trust, integrity, bringing heart into relationships, health and work-life balance.[138]

Chapter 6

Managing self: A neuroscience lens into leader-manager behaviour

by Ingra Du Buisson-Narsai

Background

Although the relationship between brain functioning and human behaviour is complex, there are neuroscientifically-founded leader-manager behaviours that can be applied by leaders across their organisational landscapes. It is important to adopt a science practitioner approach and not fall prey to the misconceptions that prevail. The most important myth is that *specific parts of the human brain have specific psychological jobs.* We now know that the brain uses large-scale networks of real-time information processing. In other words, brains don't work by stimulus and response; instead, predicting and correcting is a more effective way to run a system than continually reacting in an uncertain world. Let's dive deeper.

Why understanding the brain is helpful for leader-managers

Using a neuroscience lens is beneficial to understanding behaviour because, according to Domenico and Ryan:[139]

- the brain mediates all experience and behaviour;

- neuroscience methods enable examination of internal processes that are not accessible by self-reports of experience or behavioural observations; and

- neuroscience enables a level of sophistication and resolution rather than only experiential and behavioural methods.

The evidence base for this section mainly comes from a body of research called Social Cognitive Neuroscience[140, 141, 142] and Affective Neuroscience.[143, 144] We are also not overpromising what neuroscience can offer, as no one level of analysis can tell us all we need to know about good leader-manager behaviour. Thus, a neuroscientific lens can explain to a limited extent the underpinning biology behind human behaviour, which can result in leader-managers being more open to developing new skills in themselves and in those whom they lead and manage.[145]

The nature of the human brain

There have been many examples of long-held convictions about the world eventually being invalidated by science. We used to believe that the earth was flat and that the sun circled around the earth. One of the oldest evolutionary stories is that of the triune brain arrangement. In this story, the human brain ended up with three layers – one for surviving, one for feeling, and one for thinking. Emotions, thinking and perceptions are said to be hosted in a so-called "triune brain" that evolved like a layered cake with each new (better) processor loaded on top of the ones that came before. This is a widespread misconception which holds that:

1. as vertebrate animals evolved, "newer" brain structures (like the neo-cortex) were added over "older" brain structures (like the limbic system); and

2. these newer, more complex structures gifted humans with newer and more complex psychological functions, behavioural flexibility and language.[146]

Essentialism believes that the things within a particular category share a common nature because they share a deep, immutable core, an unchanging essence. This essentialist view also claims that we have emotional categories that are biologically hardwired via dedicated neural circuitry or their own neutral substrate. For example, the amygdala, which is part of the limbic system, is implicated in detecting fearful stimuli. The insula is associated with disgust.[147] Basic emotions like fear and anger are innate, fast, and trigger behaviour with a high survival value, making us less creative.

Though widely shared in society, these misconceptions are increasingly being challenged and stand in contrast to the clear and undisputed agreement on these issues among those studying nervous system evolution.[148] "Perhaps mistaken ideas about brain evolution persist because they fit with the human experience: we do sometimes feel overwhelmed with uncontrollable emotions and even use animalistic terms to describe these states".[149] We know from contemporary science that the brain as a whole is highly complex and intricate, with deep interconnections and cross-connections. Thus our brain is much more like a proficient accountant in which networks, hubs and chemicals are inextricably linked to all other parts of the brain. The key focus is to ensure energy efficiency to the brain and the body.

From all directions in science, there is an emerging consensus that variation is more the rule than the exception in nature and modern human society. This new, robust scientific view states that experiences and behaviours derive from populations of *time-varying, context-dependent* brain states.[150] Let's examine the brain as a predictive and pattern-seeking device.

The predictive brain

A considerable amount of your brain's activity occurs outside your awareness. In every instance, your brain must work out your body's needs for the next moment and implement a strategy to supply those demands in advance. Take, for example, a typical morning routine – as you wake, your brain anticipates the energy you'll need to jump (or crawl) out of bed and start your new day. It proactively trickles your bloodstream with the hormone cortisol, which aids in making glucose available for quick energy.

Your brain runs your body like a budget where deposits and withdrawals are precisely tracked. The budget consists of your body's resources, including water, blood, salt, oxygen, glucose, hormones, and many more biological resources, to keep your body running efficiently – this is called allostasis. The brain is not so much a singular "organ" as a metabolic process. The central argument is that it takes much energy to run a human body. The brain's number one task is to co-ordinate (or serve) the body to be energy-efficient. The brain is an organ of prediction driving a vulnerable body through an uncertain world. Serving the body means keeping body systems co-ordinated and metabolism efficient, and keeping the body alive and healthy.[151]

Each *action* that spends resources, such as going for your morning run, sitting down for a virtual meeting, and having a stressful conversation, is like a withdrawal from your account. Each *action* that re-stocks your resources, such as drinking water, eating, sleeping or laughter, is like a deposit.

The brain is always preparing what to do next (called predictive processing). To be more precise, all your neurons are firing at various rates all the time. What are they doing? Actively predicting. In every moment, your brain uses all its accessible data (your memory, your situation, the state of your body) to guess about what will happen in the next instant. It automatically predicts and prepares to meet the body's needs before they arise. If a guess turns out to be correct, your brain has a head start: it's already launching your body's subsequent actions and creating what you see, hear and feel. If a guess is wrong, the brain can correct itself, and hopefully learn to predict better next time. Sometimes it doesn't bother correcting the guess, and you might see or hear things that aren't present, or do something that you didn't consciously intend. All of this prediction and correction happens in the blink of an eye, outside your awareness.

A straightforward example is when you drink a glass of water. The water takes several minutes to reach your bloodstream, but you feel much less thirsty within a few seconds. This is how the brain "relieves" your thirst. It has learned from previous experience that water is a deposit to your body budget that will hydrate you, so your brain reduces your thirst long before the water has any impact on your bloodstream.

This budgetary explanation of how the brain works may seem plausible when it comes to your bodily functions, but it may seem obscure to compare your mental life to a bank account of deposits and withdrawals. Be assured that every clever or dull thought you have, every feeling of joy or worry or inspiration you experience, every act of kindness you show, and every insult you give or take, forms part of your brain's calculations as it guesses and budgets metabolic requirements.

This new understanding of the brain has many implications for how we, as human beings, function. First of all, the body and the mind are highly interrelated. We should not think of ourselves in psychological terms, separate from the body. We often tend to interpret our bodily sensations as emotions – for example, feeling fatigued or anxious. It turns out that the primary physical symptom of dehydration isn't thirst – it's fatigue and feeling anxious. So it is a good start to consider both the physical and the psychological in explaining our experiences.

Your body's internal state (called interoception), as perceived by your brain, directly affects how you feel day-to-day. Your affective feelings of pleasure and displeasure or calm and agitation are simple summaries of your budgetary state. If you feel generally unpleasant and/or agitated, your body budget is unbalanced; if you are feeling primarily pleasant and/or calm, your body budget is balanced (see Figure 6).

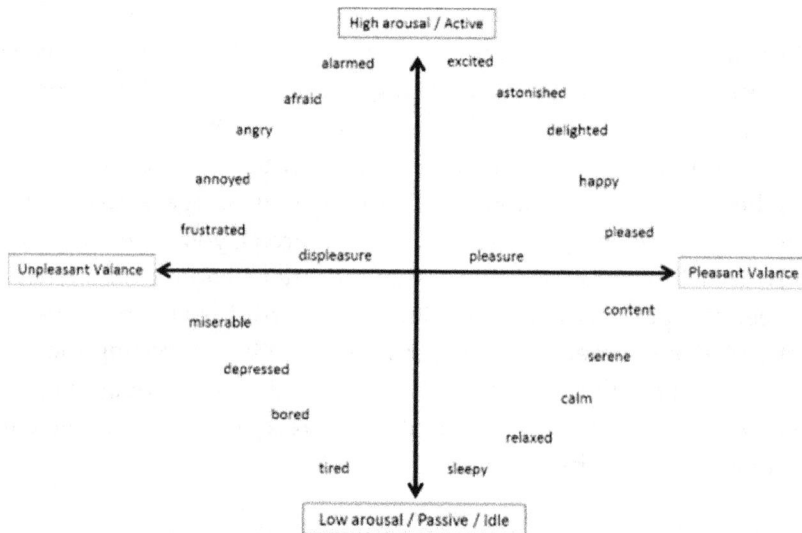

Figure 6: Affective circumplex

Source: Russell and Barrett[152] (Photo credit: Feldman-Barrett; Figure 4–5, p. 74)[153]

Everything you feel and do hinges on the state of your inner budget: The human brain is anatomically designed so that no decision or action can be free of interoception (inner sensations) and affect (raw feelings), no matter what fiction people tell themselves about how rational they are. Your bodily feeling right now will project forward to influence what you will feel and do in the future. In short, your body balance directly affects how you function, feel and think. Our moment-to-moment physiological state impacts every aspect of our existence or mental experience. Therefore taking care of your body through physical actions such as deep rhythmic breathing, changing your lacklustre diet that deprives you of essential nutrients, or getting quality sleep, can be miraculous for enhancing problem solving at work.

Your brain is a network

We now know that psychological functions do not map directly onto spatially localised brain structures in a one-to-one fashion. Rather, numerous brain areas work together in a spatially distributed way to execute a mental function, also known as a large-scale brain network.[154] A large-scale brain network is defined as "a collection of interconnected brain areas that interact to perform circumscribed functions".[155] Certain networks act as controllers or task switchers that co-ordinate, direct and synchronise the participation of other brain networks. On the other hand, other brain networks enable the flow of sensory or motor information and participate in the conscious execution of tasks.[156] The default mode network (DMN) is what the brain does when it is not engaged in specific tasks. The DMN (illustrated in Figure 7) comprises an integrated system for autobiographical, self-monitoring, and social cognitive functions. This is also called the mentalising system of the brain. The DMN is also responsible for rapid episodic spontaneous thinking (REST), which forms part of mind wandering. It turns out that the numerous brain regions which process language also control the inside of the body (the default network). This language network guides our heart rate up or down, and even adjusts the chemical messengers that are "heard" by immune cells and lead to changes in immune function, including effects on inflammation.

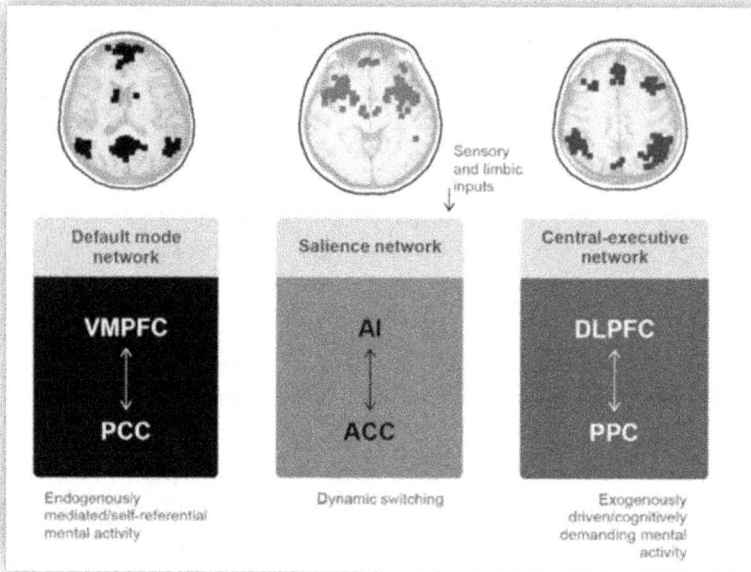

Figure 7: The brain as a network

Source: Bressler and Menon[157] (photo courtesy of Steven Bressler)

The Salience Network (indicated in Figure 7 in the centre) is a controller or network switcher. The controller decides which information is most important and which should receive priority in the queue of brain signals waiting to be sent, based on the task at hand. The central executive network (shown in Figure 7 on the right) is engaged in higher-order cognitive and attentional control. This is also called the analysing system.

When these networks are in synchrony (i.e. in simultaneous action), optimum brain performance is the result. When synchrony is poor, efficient and normal cognition and motor behaviour are compromised.

The current reality of our world at work

The core reality of today's business world is that it is virtual and global, and is increasingly becoming massively complex. The rigours of the hybrid world of work have led to a growing body of research in psychology, sociology and neuroscience that highlights the importance of "decision fatigue": attempts to make several decisions at once diminish the ability to make wise decisions at all.[158] These indeterminate challenges require the capacity to process a lot of data very deeply, be creative, and at the same time try to think in terms of people.

The inverted U-curve of performance (or the optimal arousal curve) explains the relationship between cognitive demands, arousal or stress, and levels of performance (see Figure 8). Optimal performance is achieved at the peak of the curve. A mentally stimulating state characterises this midpoint. Below the midpoint, performance declines as a result of insufficient arousal. Above the midpoint, arousal builds to levels that induce stress and anxiety caused by the task being perceived as beyond the individual's capability.

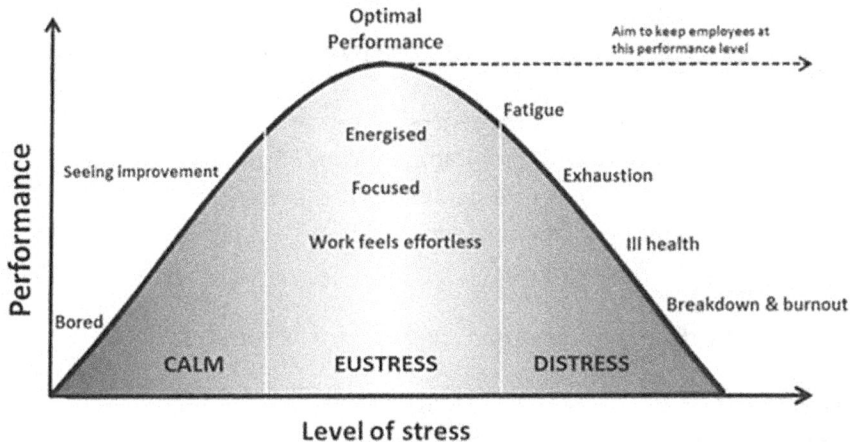

Figure 8: The inverted U-curve of performance

Source: Adapted from Yerkes and Dodson.[159]

Some leaders thrive amidst these challenges; they experience being at the top of the arousal curve or in a state of "flow".[160] Others become frazzled or choke under the perceived pressure, which leads to a decline in performance – also known as power stress.[161] In a state of high stress, the brain invokes the hypothalamic-pituitary-adrenal (HPA) axis, driven by adrenaline and cortisol, and prepares us for fight, flight or freeze responses.

As mentioned previously, "allostatic load" is the expression used to describe the wear-and-tear effects of prolonged stress on the body. High allostatic load leads to high blood pressure, impaired immune function, and loss of brain form and function in parts of the brain responsible for memory and executive functions like planning, decision making and problem solving. However, the allostatic load can be managed so that a state of "flow" can be induced through neurally-aware leader-manager behaviours.

Neuroplasticity, or *the capacity for our brain cells to change in response to our behaviour*, can help us engage more thoughtfully in activities that will contribute to our wellbeing

– no matter our age. This means that the brain can "rewire" itself throughout life – it offers a real opportunity for leader-managers and their organisations to develop and grow new ways of thinking and acting.

By becoming neurally aware through learning how the brain works, what factors affect the reward and action systems in the brain, and the way that stress and other distractions, distortions and misunderstandings lead to sub-optimal performance, leader-managers can effectively change how they lead and perform.

Towards neurally-aware leader-manager behaviour

What does this imply for leader-managers? We suggest that adopting a wellbeing protocol (using insights from neurobiology and psychology) that draws a parallel with physical fitness can help build leadership behaviour that inspires rather than deflates others. As a quick start, we suggest focusing on the following seven brain-based leader-manager behaviours:

Re-boot: the body and mind are deeply interconnected

Understanding our body's inner sensations is central to everything from thought to emotion to decision making to our sense of self. We should not think of ourselves in purely psychological terms, i.e. as separate from the body. We often tend to interpret our bodily sensations as emotion – for example, feeling fatigued or anxious. It turns out that the primary physical symptom of dehydration isn't thirst – it's fatigue and feeling anxious. So it is a good start to consider both the physical and psychological in explaining our experiences. Most of the time, we don't feel sensations from our body in an exact way. If we do, it is in simple terms like raw feelings or "affect". More intense sensations are used to make emotions, whereas less intense ones are used to make thoughts and other things.

Re-calibrate: build circadian rhythm into your life

This means giving routine and ritual to your day, like "make your bed", "unplug time" or "purposeful pauses". Also, learn to down-regulate distress by building perceived control into your life through exercise, nutrition and sleep. Exercise profoundly reduces the effects of chronic stress, which is the Number One enemy to brain performance.

Leverage the power of slumber – go to bed in a state of grace and without light-emitting devices. Gratitude primes the brain for good quality and quantity of sleep. Lack of sleep can increase inflammation in the body, which puts us at risk of getting ill. Take a *power nap* – as little as a seven-minute nap improves mood and allows for the regeneration of creative brain circuits. Both quality and quantity of sleep remove neural debris and help to consolidate memory.

Re-flect: stillness of mind = developing mindful attention awareness

The best way to develop stillness of mind is to slow down our thought processes. This is done through breath awareness and breath regulation, not through talking or thinking. Breath regulation and breath awareness calm down the mind and enable a broadened field of view, so we have many more perceived resources to cope with life. Remember to breathe when you are doing screen time, as screen apnoea (like sleep apnoea) prevents us from doing proper breathing.

Re-categorise: put feelings into words and fine-tune your emotional granularity

A way to change the way your brain makes meaning out of your bodily sensations is to increase your emotional vocabulary (known as emotional differentiating). Learn to effectively categorise your interoceptive sensations, i.e. to put feelings into words or "name it to tame it", which simply means naming a feeling. The words that we know for emotions are like tools that your brain uses to make meaning of your physical sensations, and to predict and tailor your actions to specific situations. The more emotion concepts you begin to understand, the bigger and more flexible your vocabulary of emotion concepts will become, giving you an extensive, more flexible repertoire of emotions that you can not only construct, but also perceive in other people.

When stressful feelings and bodily sensations arise, instead of letting these experiences govern attention or dictate how to behave, high differentiators can better distance themselves – a concept referred to as defusion.[162] With this psychological distance, there is greater opportunity to direct effortful behaviour toward personally valued goals.[163]

The paybacks of granularity (also known as differentiation of emotions) go beyond being well-spoken. The greater your granularity, the "more precisely" you can experience yourself and your world. For example, emotional granularity can be enhanced. If you can learn to differentiate specific meanings for "feeling great" (like happy, pleased, thrilled, relaxed, joyful, confident, inspired, appreciative, loving, grateful, blissful, etc.) or "feeling bad" (like fuming, shocked, aggravated, distressed, spiteful, irritable, remorseful, cranky, offended, uneasy, resentful, offended, afraid, envious, woeful, melancholy, etc.), your brain will have many more possibilities for predicting, categorising and perceiving emotions.

Re-connect: dial up your social engagement deliberately – imitation and intent

Social reality provides the collective agreement and language that make the perception of emotion possible among people who share a culture. The human brain creates a conceptual system into its wiring (a dependable network of concepts) within the first year of life. This "conceptual system" is responsible for all the emotion concepts you now employ to experience and perceive emotions.

To cultivate an inclusive social reality, build micro-positive actions (small gestures that act as social signals). For example, when a colleague joins a conversation, take a moment to bring them up to speed, and avoid micro-aggressions (indirect and unintentional moments of exclusion). Look for similarities not differences, do more one-on-one and small-group discussions, and dial-up in-group social inclusion.

Re-focus: develop pro-social goals that are congruent with your highest values

Goal pursuit is a strategy for surfing uncertainty, provided that these goals are clear. In essence, this means setting goals aligned to your highest values and purpose and holding the image through time. The only way to hold the image (the "why") through time is to keep it in motion (the "how"), and the only way to keep it in motion is to focus on the ever-finer details.

Episodic future thinking (EFT) can be deployed. This means imagining doing something specific in the future in a vivid, detailed way. Engaging EFT with high imagery can significantly change the ability to focus on and achieve future goals. It strengthens connections between the anterior cingulate, amygdala and hippocampus.[164] Pursuing your dreams and changing behaviour is not easy, but is highly rewarding if it is aligned with organisational, team and individual purpose. This equates to being inspired from within (intrinsic motivation) as opposed to having to be motivated from without (extrinsic motivation).[165]

EFT is essential for adaptive functioning[166] as it helps us preserve mental and body bandwidth, especially when swimming in a sea of uncertainty like now. Being clear and positive about the future allows the brain to construct an internal model of itself and the body in the world, minimising adverse effects on energy efficiency (allostasis). Being clear about our future goals with daily action steps prevents us from giving in to anxious fixing, where we jump into action and try to get done as many small, low-priority tasks as possible.

Re-flect: mirroring the good, the bad and the ugly

The emotional states and regulation strategies of others, especially those in positions of power (such as leader-managers), can have a real and enduring effect on individuals and groups. The existing evidence shows that while all emotions can be contagious, "negative" emotions have greater power to influence. This can lead to a negative organisational culture. The aim is to create a safe environment for all individuals within the organisation.

The brain's *mirror neuron system* or *resonance circuitry* underpins the construct of emotional contagion. Mirror neurons fire both when we are performing a particular action and when we observe that action. Thus, people in relationships become more emotionally similar over time. This similarity helps co-ordinate the thoughts and behaviours of the partnership, increases their mutual understanding, and fosters their social cohesion. Relationship partners with less power (such as team members) make more of the change necessary for convergence to occur. Thus emotional contagion and convergence are of central importance to relationship formation, functioning, and long-term outcomes.

Activity: The quality of your life depends on the quality of your questions

To be in the optimal performance zone, we need to become more aware of our conceptual or mental models. Often, this is obvious to us only after an interpersonal transaction. Next time you experience a perceived emotional dilemma at work, reflect on what happened by adopting a "predictive processing" or "constructed emotions" interpretive frame of your behaviour (see Figure 9). This means you need to ask a different set of questions to understand and explain your behaviour. By being aware of how your brain is making meaning out of sense data in particular situations, you can take an active part in your own constructions. Know that positive experiences create new predictions. Negative experiences do as well. Ruminating on negative experiences puts more negative experiences in the pool from which the brain searches.

Start asking yourself, "What am I making up about this situation?" Also, asking how you feel about something is a way of understanding what you are simulating and predicting.

Alternatively, ask yourself "What happened and is it what I expected?" This is a way of opening the conversation for comparison. Asking "What do I make of that?" is helpful to resolve any errors.

Finally, re-categorise any discomfort, which is *physical*, away from *suffering*, which is subjective, because it's the affect that transforms the sensation into something we've predicted based on our past experiences. For example, if you feel nervousness in your stomach because you're about to present on an important topic, try to re-categorise it as being excited to share your knowledge on a topic into which you have put in a lot of effort.

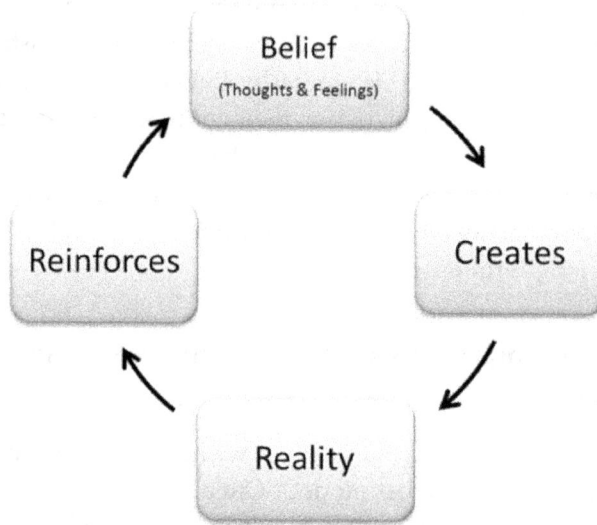

Figure 9: Focus creates reality

Source: Adapted from Whitecloud.[167]

Conclusion

Whatever you attend to as a leader-manager results in the tweaking of your conceptual model, thereby reinforcing concepts about interpersonal experiences, thoughts, feelings, perceptions, emotions and cognition. This "attending to" makes any mental representation salient in your mental model of the world. Every experience you construct is an investment, so invest wisely. Nurture and grow the experiences you want to construct again in the future. Dial up the positive, spot the good, find the benefits. It's even better if you write down your experiences because, again, words lead to conceptual development, helping you predict new moments which cultivate positivity, and as a leader-manager developing new inspiring habits for the future.

Chapter 7

Managing others: Creating a thinking environment and transforming meetings

Leader-manager as coach and thought partner

When working one-on-one with each of your direct reports, a good leader-manager will be a "thought partner" for their team members, helping them to think clearly about the issues they need to address. This coaching conversation is a thinking partnership, where leader-manager and direct report reflect on the direct report's experience, transforming it into potential for learning and action. Your job is to help your direct report to think clearly about the core issues which are currently challenging them – in their job, career and daily working life. You are to encourage them to think for themselves and to develop an awareness of their own conscious and unconscious behaviours, which may influence performance and behavioural change.

By asking the right questions, in the right way, at the right time, you as the manager can help your team member to find their own solutions. Working within a coaching conversation literally provides a "thinking environment" where business leaders develop self-awareness and a depth of understanding about themselves and others. Your job as manager-coach to your team is not to provide answers or solve their problems for them. The greatest gift you can offer is to help them consider their experiences, approaches, ideas, strategies, behaviours, and actions they have not previously considered.[168]

The most important issues you could help your harassed executives or managers to reflect on, and develop clear strategies for, would probably include:

- developing strategic management and leadership competences;

- sustaining complex but rapid decision making processes;

- effectively motivating, developing and managing the performance of their direct reports;

- managing complexity within their teams, their division and the overall organisation;

- effectively addressing diversity issues (particularly around gender, race, and age) in a sector historically dominated by middle-aged white males;

- effectively dealing with workplace conflict, and managing difficult people and situations;

- transitioning into a new position and role(s);

- gaining insight into their own intrinsic personal and professional drivers;

- dealing with corporate stress levels; and

- balancing business and personal life demands.

For any busy executive, under pressure to deliver big results in a competitive industry under difficult economic, financial and systemic circumstances, real help in getting to grips with these issues can be absolutely priceless.[169]

Goals and motivation

If you wish to help your team members or direct reports to improve their behaviour and performance, it is useful to understand the psychology behind adult behaviour, goals and motivation. Alfred Adler, who worked with Freud for ten years, reasoned that adult behaviour is purposeful and goal-directed, and that life goals provide individual motivation. He focused on personal values, beliefs, attitudes, goals and interests, and recommended that adults engage in the therapeutic process using goal setting and reinventing their future, using techniques such as "acting as if", role playing and goal setting.[170] All these tools are utilised and recognised by well-qualified business coaches worldwide.

Motivational theories primarily focus on the individual's needs and motivations. I have typically worked with executives and managers to help them understand more fully their intrinsic motivators (internal drivers such as values, beliefs, and feelings), and how to use extrinsic motivators (external drivers such as relationships, bonuses, the work environment, and job titles) to motivate their teams. If an individual's goals are not in alignment with their own internal, intrinsic drivers, there will be difficulties for them in achieving their goals.

A study by Griffiths and Campbell[171] confirms that coaches often assume leader-managers are aware of their own values, but within the confines of the study this assumption appeared to be incorrect. The individual executives interviewed indicated that they were not aware of their own values, and that acquiring a process of awareness and reflection led them to become more aware of their emotions and values, and of the need to clarify their goals and align these with their values, beliefs and feelings. Whitmore[172] supports this, and states that the goal of the coach is to build awareness, responsibility and self-belief. We would add that it is also a role for the leader-manager.

Ryan[173] talks about how coaching can support motivation for change. He asks "What do people really need to flourish?" and explains that, like a plant which needs water and sunlight to thrive, the human psyche has some nutrients that it needs to survive. It is in our nature to flourish – to flourish is to develop, to become both more differentiated and integrated, and to become fully functioning; but it is by no means automatic. It requires nutrients. And those nutrients are the three conditions that facilitate intrinsic motivation:

- *autonomy* – which means absence of pressure, goal choice, strategy choice, task involvement, and promotion of task interest;

- *competence* – which indicates optimal challenge, positive feedback, and informational rewards; and

- *relatedness* – which includes empathy, warmth, and acknowledgement of emotions.[174]

He explains that outcomes associated with high *autonomous* motivation include greater persistence, more flexibility and creativity, better heuristic performance, more interest and enjoyment, better mental health and wellbeing, better physical health, and a higher quality of close personal relationships. These functional effects are apparent across lifespan, across genders, and across cultures.[175]

However, relationships, which are universally rated as the most important value, are often neglected in schools, medical clinics and work climates. Ryan[176] explains that "relationships are enhanced by supporting another's autonomy and competence. When in good relationships you want to do well. It's so important to motivation."

Why do leader-managers feel great when motivating, helping and encouraging their direct reports? Ryan explains that receiving autonomy support improves your wellbeing, but if you are the one giving the support, then all three of these basic needs (autonomy, relatedness and competence) are met. Helping studies also indicate that the helper feels more positive, more vitality and more self-esteem. And the recipient of help somehow picks up on that willingness to help and feel more vitality. If someone helps you resentfully, then you don't feel good about yourself.[177] These three basic psychological goals are crucial to intrinsic motivation, whether you are coaching or mentoring your team members.

Coaching Framework 1: Intrinsic drivers – values, beliefs and feelings

The team and the organisation depend on the individual achieving their goals, so goals must be in alignment with internal drivers or motivators, otherwise there will be internal conflict or stress.[178]

Activity: Intrinsic drivers – values, beliefs and feelings

You as manager-as-coach can use the following coaching question framework to help your direct report discover their own intrinsic drivers or motivators, and to help both of you identify whether their personal and organisational goals are in alignment with their personal and professional internal drivers:

1. What is important to you professionally? What is important about that? Anything else?

2. What is important to you personally? What is important about that? Anything else?

3. Help your team member to finalise their list of values ensuring they are not measurable – if they are measurable they are goals.

This is a much deeper exercise than it seems at first glance. This is because you as manager will be helping to uncover the individual's core feelings, values and beliefs. These can touch on individual existential anxieties. However, it will be difficult for an individual to achieve their goals without harnessing their intrinsic drivers.

All goals given to the direct report needs to be in alignment with their underlying values, beliefs and feelings in order to keep up their own sense of motivation.

This process is important, as the individual's motivators must be aligned not just to their own goals, but also to the goals of the team and the organisation. Typical responses are intangibles which cannot be measured, e.g. achievement, balanced life, peace of mind, recognition and acknowledgement, a higher purpose, affiliation, financial security, honesty, integrity, balance, freedom to choose to do something of value, and giving something back, receiving support and teaching.[179]

If you use this question framework, know that external motivators come into effect when someone tries to "engage" our internal motivators, to encourage us or make us want to do something. Examples of extrinsic motivators are the working environment, feedback, recognition and titles, salaries and bonuses, personal health plans, holiday leave, education and training, an overall salary package, and benefits such as a company car or share options.[180]

To understand oneself, and to understand what drives you before setting goals, it is important, firstly, to understand the values, beliefs and feelings that underpin your individual behaviour. As a leader-manager, you are helping your team members to look for the intangibles, the un-measurables. If the individual replies with a measurable goal (such as a specific salary or titled position in the organisation), ask "What is important about that?" (you are helping them to search for an intangible such as financial security, recognition or acknowledgement). For each motivator, you can ask, "What's important about that?" Another important question to ask is, "Anything else?" At the end of this framework, ask the direct report which motivator, if achieved, would allow the rest to follow. This is to check whether there is a top value from which all the others flow.

Other applications of this framework are to ask questions relevant to a particular project or issue, such as:

1. What is important to you about your job / this project?

2. What is important about that?

3. Anything else?

Types of goal

This section is adapted from Stout-Rostron.[181]

Businesses place great emphasis on clarifying and achieving goals, and the leader-manager is responsible for ensuring that goal-setting conversations get the best results. Within the complexity of the organisational environment, the manager's overarching goals may often be set by a more senior executive and passed on to the latter's own direct reports. However, that senior executive may have different worldviews, different paradigms, and differing limiting and empowering assumptions. It is therefore important that, as goals are set, they be related to the intrinsic and extrinsic drivers of the direct report themselves.

A secondary consideration is that goals change for the individual over time as the relationship develops. For example, as he grew in competence and confidence over a two-year period, one of my clients working in an international organisation changed his overarching goal, from that of developing strong leadership competence, to being considered one of the most competent business leaders – not just within his own country, South Africa, but in the entire sub-Saharan African continent!

To develop the relationship effectively, the principles and concepts of the Rogerian, person-centred approach is useful to us. This is a relationship-oriented experiential approach, requiring the leader-manager or practitioner to listen with acceptance and without judgement if clients are going to be able to change.[182] If one of the aims of the coaching intervention is to help team members understand and manage themselves and their own interpersonal communications, and if we as leader-managers are going to enable rather than disempower our direct reports, then our coaching and mentoring interventions constantly need to have goals in mind, and be able to clearly define the types of goal. I would, however, encourage you to take part in a reputable and certifiable coaching programme to enable you to understand all the nuances of coaching within the working environment.

O'Neill differentiates between two kinds of managerial goal, business and personal, and links the coaching effort to a business result, highlighting and prioritising the business areas that need attention. Business goals are about achieving external results; personal goals are what the leader-manager or direct report must do differently in how they conduct themselves to get the business results. O'Neill[183] describes three types of goal:

- *bottom-line goals* – aligned to the reason the organisation exists;
- *work-process goals* – how the work is accomplished; and
- *human relations goals* – how people collaborate to accomplish goals.

In setting goals, O'Neill's[184] interventions are:

1. Which business results are needed?
2. What team behaviours need to be different to accomplish the results?
3. Which personal leadership challenges is the manager facing in improving these results and team behaviours?
4. What are specific behaviours the leader needs to enhance or change in themselves?

Yalom talks about two types of goal: *content* goals (what is to be accomplished), and *process* goals (how the coach, or in this case the leader-manager, wants to be in a session). He describes the importance of setting concrete attainable goals – goals that you as manager (if being coached) or your direct report have personally defined, and which increase your or their sense of responsibility for their own individual change.[185]

Other types of goal are:

- *Extrinsic life or professional* – financial success, social recognition (popularity, fame), being physically attractive.

- *Intrinsic life or professional* – meaningful relationships, community contribution, personal growth, learning.

Developmental goal setting – working with the development pipeline

If the team member is to learn how to learn, they need to cultivate self-awareness through reflection on their experience, values, intrinsic drivers, the impact of these on others, the environment, and on their own future goals. This process is often implicit in the coaching relationship through the process of questions that develop critical reflection, and subsequent actions that develop practice. As a leader-manager working with a coaching approach, you will be asking questions of your team members and direct reports to help them to reflect, review and gain useable knowledge from their experience. A useful structure for your work with them is along the continuum of a development pipeline.[186] Your questions and challenges in your one-on-one sessions can help your direct reports reflect in each of these five areas:

- *Insight* – How are you continually developing insight into areas where you need to develop?

- *Motivation* – What are your levels of motivation based on the time and energy you are willing to invest in yourself?

- *Capabilities* – What are your management and leadership capabilities; what skills, knowledge and competences do you still need to develop?

- *Real-world practice* – How are you continually applying your new skills at work?

- *Accountability* – How are you creating, defining and taking accountability?

It is crucial that the individual being coached (whether you or your direct report) has a "living sense" of what their goal may be.[187] In other words, goals must be aligned with the values of the individual, as much as with the values of the organisation, if they are to be achieved. I would recommend working with this model which helps the coachee to dig deeper into their own levels of inspiration and motivation.

Kline's Thinking Environment® – Thinking Pairs and Transforming Meetings

My work has been widely influenced by Nancy Kline's Thinking Environment® philosophy and methodology. The underlying premise of Kline's Thinking Environment® processes is that the individual is best able to do their own thinking, and it provides a rigorous approach for leaders and managers to help their team members to explore their own thinking and ideas. In this chapter we will explore Thinking Pairs for use in a coaching approach with individual members of your team. Thinking pairs can also be used for colleagues within the team to co-coach each other.

We will also work with the Transforming Meetings process, as facilitating meetings is a core competence for managers. Kline's Transforming Meetings process provides us with a set of meeting tools that ensure all of the voices are heard – and that the agenda is covered. The tools are those of *Rounds, Open Discussion, Thinking Pairs,* and *Dialogue*. All Thinking Environment® processes are underpinned by the Ten Components, ten specific behaviours that help individuals and teams to think for themselves and together. All of the tools can be found in her books *Time to Think* (1999), *More Time to Think* (2009), and *The Promise That Changes Everything* (2020).

Both processes are practical and useful to help your team members learn to think together and to make clear and strong decisions. Part of this work includes working with limiting and liberating assumptions to help unblock any limiting thinking that might be sabotaging their best efforts to deal with challenging issues or people. First we will discuss working with catalytic attention, limiting assumptions and understanding the ten components or behaviours that help us to be together when thinking.

Giving catalytic attention – in Thinking Pairs

Focused attention on the other while they speak, or giving time to hear out another's viewpoint and arguments, is rare in the working world. And yet, without giving each other attention and being willing to hear a different viewpoint, it is hard to understand all of the perspectives needed to think through difficult issues. Attention is not a technique; it is a way of being with a person. And it is an attitude driven by several assumptions, that:

- the other person is inherently intelligent and can think well;

- the other person is inherently able to come up with ideas for themselves;

- the other person is inherently worth giving your time and attention to; and

- the other person is inherently good and compassionate, and able to figure things out and to cope.[188]

The Ten Components

Kline's work is based on the philosophy that "everything we do depends on the quality of the thinking that we do first. The quality of our thinking depends on the way we treat each other while we are thinking".[189] The Ten Components are essential "behaviours" which help people to think for themselves. They represent ten ways of being together, and ten ways of treating one another which offers catalytic attention and focused listening. These ten behaviours are powerful in themselves individually, but when all ten are present in any process they have a transformational impact on both the Thinker (direct report) and the Thinking Partner (manager).

The Ten Components are as follows:

1. *attention* (listening without interruption and with interest in where the person will go next in their thinking);

2. *equality* (regarding each other as thinking peers giving equal time to think);

3. *ease* (discarding internal urgency);

4. *appreciation* (noticing what is good and saying it);

5. *encouragement* (giving courage to go to the unexplored edge of our thinking by ceasing competition as thinkers);

6. *feelings* (welcoming the release of emotion);

7. *information* (supplying facts, recognising social context, dismantling denial);

8. *difference* (championing our inherent diversity of identity and thought);

9. *incisive questions* (freeing the human mind of an untrue assumption lived as true); and

10. *place* (producing a physical environment – the room, the listener, your body – that says, "You matter".

Working with Thinking Pairs

Our work with Thinking Pairs is underpinned by the Ten Components, or behaviours, and they are a key process used in the Transforming Meetings process. When we work in a Thinking Pair, one person is the Thinker, and the other is the Thinking Partner. This is a brilliant process to use in working with members of your team, and for them to use in working with each other as co-coaching peers. You can work with a series of questions or simply ask, "What do you want to think about and what are your thoughts?" You listen without interrupting, and only ask, "What more do you think or feel or want to say?" Each person speaks for five, ten, 20 or even 30 minutes in this way while the other gives focused attention. Boundaries are set by agreeing who will be the first Thinker, and who the first Thinking Partner. When their turn is finished you switch roles. This is the most powerful way to give another person time to think through an issue they have been struggling with for a while.

As a Thinking Partner it is important to be present to allow the human mind in front of you to be ignited – and it lets them know they matter. Your eyes are on their eyes, and even though they may look around, when they come back to you – you are still there with them, looking at them, interested in what they think and in what they are saying.

The Thinking Pair requires all ten components to be present. They are like a system and, as Kline often says, the brain loves to be attended to in this way. It allows the higher thinking cortex to work with the Limbic System. The Partner asks a question and sits back with their full attention on the Thinker for five minutes, or other time limit that you have agreed for each of you to think out loud. You can set up a Thinking Pair for any length of time that suits the two of you. However, be careful not to interrupt each other, and instead listen catalytically for the entire length of time agreed to.

It is largely unsettling that change can happen through what we do not say as the Thinking Partner. This should be the place where we actually start our coaching conversations, the purpose being to generate independent thinking. The human mind in front of you can do the job better than we can think for them. This is important to understand if you are a manager who does all of the thinking and talking in your meetings! It means getting better at attention, listening and asking fewer questions. What is particularly weird about Thinking Pairs is that there is no "content" response from you as the Thinking Partner. It is relatively easy, because the strangeness of the process keeps the discipline in place.

Understanding and working with assumptions

According to Nancy Kline[190] team effectiveness depends on the calibre of thinking the team can do. Yet most teams do not operate within a thinking environment with Kline's ten components to enhance quality thinking and decision making. Teams are the most strategic place to begin organisational change, but the limiting assumptions of each team member, and the limiting assumptions of the group as a whole need to be identified and replaced with empowering assumptions.[191]

An assumption is a proposition that is taken for granted, as if it were "true" without the facts. And it is based on the possible, either positive or negative. Kline identifies assumptions as limiting or liberating assumptions about "self" (I can, I cannot), and "how life works" (they will let me, they will not let me). The ongoing narrative in your head tends to be organised by three general levels of thought:

- *Automatic thoughts* are on the surface and are like short tapes that flash through your mind; they are a form of "self-talk" which you use throughout the day.

- *Assumptions* are positioned midway between automatic thoughts and your core beliefs; they act as a translation between the two. Assumptions are not as fundamental as core beliefs, yet they aren't as superficial as automatic thoughts. Assumptions are one of the prime targets of cognitive behavioural therapy (CBT), which aims to restructure a person's thoughts to reflect adaptable and constructive thinking. It is at the level of assumptions where we as leader-managers and coaches can work with behavioural change and improving performance.

- *Core beliefs* develop over time, usually from childhood and through the experience of significant life events or particular life circumstances. They are the very essence of how we see ourselves, other people, the world, and the future. However, we are not trying to change our team members' core beliefs, but rather to identify assumptions that might be limiting their thinking and performance.

Coaching frameworks to use with your direct reports

You can work with coaching frameworks in Thinking Pairs. In addition to "Coaching Framework 1: Intrinsic drivers" described above, you as manager-coach can use the following coaching frameworks (adapted from Kline[192]) with your direct reports.

Coaching Framework 2: Goal setting

1. What is one thing at work, or in your professional life, that you would like to do better?

2. What do you need to learn or positively assume to make the change?

3. How will your new thinking and feeling impact on your behaviour? What new thinking and feeling might you experience?

Coaching Framework 3: Assumptions

(You can work on this on your own as well.)

1. What are you assuming about yourself as a leader-manager (or whichever role you play) that motivates and inspires you?

2. What are you assuming that gets in your way?

3. What would be a more credible, liberating alternative that would take you the next step in your role?

Coaching Framework 4: Working with a goal and understanding limiting assumptions

1. What challenging step do you want to take in your life or work right now?

2. What might you be assuming that is stopping you from taking that step? ("I am assuming that …")

3. What else might you be assuming that is stopping you from taking that step? ("I am assuming that …")

4. What are you assuming that is most stopping you from taking that step? ("I am assuming that …")

5. What would you credibly have to assume instead to take that step?

6. If you knew that [new assumption], how would you take that step?

The Thinking Environment® meetings process

Chairing a meeting is one of the most important skills for you to develop as a leader-manager – and one of the most difficult. Meetings require open discussion and debate, decisions and actions agreed to be taken. However, decisions are a skill and an art for the leader-manager. Decisions can be a lonely act: they not only force the individual to face the limitation of possibilities, but encourage one to accept personal responsibility and existential isolation.[193, 194]

For this reason, most executives choose to work with their team to make decisions about the business, people, and processes. However, to make decisions in meetings we need structure – this will include all the voices and give free reign to thinking, and yet set boundaries around the process. Kline calls this process Transforming Meetings, which allows people in a meeting to be able to "think for themselves with rigour, imagination, courage and grace". When all Ten Components of a Thinking

Environment® form the culture of a meeting, "people's thinking, and engagement improve dramatically".[195]

In Kline's book, *The Promise That Changes Everything: I won't interrupt you*, she shares the thinking of CEO, Charles: "'I won't interrupt you' changed the way I lead. It also changed the way I develop young leaders. As Chief Executive I have generally been a good listener. But understanding the promise of no interruption moved me from good listener to generator of independent thinking, almost overnight."[196]

This phenomenon moves the standard way most leader-managers chair their meetings, moving them away from hours-long, interminable presentations of figures and statistics with no creative or critical thinking (or perhaps no thinking at all), and with only a few people dominating the meeting. If you can bring yourself to try to work with the Thinking Environment® meetings process just as an experiment, you may be surprised to discover that you can move the culture of all your meetings, from one of interruption and domination by a few voices, to one where all voices are heard, allowing you to move through the agenda more quickly and succinctly. You will also have to decide how much technology (if any) is allowed in the meeting, if team members tend to focus on their email when it is not their turn to present. You can choose to create an environment where creative thinking can blossom, and issues can be addressed more decisively and thoroughly.

Chairing a Transforming Meetings process

In Alex Pentland's *Harvard Business Review* article, "The new science of building teams", he says core guidelines for meetings are that:[197]

1. Everyone in the team talks and listens in roughly equal measure, keeping contributions short and sweet.

2. Members face one another – and, even online, keep their eyes on the eyes of the person speaking.

3. Members connect directly with one another – not just with the team leader.

4. Members do not carry on back-channel or side conversations within the team.

5. Members periodically break, explore outside the team, and bring information back.

These guidelines are in alignment with Kline's Transforming Meetings process. The work to be done to prepare for a meeting is just as important as chairing the meeting itself, with all the right information. Your tools for the meeting are:

- an *Agenda* in the form of questions;

- *Rounds* with equal input from all;

- *Thinking Pairs* to generate new ideas on the Assumption question ("What might we be assuming that could limit our thinking on this issue?");

- *Dialogue Pairs* (Thinking Pairs on the same question, where they have a "thinking" exchange); and

- *Open Discussion*.

The Transforming Meetings process includes what I consider the best tools to be used by a team leader when designing team coaching sessions or team meetings. All my team coaching sessions work with the basic principles of Thinking Pairs, and often with the applications from the Transforming Meetings process. That is, *how much further can the other person go in their thinking before they need my or anyone else's thinking?*

Rounds – Each one speaks once before anyone speaks twice

A core principle when working with Transforming Meetings with teams is how to help each one in the group to think in a wave, and to pass the baton over to another for them to think in a wave, and so on. One way to facilitate this process is to work in rounds to generate the group's thinking: that is, each one speaks *once* before anyone speaks *twice*, and no-one speaks *twice* before everyone speaks *once*. Only then do you move the group into Open Discussion.

Rounds are a very dynamic way to open a team meeting, setting a positive tone and bringing everyone's voice into the room. Once everyone has spoken on the issue at hand, the leader or team coach can facilitate an Open Discussion. Each of these processes are underpinned by the Ten Components of a Thinking Environment® – that is, the ten behaviours which enhance listening, attention and dialogue. The group can break into Thinking Pairs, Dialogue or Small Groups to focus on a particular issue or to generate more innovative thinking before bringing those new ideas back into the plenary group.

Outline of a Transforming Meeting

The Kline Transforming Meetings process can be outlined as follows:

1. *Welcome and purpose of the meeting*.

2. *Opening Round question*.

- Positive reflection on the business; or on a work team, group or project issue. Each team member answers the question, and their response is timed – each person has the same amount of time (about 60 to 90 seconds). This sets a positive tone for the meeting.

3.   *The agenda.*

- Agenda item questions are confirmed or amended in a Round.

- First agenda item:

    –   Round on agenda item question.

    –   Open Discussion (with set boundaries for the entire discussion, no interruption of the speaker).

    –   Round on a refreshed question.

    –   Open Discussion.

    –   Round if needed on refreshed question.

    –   Open Discussion.

    –   Decision, action, next steps.

- Next agenda items:

    –   Same process as above.

4.   *Burning issues round.*

- Identifying the issues to be considered for a future meeting.

5.   *Closing round.*

- Appreciation of the meeting, colleagues, and the Chair.

Critical Transforming Meetings tools

The Thinking Environment® tools which are used in Transforming Meetings can be explained as follows:

- *Pre-meeting components* – Agenda, participants, reading material, presentation material, minutes for the previous meeting.

- *The agenda* – Each agenda item is put into the form of a succinct question. The Chair confirms the agenda and ensures all items are in the form of a question, and asks in a round if there are any amendments to the agenda.

- *The opening round* – This must be a short Round, with each person speaking for only one or two minutes, and the question must be a positively-focused question. For example, "What is going well for you in your team right now?" or

"What is going well in your work life / team / unit right now?" or "What do you think is going well in your project?" Each one speaks once before anyone speaks twice, and the Chair asks who would like to start (going either right or left of the first speaker until everyone has spoken once). The input from each speaker must be given equal time.

- *First agenda item, and every subsequent item* – First have an input round where each one speaks once before anyone speaks twice. In this round the Chair asks everyone to give their thinking on the item. Time each person's input equally.

- *Open Discussion* – After the first input round there is Open Discussion ("popcorn"). Timing is set for the discussion overall. Each person must manage how much time they use, giving one wave of thinking, then passing the baton on to others. This is facilitated by the Chair who ensures that no one is interrupted. The Chair or a timekeeper manages the overall time for the discussion.

- *Thinking Pairs (or Dialogue Pairs)* – At useful moments when the team gets stuck, or is cycling around an issue, or a few people are dominating the discussion, the Chair breaks the group into pairs. This is for a five-minute think by each, without interruption by their partner, on the question being addressed. Each thinking pair reports back in a Round. Instead of a Thinking Pair, you can work with a ten-minute Dialogue Pair, where the pair answers the question but hands the baton back and forth to each other for a prescribed period of time – being sure not to dominate the dialogue. Then the pairs go back into the meeting and share their new thinking with the team. Dialogue is different from conversation, which is two people talking together. A Dialogue Pair is actually two people thinking together. Both Thinking Pairs and Dialogue Pairs need the boundary of setting the length of time to think together.

- *Removing assumptions* – At strategic points in the discussion, the Chair can ask, "What might we be assuming that is limiting our thinking on this issue?" And, "If we assumed something more liberating, what would it be?"

- *Open Discussion* – No one is interrupted after the five-minute thinking or Dialogue Pairs, and the Chair can refresh the question if needed. The group goes back to Round – Discussion – Round.

- *Actions and issues* – The Chair clarifies all action agreed before moving to the next agenda item.

- *Burning issues round* – At the end of the meeting, the Chair asks the group, "Is there a burning issue we should address at our next meeting?"

- *Closing round* – The Chair asks everyone a positive reflective question. For example, "What do you think went well in this meeting?" Or "What was positively challenging for you today?" or "What will you commit to going forward?"

- *Appreciation* – The Chair asks each member in a round to appreciate the person (either on their left or right). What quality or characteristic do you appreciate in the person sitting on your left? And the meeting is closed.

Conclusion

Businesses place great emphasis on clarifying and achieving goals, and you as the leader-manager are responsible for ensuring that goal-setting conversations with your team members get the best results. Increasing your skill and competence in the role of manager-as-coach will help to get the best thinking and performance out of people, giving you time to take on the strategic areas of the business where you are most needed.

Working with developmental goal setting, you will begin to develop your coaching competence as a leader-manager. This takes practice, but it is ultimately liberating for the team member to learn the importance of thinking independently for themselves. This contributes to the creativity and decision making of the team.

The underlying premise of Nancy Kline's Thinking Environment® work is that the individual thinker is best able to do their own thinking, with the implication that all direct reports have the internal mental resources they need to learn or think for themselves. Also, managers can let go of doing all the thinking, instead, encouraging innovative, clear, unfettered thinking by their team members. One of the key results of this is that you begin to develop your leadership pipeline.

As important is the ability to chair a successful meeting. Most meetings in the business world are not effectively chaired, which leads to poor decision making. Trying your hand at a Transforming Meeting will change the ability of your team to think together, take decisions, and execute on their goals. Wishing you an enjoyable journey, opening up the thinking capabilities of your team and the organisation.

Part Three – Managing people

Chapter 8

Managing people: Motivation

The importance of values and motivation

One of the reasons that leaders and managers often work with a business coach is to help them to think clearly about the core issues which present challenges to them in their career, their organisation, their job, and their daily working life.

The focus of a coaching conversation is to help leader-managers work towards achieving their desired outcomes. It is in this process of reflection – where coach and manager reflect on the manager's experience – that potential for learning and action emerges. With a coach you can also explore what it is that is holding you back or preventing you from achieving your goals.

This raises an important question for leader-managers: if goals are to be motivationally achieved, are they in alignment with your own individual values, beliefs and feelings? Organisations often pay lip service to organisational values, and do not necessarily create them as a synthesis of the core individual values which make up the culture of the organisation. Ethical dilemmas can arise during the coaching process if you as a leader-manager, or one of your direct reports, need to make difficult choices which are incompatible with your or their own value system.

Motivational theories focus primarily on the individual's needs and motivations. We have typically worked with leaders to help them understand more fully their intrinsic motivators (internal drivers such as values, beliefs and feelings), and how to use extrinsic motivators (external drivers such as relationships, bonuses, the environment, share schemes and titles) to motivate their teams. If an individual's goals are not in alignment with their own internal, intrinsic drivers, there will be difficulties for them in achieving their goals.

Leader-managers need to understand how they learn and begin to cultivate self-awareness through reflection on their own experience, values, intrinsic drivers, the impact of these on others, on the environment, and on their future goals. The development of self-awareness is often implicit in the coaching relationship through the process of questions that develop critical reflection, and subsequent actions that develop practice. As a leader working with a coaching approach, you will be asking questions to help your direct reports to reflect, review and gain useable knowledge from their experience.[198]

Learning, and particularly learning from experience, is one of the major components which drives motivation. The significance of your own experience and your own stories – and the interpretation and significance you give to them – will help you to develop self-awareness and continue to grow, develop and become the leader you want to step into being. This is also how you can work with your direct reports and team members.

Intrinsic and extrinsic motivation

Motivation has fascinated researchers for over 100 years. There is internal motivation which comes from within, which we call intrinsic motivators. Extrinsic motivation comes from the external environment: one's boss, colleagues, the environment, and the rewards offered to the employee to try to get them to do a good job. What we do know is that we cannot force people to do a good job. People have different needs and goals. Many managers unfortunately believe in rewards to such an extent that they believe people will do a better job simply if they have been promised some sort of incentive. However, a reward or incentive will work only if it touches on one of the individual's own personal intrinsic motivators.

Motivational theories focus primarily on the individual's needs and motivations. Managers need to understand more fully their direct reports' intrinsic motivators, and to recognise how to use extrinsic motivators to motivate their teams. If an individual's goals are not in alignment with their own internal, intrinsic drivers, there will be difficulties for them in achieving their goals.[199]

Activity: Determine your own intrinsic motivators

1. Make a list of what is most important to you at work that cannot be measured (for example, work/life balance, good relationships in the workplace, challenging tasks which stretch you). If it can be measured, it would be a goal – such as getting a promotion, a salary increase, or to work in a new organisation.

2. Make a list of what is important to you personally – and that cannot be measured (for example, family, friendship, stability at home and love).

3. Rank all the items in both lists in terms of importance in one list – and you will find yourself integrating the two lists. What you will end up with is a list of your own intrinsic motivators.

How to use your list of intrinsic motivators

If you ever find yourself not motivated or demotivated for some reason, take a look at the list. Those items need to be in place for you to stay motivated and inspired personally and professionally. They need to be aligned with the life goals you are currently pursuing, and the goals you are trying to achieve at work. If they are not aligned, it can lead you to feeling demotivated. It is worth carrying out this Activity every few years, as your intrinsic motivators change while you go through the psychological stages of life development.

Motivation theory and practice

Motivation is the drive to satisfy desires that are deeply rooted in our physical, psychological and emotional make-up. We need to be aware of what is motivational to ourselves, and what demotivates you and can stop you from clearly visioning your goals and aspiring to accomplish them. What we know about motivating people is that:

- *Behaviour is the result of forces in the individual and in the environment.* As a leader-manager you need to understand your individual team members' intrinsic and extrinsic motivators, and most importantly you need to analyse your own behaviour to see if it is creating or impacting their demotivation.

- *People make conscious decisions about their behaviour.* You cannot force people to do good work.

- *People have different needs, desires and goals.* You cannot deal with everyone on the same basis – they do not all want the same things.

- *People do what they see is rewarded.* In other words, they avoid behaviour that leads to negative consequences.

Activity: Practical motivation

1. Think of the last time you felt really motivated at work, and why. In the left-hand column below, make a list of the ten most important factors that motivate you to do a good job, or that help you to aspire towards accomplishing something new or challenging.

2. Think of a time when you felt really demotivated, and why. In the right-hand column below, list the ten most important factors that are currently demotivating you and preventing you from aspiring to what you wish to achieve.

My top ten motivators	My top ten demotivators
1.	1.
2.	2.
3.	3.
4.	4.
5.	5.
6.	6.
7.	7.
8.	8.
9.	9.
10.	10.

Examples of motivators include the following:

- Being given the opportunity to prove yourself.
- Working with like-minded people.
- Completing tasks, projects or delegated work that helps you grow.
- Being given a chance to make a difference.
- Positive results of legislation.
- Your values and beliefs match those of the organisation.
- Recognition and acknowledgement.
- Success against the odds.
- Seeing results and your team in action.

Examples of demotivators include the following:

- Questioning your chance of success.

- Expectations of others not being met, perhaps due to differing values.

- Being prevented from achieving or from advancement.

- Being blocked from advancing within the organisation.

- Being overloaded or overwhelmed with projects.

- Negative feedback, with no positive reinforcement for jobs well done.

- People not taking responsibility, which impacts your work.

- Loss or alienation within the workplace or community.

- Not being heard or asked for your opinion or thinking.

Five major theories on motivation

There are five major theory areas on motivation that are useful to you as a leader-manager:

- Maslow's Hierarchy of Needs;

- McGregor's X and Y Theory;

- Herzberg's Motivation / Hygiene Theory;

- McClelland's Need for Achievement Theory; and

- Deci and Ryan's Self-Determination Theory.

Maslow's Theory of Sequential Development

Maslow's theory explains that people are motivated by unmet needs. These needs are in a hierarchical order. They can prevent people from being motivated if the lower-level needs have not been met or are threatened. Abraham Maslow, like many other psychologists, believed that we need to resolve certain issues before we can move on to the next ones which need resolution (from physiological needs, to safety needs, to social needs, to esteem and self-actualisation needs). Maslow broke the mould of exploring pathology to understand human nature.[200] He looked at motivation and at motivators, believing that "individuals naturally actualise themselves unless circumstances in their development are so adverse that they must strive for safety rather than for growth".[201] Maslow says that we live in order to fulfil our potential, and he identified the following hierarchy of five needs that must be satisfied for us to achieve that:

1. *Physiological needs,* e.g. food, water and sleep.

2. *Safety needs,* e.g. security, order and protection.

3. *Social needs,* e.g. a sense of belonging, identification, and love and affection.

4. *Esteem needs,* e.g. prestige, success, status, recognition and self-respect.

5. *Self-actualisation needs,* e.g. the desire for self-fulfilment and accomplishment.[202]

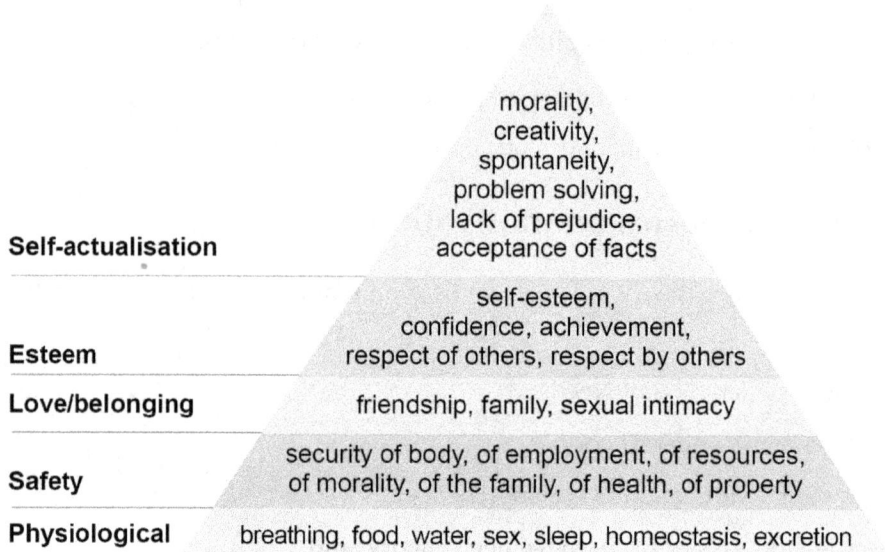

Self-actualisation — morality, creativity, spontaneity, problem solving, lack of prejudice, acceptance of facts

Esteem — self-esteem, confidence, achievement, respect of others, respect by others

Love/belonging — friendship, family, sexual intimacy

Safety — security of body, of employment, of resources, of morality, of the family, of health, of property

Physiological — breathing, food, water, sex, sleep, homeostasis, excretion

Figure 10: The Motivation Pyramid

Source: Clipartkey.com.[203]

Maslow later identified primary and secondary needs (see Figure 11):

1. *Physiological needs* (primary).

2. *Safety needs* (primary).

3. *Love and belonging needs* (secondary).

4. *Esteem needs* (secondary).

5. *Cognitive needs* (secondary).

6. *Aesthetic needs* (secondary).

7. *Self-actualisation needs* (secondary).

Figure 11: Primary and secondary needs

Source: Maslow.[204]

Indicators of low motivation and demotivation

Factors to watch out for in your team which indicate low motivation are:

- Low-quality output.

- High labour turnover.

- High accident rate.

- High or abnormal absenteeism.

- Poor time-keeping.

- Lack of structure and discipline.

- Failure to make use of the social activities provided.

Factors to watch out for in your team which indicate demotivation are:

- Aggression.

- Conflict.

- Obsessiveness.

- Submissiveness or resignation.

- Reluctance to take on responsibility and accountability.

- Poor standards of client service or customer service.

- A lack of respect for senior management.

- Wasting time and lack of interest in the job.

- Putting in the minimum amount of time or effort.

McClelland's Need for Achievement Theory

In 1961 David McClelland built on Maslow's work in his book *The Achieving Society*. McClelland's Need for Achievement Theory is underpinned by Maslow's self-actualisation theory. In response to the early criticisms of the leadership trait approach, academics began to research leadership as a set of behaviours, evaluating the behaviour of successful leaders, and identifying broad leadership styles. McClelland[205] held that leadership needs a strong personality with a well-developed and positive ego, and that to lead, self-confidence and high self-esteem are also useful if not essential.

McClelland's Human Motivation Theory explains that every person has one of three main driving motivators – the need for achievement, affiliation, or power – and that one of these will be our dominant motivating driver. These motivators are not considered to be inherent; we develop them through our culture and life experiences. McClelland's[206] Needs-Based Model suggests that a manager's motivational style and behaviour is a combination of the need for achievement, the need for authority and power, and the need for affiliation.[207, 208]

It is important with all these theories to understand that extrinsic reward systems must correspond to intrinsic factors if you are going to be able to motivate your team members. Many organisations often make the mistake of focusing only on extrinsic factors to motivate employees, ignoring the fulfilment of intrinsic motivators. This is because they do not take the time to build relationships with staff, learning to understand what motivates them to do more than an adequate job.

Activity: Where motivation can go wrong

Let us think about your team. Recently one of your direct reports produced a monthly report that was excellent in every way. It was thoroughly researched and well-written, and produced in a superior format to the run-of-the-mill reports produced by your team, with all the information accessible to everyone in the team. You decided to acknowledge your team member in front of the entire team – and it backfired. She looked at you in surprise and frowned, and as soon as the meeting was over, she left the room.

What happened?

What happened is that you were not aware of her intrinsic or extrinsic drivers, nor how she would respond to public acknowledgement. This is why it is so important to understand what motivates every one of your team members. This team member happened to be very reserved, and was consequently embarrassed to have been singled out in front of the entire team. It would have been useful to acknowledge her work face-to-face first, and to enquire whether she was happy to be commended during the meeting in front of the entire team. This would have indicated whether she was more motivated by Affiliation than by Achievement or Power. Everyone is motivated differently. Therefore, it is important that you understand each team member's underlying values and intrinsic motivators. That means having regular conversations with them about what is motivating or demotivating them at work.

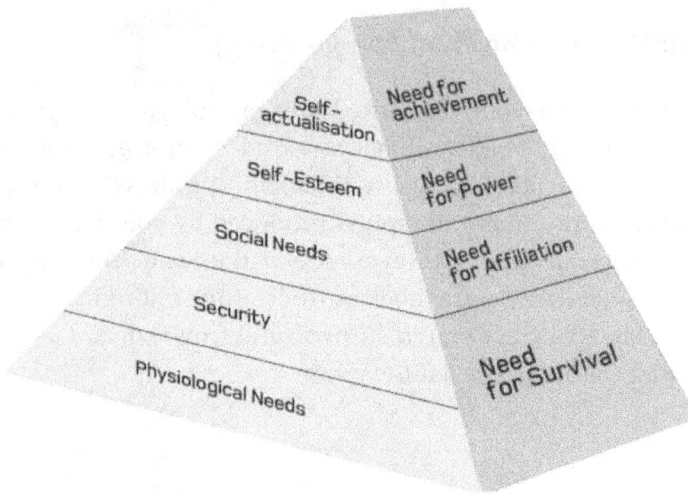

Figure 12: McClelland's Need for Achievement Theory

Source: TutorRoom.[209]

You can use McClelland's theory to help identify what motivates each of your direct reports or members of your team. Determining which motivating factor is dominant for each member of your team can help you to define specific key performance indicators (KPIs) that are in alignment with their needs:

- *Achievement* – If your team member is motivated by achievement, they will be motivated to personally create and accomplish their goals successfully. They will be driven by their intrinsic need to be proud of their work at the end of the day. With an achievement-oriented staff member, they often prefer to work alone, and will need acknowledgement, praise and constructive feedback on their work.

- *Affiliation* – This member of your team will be more motivated while working as part of a team or a group with whom they can share a sense of accomplishment once the project is complete. They need "inclusion" in the team or group, and want to be accepted by the other team members for the work they do. In this day and age where team-work is the norm, an affiliation-driven team member can be cohesive for the team.

- *Power* – This member of your team will be intrinsically motivated by being in charge, and will appreciate any opportunity to be in control or to be the leader. They will thrive in a competitive working environment, and may compete for the position of team leader in a group or a team. This team member wants recognition and praise for taking the team to success.

Activity: Your team

1. Think about all your direct reports and who is motivated by each of the above needs – for achievement, affiliation or power.
2. Make a list of those motivated by achievement, affiliation or power – or all three.
3. Think about what this means in terms of you managing them. What can you do differently from how you have been managing and helping them to maintain their motivation?

Case study: *Managing the new boss*

This is the story of a fairly senior leader-manager, Jacqueline (not her real name), who is one of the General Managers of the IT Division of a large corporate. She was originally head-hunted from another company, and had developed a great relationship with her new boss, who was an excellent role model and had built up good relationships with all of her direct reports. However, Jacqueline has just begun to report to a new boss who is domineering, demanding and uncompromising. He is not used to women debating with him, and has begun to build relationships with all the General Managers except Jacqueline. She is trying hard to work more comfortably with him, but is not winning on this score. She is finding it hard to influence him, has found herself side-lined, and is being given projects far below her level of work.

Activity: Managing the new boss

1. In this study of Jacqueline and her new boss, at what level is Jacqueline motivated (achievement, affiliation or power)?
2. How might Jacqueline work more effectively with her new boss?
3. How does the boss need to change, which will encourage Jacqueline to stay in her current role or even stay in the company?

Herzberg's Motivation / Hygiene Theory

In Maslow's hierarchy, people are more motivated the higher up the ladder they move. Maslow's five needs help us to understand where we are in our life, and the importance of understanding the people who work for us. Frederick Herzberg caused some controversy with his slightly different approach to motivational needs.

Herzberg believed that there are two complementary factors to motivation at work, Motivators and Hygiene Factors. Ideally, both factors need to be satisfied.[210]

Herzberg recognised that the "Motivators" or "Satisfiers" are the factors that can actually motivate people. On the opposite side of the coin are Herzberg's "Hygiene Factors" or "Dissatisfiers". The Hygiene Factors don't motivate, but they can demotivate if they are not right. However, both Hygiene Factors and Motivators need to be in place for motivation to happen. And money is only a short-term motivator! When was your last pay rise – and are you still motivated by it? People respond in different ways to both work content and the working environment. Herzberg said that satisfaction and dissatisfaction are not on the same continuum, and are therefore not opposites.

The first factors are the Motivators or Satisfiers, such as:

- sufficient job interest;
- personal achievement;
- recognition and acknowledgement;
- responsibility and accountability;
- work and job satisfaction (including pleasure in the work itself);
- advancement or promotion opportunities; and
- possibility of personal and professional growth.[211]

The second factors are the Dissatisfiers or Hygiene (environmental) factors, such as:

- conditions of work;
- company policies, administration and bureaucracy;
- suffocating management or over-supervision;
- salary concerns;
- interpersonal relationship problems;
- concerns about job security; and
- inadequate personal status in the role.[212]

Activity: You and your team

1. Identify the motivators or satisfiers that keep you in your job.

2. Identify the hygiene factors that are negatively impacting your motivation to be the best you can be as a manager or people.

3. Which of the two sets of factors are motivating or demotivating your direct reports?

According to Herzberg, both Motivators and Hygiene Factors need to be in place for motivation to happen. Some people say that they are "simply in the job for the money". But if they are given low-quality work with little challenge or recognition, they are more likely to be demotivated.[213] As a leader-manager, you can have the most influence working with the top list, the Motivators. The second list, the Hygiene Factors, will help you only to maintain the *status quo* – they will not tap into intrinsic or extrinsic drivers.

Ways to motivate are to listen, give people feedback, set an example, and be an exemplary role model. Also, use open appraisal systems, communicate with your team throughout the year, have regular team meetings and team briefings, and talk to your staff about what can be realistically achieved. Finally, sandwich discipline between layers of praise, and always leave your staff members on a high note – including discussing how they can improve, and particularly how they can help themselves.

Activity: How motivated are your staff?

Think of each member of your team individually. For each one, write down whether they are motivated or not, and give at least one reason why. Using your instinct and your judgement you can identify some of the signs of both poor and healthy motivation.

Name	Motivated? (Y/N)	Why?
1.		
2.		
3.		
4.		
5.		
6.		

7.		
8.		
9.		
10.		

Self-Determination Theory

Good leaders motivate people by giving them valuable and interesting work. This section examines the psychology of goals and motivation, and explores new thinking about setting goals and motivation.

Edward Deci and Richard Ryan are the creators of Self-Determination Theory[214] which is an internationally researched theory of human motivation, personality development, and wellbeing. Self-Determination Theory is a theory of motivation concerned with supporting our natural or intrinsic tendencies to behave in effective and healthy ways. "To be self-determined is to endorse one's actions at the highest level of reflection. Self-determined people experience a sense of freedom to do what is interesting, personally important and vitalising".[215] Deci and Ryan[216] expanded on their earlier work, differentiating intrinsic from extrinsic motivation, and proposing three main intrinsic needs involved in self-determination: autonomy, competence and relatedness.

Volitional motivation and wellbeing as basic needs

Ryan[217] talks about the basic psychological needs which underpin volitional motivation and wellbeing. He says that our most basic list of nutrients includes *autonomy*, *competence* and *relatedness*, and that these three things lead to volitional motivation and wellbeing, as follows:

- *Autonomy* supports volition. According to Ryan, autonomy is when behaviour is in alignment with the individual's values and interests, and that individual's actions at work are self-endorsed, and are congruent with implicit and explicit motives. If you have autonomy, you want to do your work, and you believe in what you are doing. Autonomy is not about independence, individualism or self-interest, but is instead an endorsement of them. Autonomy means that your actions and behaviour are self-endorsed, and in alignment with your values and interests.

- *Competence* is about controlling the outcome and experiencing mastery. Competence supports structure and positive feedback and means that you have a sense of effectiveness and competence within your working context.

- *Relatedness* is the collective wish to interact with others, to be connected to others, and to experience caring for others. Relatedness supports inclusion, empathy and care. It also means feeling cared for, connected to, and having a sense of belonging with others.[218]

If deprived of any one of these conditions, people will probably go downhill. But when people experience all three of these basic needs, they will be optimally motivated at work. In other words, when people are satisfied at work – and these three basic needs are activated – they will thrive. If this is critical, then leaders need to have the relational skills to motivate followers using autonomy, competence and relatedness.[219]

Ryan talks about how these conditions facilitate intrinsic motivation:

- *Autonomy* means there is an absence of pressure, and there is individual goal choice, choice of strategy, involvement and interest in the task.

- *Competence* means there is optimal challenge, with positive feedback and rewards.

- *Relatedness* means there is empathy and warmth which acknowledges the individual's emotions.[220]

However, certain aspects of these conditions can also undermine intrinsic motivation:

- *Autonomy* is undermined by pressure toward outcomes, punishment contingencies, goal imposition, deadlines, controlling rewards, ego involvement, and surveillance.

- *Competence* is undermined by non-optimal challenges and negative feedback.

- *Relatedness* is undermined by lack of collective interaction and positive involvement, and even watching somebody closely.[221]

Ryan[222] explains that autonomy supports minimal external pressure and provides maximum choice, and the internal frame of reference is shared; competence supports optimal challenge, and the development of appropriate demands with relevant feedback; and relatedness supports warmth and involvement which conveys belongingness. The more aware a manager is, the more likely they will create these three conditions for people. Ryan discusses the following behaviours that are useful to managers to support these three conditions of motivation:

- *Autonomy-supportive environments*:
    - understand the other's perspective;

- encourage self-initiation and self-reflection;

- offer meaningful choices;

- provide a rationale for requested behaviour; and

- minimise use of controlling language or rewards.

- *Competence-supportive environments*:

- design activities so that mastery is the dominant experience;

- provide enough structure for active development;

- give informational feedback rather than controlling feedback; and

- focus praise on effort and specific accomplishments – not on ability or comparisons.

- *Relatedness-supportive environments*:

- convey respect for the individual;

- ensure the individual feels valued and significant;

- offer care and concern when facing challenges;

- radiate warmth; and

- let the individual know that their boss likes them.[223]

Activity: How are you impacting the workplace?

- As a leader-manager, in what way do you embody each of these three conditions of *autonomy*, *competence* and *relatedness* in the way that you lead and manage your staff or team?

- In what areas can you improve?

- What will you do differently going forward?

Key motivating questions for you as leader-manager and your team

Having explored the major important theories of motivation, please find below a rich array of questions which emerge from these theories, that will help you and your team reports to be aware of what is motivating and demotivating for both you and them. Use these in your one-on-one sessions with your direct reports, and create a bookmark for your team members.

Leading and managing people

- What is your purpose as a leader-manager?

- What perspectives inform your work as a leader and a manager (cultural background, education, work and career experience, family life, spiritual life, relationships)?

- How does your team and the organisation experience you? What do you need to change?

- In team coaching workshops or in your coaching sessions, are you asking your team members to share their stories – of their lives, their learnings, their failures and their successes?

- What style of management do you work with – an authoritarian management style (X) relying on coercion and threat, or a management style (Y) that assumes people are self- motivated and can exercise self-control?

- How would you describe your collective engagement with people in the workplace (relatedness)?

- What keeps you connected and engaged with others?

- What is your impact on your workplace – and how does that influence your own self-motivation?

- How are you holding yourself accountable?

- How are you developing accountability in others?

Motivation, behaviour and demotivation

- What are your levels of motivation based on the time and energy you are willing to invest in yourself?

- Is your behaviour in alignment with your own values and interests (autonomy)?

- How has your own behaviour changed when you have been motivated?

- What are your top five motivators?

- What are your top five demotivators?

- What are the higher-order needs (see McGregor's Theory X and Y) that will motivate their creativity, willingness to learn and to create a sense of belonging?

- What are the motivators or satisfiers that keep you in your job?

- Which factors are negatively impacting your ability to be the best manager that you can be?

- What drives your own level of motivation and those of your team – achievement, affiliation, power, autonomy, competence or relatedness?

- Your direct reports – what happens to your and their behaviour when they are not motivated?

- What extrinsic motivators are alive and well in your own organisation – and do they work?

- What are the lower-order needs (see McGregor's Theory X and Y) that people in your workforce need to be met in order to stay in their job?

- Where do you most need to work to increase your levels of motivation and those of others?

Goals and values

- Are your goals in alignment with your own individual values, beliefs and feelings?

- Are your goals in alignment with the values and goals of your organisation?

- How does your work tap into your passion for life itself, and for who you want to become?

- What are your short-term, medium-term, and long-term goals – and how are you using them as motivators?

- Of all the values that most matter to you, which are most important in your professional life?

- Which values do you leave at home that you could use at work? And which values do you leave at work that you could use at home?

- What challenging step do you want to take in your life right now?

- What are you assuming that is stopping you from achieving that challenging step?

- What would you have to credibly assume instead in order to take that challenging step?

- What drives each member of your team or ExCo from the inside? Identify that as a value rather than as a goal – in other words, it is intangible and cannot be measured.

Learning to develop mastery

- What are your leadership capabilities and what skills, knowledge and competence do you need to develop?

- How are you continually applying your new skills in your professional life?

- What gives you a sense of experiencing mastery, and how do you continue to build your competence?

- How do you celebrate achievement, mastery and new learning?

- Learning from experience:

  - What's working for you personally and professionally?

  - What, if anything, is not working for you?

  - What might you do, think or feel differently to create change or make a shift?

- Continually developing insight into the areas you need to develop:

  - What are you doing to develop a deep understanding of yourself – as well as understanding how others experience you – and how would you articulate who you are right now, as a manager, as a leader, as a human being?

  - Who do you want to step into becoming in your life in this world – and how will that create a shift in you and in those you are leading and managing?

Working with intrinsic and extrinsic motivation

The Motivation Model below looks at intrinsic motivation (being driven from something inside of you) versus extrinsic motivation (being motivated from something outside of you). Although they are the two main categories of motivation, intrinsic being driven by internal reward, and extrinsic driven by external reward, there exist many different types of motivation within each category.

Other types of intrinsic motivation are competence and learning motivation, attitude motivation, achievement motivation, creative motivation, physiological motivation. Other types of extrinsic motivation are incentive motivation, fear motivation, power motivation, and affiliation and social motivation.[224] All are useful in business.

Although we need both types of motivation, intrinsic motivation tends to be the more sustainable, as it focuses on the positive and things you can control. Extrinsic motivation focuses on what is given to you by another, and is not directly within your control. Both types of motivation can be negative if they are motivating you out of fear or punishment. Leaders can access another person's internal motivation through external motivators if they understand the values driving that person and understand what most matters to them. External motivators can then be used to tap into those internal motivators.

If an individual clearly understands what drives them internally, they can easily adapt external motivators to become part of their own internal satisfaction. Internal motivation comes from doing what you are passionate about, and that sense of feeling satisfied or proud knowing you have done something well. Extrinsic motivators can, however, be used to give you internal momentum. If you want to understand what drives someone, find out what are their underlying values and what matters most to them. Just be careful you do not confuse the two. For someone who is internally motivated, they might not always need an external motivator. Too many motivators can get in the way. It is important to understand what are the individual's underlying values, and what makes them strive to do their best.

Motivation underpins purposeful behaviour, and can be useful in understanding behaviour change and in moving between adaptive or maladaptive outcomes. Self-determination theory proposes motivation to be multi-dimensional.[225, 226] This starts on a continuum of self-determination which includes amotivation (when an individual lacks the motivation to act), to extrinsic motivation (when a person acts to attain separable outcomes), through to intrinsic motivation (when a person acts for their own interest inherent in a particular activity). There are four types of external regulation which vary according to how self-determined the individual is. From the least to the most self-determined are:[227]

1. External regulation: acting to avoid punishment or gain rewards.

2. Introjected regulation: acting to avoid feeling guilty, or to obtain contingent self-worth.

3. Identified regulation: acting because it feels personally important.

4. Integrated regulation: behaviours that contribute to defining who one is.

Beyond childhood, it is argued that the majority of our behaviours are extrinsically motivated as few activities are taken solely for pleasure.[228, 229] However, extrinsic motivation can still result in positive outcomes if the motivation is more towards the self-determined end of the continuum, which tends to be self-endorsed; and if the behaviour is considered to be personally valued and meaningful. Becoming more self-determined in your behaviour and actions is called *internalisation*.[230, 231]

Intrinsic motivation

This refers to motivation that comes from inside of you, and is a result of your values either being in alignment with the action to be taken, or a personal satisfaction of achievement. For example, being recognised for something worked hard for, or alignment with your sense of helping others. For example, mentoring a colleague to help them succeed at something, or simply managing a difficult challenge that no one else has dealt with successfully before.

Extrinsic motivation

This involves an external motivator to encourage an individual to behave or take action in a particular way. External influences can be salary increases, promotions, company cars, prizes, incentives, or more holiday or vacation time. The downside is that this can lead to expectations for consistent rewards. Also, if extrinsic rewards do not tap into internal motivators, those rewards remain meaningless.

Introjected motivation (external regulation)

Introjected motivation accompanies high levels of self-determination. This can be related to social factors such as social disapproval or the need for ego enhancement. For example, to strive to maintain approval by peers which leads to self-worth. This is valuable because it leads to personally meaningful and important goals, and the internalisation of external regulation.[232] Introjected motivation can also be about avoidance. For example, being bullied, manipulated or managing a passive-aggressive boss or colleague, which means the individual is internally motivated to either avoid that person because they receive negative feedback, or to avoid the other person's challenging behaviour. This type of motivation can lead to inaction and anxiety.[233] Introjected motivation is more controlling when behaviour is regulated either by internal sanctions, and/or pressures directed towards gaining feelings of self-worth and ego enhancement, or avoiding punishment (e.g. feelings of guilt, shame or anxiety).[234]

Identified motivation (acting because it feels important)

This is when an individual feels the need to take part in or seek to achieve some form of activity or task from something they are spurred to do. This type of motivation is from the perceived importance of the activity. For example, being told that you only have a specific period of time to live if you do not give up drinking and smoking or adopt a more balanced diet and lifestyle. Or taking more exercise due to its perceived importance for your own personal health. Any one of those might spur someone to action. But this type of motivation means that something outside of them spurs them to action, often out of fear.[235]

Four motivation archetypes

See the four-quadrant model in Figure 13 outlining four archetypes, to help understand your team members in terms of intrinsic and extrinsic motivation.

	High intrinsic motivation	Low intrinsic motivation
High extrinsic motivation	Drivers	Followers
Low extrinsic motivation	Survivalists	Foot soldiers

Figure 13: Four-quadrant Motivation Model

The four archetypes positioned within the Motivation Model in Figure 13 can be explained as follows:

- *Drivers* have a strong inner desire and determination to succeed, with high internal and external motivation. Drivers are highly motivated, determined, ambitious, self-starters and very motivated. The benefits of being self-motivated are that they often have vision, are willing to overcome negative influences, tend to be more positive and open when engaging with others, and try to avoid petty differences with people. They are seen as competent, usually thrive in situations where they have autonomy, and can be driven to build relationships to succeed. As they are internally and externally motivated, they try to align their underlying values and intrinsic motivators with their external motivators.

- *Followers* are not internally highly motivated, but they are motivated to align themselves to a leader and to show their competence for that leader. The stimulus for their motivation is to align themselves to a leader who will guide them through the organisational labyrinth and ensure their success in some way. They can bathe in the success of their leader without necessarily showing any need for autonomy themselves. Their goal is not necessarily self-actualisation, but more safe passage to stay in their role or move up with the leader. They will build relationships with those who will keep them safe in their corner. External motivation is useful to persuade them to take on a role or complete a job. This means the decision making is often made by the external motivator.

- *Survivalists* are not about being passionately motivated to take action to achieve their goals, but are doing something to survive within their current role. They have high internal motivation for self-protection and survival. For example, they might take on a job or task simply to keep their job, but they won't go all out to do their utmost best. They will do it so that they survive and look as if they have done what was necessary to their superiors. But they may have frustrated their colleagues. This doesn't build good engagement or good relationships, but can ultimately keep some kind of engagement in place.

- *Foot soldiers* can be seen as apathetic, indifferent and unenterprising, and others may assume that they are undependable, unconcerned about others, without purpose and not thoughtful about others. Although both motivations are low, they will always find a way round the problem, even if taking action only at the very last minute. It means doing something not for the sake of inner fulfilment, nor even to gain something positive such as a reward, but instead to avoid a punishment or simply to keep their job. This can be damaging to relationships. It may mean that it takes time for an external motivator to move them to action. They are typically not seen as particularly competent, pursuing autonomy, highly engaged, or motivated to build relationships.

Conclusion

One of the primary roles of a leader-manager is to motivate and inspire their individual team members and the team as a whole. However, it is difficult to do so until you understand what actually motivates you first. What are those values, beliefs and feelings that inspire you to step up the pace when needed, to get on with a difficult job, to handle difficult people as those situations arise?

Once you understand yourself, you can begin to try to understand those you lead and manage. This means you need to understand your people at a deeper level – what are their drivers, internal and external, and how can you tap into those? Most organisations throw external, or extrinsic motivators at people, without understanding what are their people's internal, or intrinsic motivators, that if tapped into would lead to heights at which even they might be surprised. Understanding motivation in all of its component parts will help you to deepen your awareness of yourself and others and help you to become the leader-manager you want to be.

Chapter 9

Managing people: Coaching, mentoring and goal setting

Part of motivation includes goal setting, which is a very important part of building your succession pipeline. Not only is it important to understand how to create a SMART goal, but also to have a goal-setting model to work with when developing your team members. GROW is an excellent tool to coach your team, and for them to use to develop their own direct reports. This is a very practical section that not only helps you to think about your own goals, but also uses a real coaching session to highlight how to work with GROW. Leader-managers, however, need to be able to both coach and mentor their direct reports, which means understanding the difference between the two, and having some training in both. It is also important to remember that mentoring in Africa has always been a way to develop young leaders.

Mentoring: a domain-specific expertise

Mentoring and coaching are often confused, although they involve very different approaches. The role of a mentor is to directly share their experience, expertise, advice and wisdom with the "mentee"; to support the "mentee's" learning and development; and to introduce the "mentee" to their network. One of the key differences between mentoring and coaching is that in mentoring it is acceptable for the mentor to share advice and expertise regarding their previous handling of a situation – while this is not commonly accepted in best-practice coaching. Also, coaches work with a coaching process that has adult learning and experiential learning as its foundation, and most coach education programmes worldwide support the view that the coach's job is to help the client or team member to think through situations in terms of their own thinking, feeling and behaviour – not the coach's thinking, feeling and behaviour.

When combined with appropriate training programmes or qualifications in specialised competences, mentoring can be a particularly useful form of support for younger managers learning the ropes. Mentoring is often domain-specific, the mentor working either within the organisation and introducing the mentee to the politics and machinations of that organisation; or the mentor, working within the same field as the mentee, introduces the mentee to their network and professional bodies, which can be very important.

Until recently, with the explosion of technological media, it was accepted that the role of mentor needed to be fulfilled by an older person with greater experience in the same industry and job type as the younger mentee. Today, some mentors are a generation younger than those they are mentoring due to their specific technical expertise. Domain-specific expertise and experience therefore need to be carefully matched between the two parties if mentoring is to work – in addition to compatibility or "chemistry", mutual respect and trust on a personal level. Because today some of the elder, wiser professionals in the business community are being mentored by the younger, technically smarter and more adept newcomers into the workplace, this brings a new challenge to mentoring across every industry.

Within the organisation, mentors focus on the development of the learner, and convey knowledge of organisational values and routines, plus the managerial system, thus helping the mentee to navigate the organisation's political system. Mentoring is personalised and domain-specific, and creates an atmosphere in which to acknowledge and recognise people.[236]

The business coaching process

Coaching tends to be more goal-directed, working within or towards an overall development plan. We see the business coaching process as one that helps business leader-managers to develop a clear understanding of their roles and responsibilities. Business coaching, like sports coaching, is about high performance, and is ultimately about sustained behavioural change and breakthrough results. The coaching conversation provides a "thinking environment" where business professionals are able to develop self-awareness and a depth of understanding of themselves and others – embedding newly-acquired skills, competences and attitudes which subsequently impact the actions they take, visibly demonstrating new behaviours.

We define coaching as "a process that creates sustained shifts in thinking, feeling and behaviour – and ultimately in performance. By asking the right questions, coaches help clients find their own solutions". Cavanagh and Grant[237] define coaching as a "solution-focused, results-oriented systematic process in which the coach facilitates the enhancement of performance, self-directed learning and personal growth of other individuals". The AMA/Institute for Corporate Productivity defines coaching as: "a short- to medium-term relationship between a manager or senior leader, and a consultant (internal or external) with the purpose of improving work performance".[238]

It has been challenging to find one authoritative definition of coaching in the marketplace, not just because every professional body has its own slant on the coaching process, but because there is no agreed global definition available. So what do business coaches do? The critical value of business coaching is in helping the individual manager to think clearly about the core issues which present challenges to them in their job, career and daily working life. Coaching is unique, helping individuals to systematise their conscious thoughts about the immediate actions needed to address specific practical issues, and to understand the unconscious processes that may be sabotaging their success.[239]

In our own practice, when we coach, we utilise a "blank page" approach. This means that, rather than "talk at" an executive, we listen actively with an open mind in order to explore fresh and exciting future possibilities. We ask incisive questions that unblock difficult and challenging issues. An individual's past is viewed as an indicator of their decision making and experience, rather than an excuse for pathological labelling.

Creating a development plan with goals

To ensure that coaching achieves the intended results, it is useful to create a development plan with the team member's overall purpose, strategy, developmental objectives, developmental actions, strengths, areas for improvement and obstacles to achievement. As a leader-manager you will want to ensure that your goal-setting conversations get the best results. Mary Beth O'Neill[240] differentiates between business goals and personal goals, and links the coaching effort to a business result by highlighting and prioritising the business areas that need attention. Business goals are about achieving visible external results in the work place; personal goals are less visible, and reflect growing self-awareness and an understanding of what the team member has to do differently in how they conduct themselves to get business results.[241]

Setting SMART objectives

SMART objectives are goals that are designed to be **s**pecific, **m**easurable, **a**chievable, **r**ealistic and **t**ime-bound. This may include process goals such as setting a budget, or end goals such as the launch of a new product or service:

- *Specific* – Noticeably clear and concise explanation of the task, broken down into manageable steps or chunks.

- *Measurable* – Time, quality, quantity, and cost. Must have at least two criteria to be an action objective.

- *Achievable* – Yet challenging. Staff must be able to complete a task, otherwise they will feel demotivated and unwilling to try a similar task again. The more staff achieve, the more you can develop the team and the team members.

- *Realistic* – Yet challenging. Even when you select the right people for objectives and tasks, they must be given help from time to time. For example, this might mean re-prioritising their existing workload or giving them additional training.

- *Time-bound* – Goals are unlikely to be achieved if there is no time limit to them, and they are achieved only if, within a team, there is a champion for that particular goal. Also, goals can be set as overarching goals to be achieved, with sub-goals which are the steps to move towards that end outcome.

Activity: Setting objectives

1. What is the purpose and what are the objectives of your company or organisation?

2. What are the overarching objectives of your division or team?

3. Are they specific, measurable, achievable, realistic, time-bound, clear, written, challenging, agreed, consistent, worthwhile, and participative?

4. Choose one overarching goal, and set the steps to achieving it against the factors in Item 3 above.

Activity: Short-term and long-term goals

1. What are your current business or job goals?

2. What are your short-term career goals?

3. What are your long-term career goals?

4. What are your short-term personal life goals?

5. What are your long-term personal life goals?

Working with the GROW Model

John Whitmore[242] developed the GROW model as an excellent goal-setting process for managers and coaches alike. GROW is a metaphor for the growth which you hope your staff or team members will experience when you are coaching or mentoring them. It uses a goal-setting framework of questions that hopefully leads to awareness, responsibility and change. GROW can be used as a goal-setting process: identifying a goal, discussing the team member's current reality, exploring their options, and summarising outcomes and what they will actually do differently.

John Whitmore's GROW model is a basic four-stage coaching process which easily structures a goal-setting session, and adds greater depth to the coaching conversation. It is useful for you to develop a coaching approach as a manager, learning to understand the importance of structure, deep listening, and how to ask questions. Although it is primarily a goal-setting tool, it can be used in many different formats. The essence of Whitmore's four-stage question framework is "to unlock a person's potential to maximise their own performance".[243] It is helping them to learn rather than teaching them:

1. Stage One: What is your _Goal_?

2. Stage Two: What is the _Reality_?

3. Stage Three: What are your _Options_?

4. Stage Four: _What_ will you do?

Although some master coaches and senior managers think the GROW model seems simplistic, its importance derives from the fact that Whitmore identified three essential concerns of coaching: developing self-awareness, taking responsibility for learning, and the use of questions as the coach's primary tool. The questions that can be used in each of the four stages are useful, not just for setting goals, but also for developing an understanding of the very basics of a coaching question framework. Whitmore's rationale behind the GROW model is fundamental: to build awareness and responsibility in the team member. Using this model can ensure that the individual is kept very focused on their goal.

Stage One: What is your _Goal_?

Outline the team member's key goals for the year, their overarching goals, and then the goal for this particular coaching conversation. GROW is about working with the elimination of external and internal obstacles to goal achievement. Furthermore, help the team member to identify the type of goal they wish to work with: i.e. performance goal, end goal, dream goal:[244]

•   What would you like to get out of this session?

•   Where do you want to be by the end of our time together?

•   What would be the most helpful thing for you to take back into the workplace?

Stage Two: What is the _Reality_?

Here the manager invites the team member to tell their story as it relates to this goal. The manager should invite self-assessment, and the question could be,

"What is happening for you right now as it relates to this goal?" At this point, the manager may take the team member back to redefine the goal if it is not specific enough, then carry on to clarify the current situation. Whitmore suggests the reality questions provide the most straightforward means of self-assessment. He suggests rarely using "how" and "why" because they invite analysis and opinion. Although he suggests that asking "why" invites defensiveness and keeps the individual in the conscious thinking process, there are times when "why" is the right question. Whitmore[245] suggests that current reality questions emphasise the value of action and the difference between action and thinking:

- What action have you taken on so far?
- What were the effects of that action?
- What are the internal obstacles?
- What are the internal blocks?
- What are the external obstacles?
- What assumptions could be limiting your thinking?

Stage Three: What are your Options?

This focuses on what the individual could do. It will encompass possible action plans and strategies, a development of some alternative perspectives, and brainstorming options. What could the team member do, moving from realistic to fantastic thinking? The options stage of GROW is not about finding the right answer; it is about creating as many courses of action as possible. Whitmore focuses on what he calls "implicit assumptions" that people carry around with them. Nancy Kline has a different way of working with assumptions, which tend to be positive or negative assumptions about "self" and "how life works" (see Chapter 7). Some examples of implicit assumptions as Whitmore identifies them also tend to be, "I/we can or cannot", "they will or will not let us):

- I can't do it (self).
- We've never done it like that before (self/us).
- I will never get permission to do it like that (how life works).
- They won't give me the budget to spend (how life works).
- No one in the team has the time to fix it (self/us).
- I expect the competition have already thought of it (how life works).

The options phase aims to move the individual from finding reasons why not to do something, and to transform that into a credible liberating assumption allowing them to move on. This phase encourages the brainstorming of options without judgement, and transforming assumptions into helping them to achieve. It is important to help the coachee to think about what might be a credible liberating alternative that would open the doors of possibility. Some alternative questions for the options phase are:

- What if you had a large enough budget?

- What if you had more staff?

- If you knew the answer, what would it be?

- If you knew how to do it, what would you do?

- What if that obstacle did not exist – what would you do then?

- What do you really want?

- What are all the different things you could do to achieve it?

- What have you not yet thought of?

- What are you willing to commit yourself to?

- What are the advantages and disadvantages?

Stage Four: What <u>Will</u> you do?

This refers to what the team member or direct report will do. What did they learn? What are they going to do differently? What can they change? This stage involves the practical, i.e. summing up and writing down of the action steps to be taken to achieve the goal. It moves the individual into decision mode with precision and detailed timelines.[246] It is about "will" – what *will* they do? Hence the questions:

- What are you going to do?

- When are you going to do it?

- Will this action meet your goal?

- Which obstacles might you meet along the way?

- Who needs to know?

- What support do you need?

- How and when are you going to get that support?

- What other considerations do you have?

- Rate the percentage of certainty you have that you will carry out the actions as agreed.

GROW Model coaching session

One of the primary roles of a leader-manager is to develop direct reports and team members through coaching and mentoring in the workplace.

Below is a coaching session with one of my clients, Zack (not his real name), working with John Whitmore's GROW model at my client's request. I have trimmed back the conversation, taking out extraneous comments and leaving in only what is relevant for each of the four sections: Goal, Reality, Options and Will. I have changed my client's name for reasons of confidentiality. He is a leadership consultant working with a range of organisations across the globe.

Step One: What is your Goal for this session?

S: What would you like to work on today?

Z: I would like to use the GROW Model to explore something I've been thinking about for years – relocating my business from Johannesburg to Cape Town. I want to talk it through, because it's difficult thinking it through on my own. I go round in circles, and am struggling to make a firm decision. Will the Grow Model work for this?

S: Yes, absolutely. We can spend some time creating the *Goal* and getting it right. We'll look at where you are now, and the context in which you are working – that would be your *Current Reality* – and we will identify what your motivations are for moving the business to Cape Town, and what assumptions you are making that are empowering or disempowering you. From there we can brainstorm your possible *Options*, and you can then think through what you *Will* do.

Z: Sounds great.

S: How would you frame the way you're thinking about this move? Think in terms of a goal and the context for that.

Z: The issue is around whether I move the business to Cape Town to be based there, and what are the implications of that. Things are pushing me in that direction. My daughter is going to move overseas next week, and she will no longer be with me. Also, the COVID situation has stimulated my thinking, because it's proved we can work from anywhere. I've seen only four or five clients face-to-face in the last 18 months, and the business has grown reasonably well during that time despite the pandemic.

My sense is that it doesn't really matter where I operate from, and that it might be a good time to move. Of course, my business partner is down in Cape Town. We have trial-run quite a few two-day team coaching sessions with big teams, and it has worked well with us physically together but working online with the team. It seems like it should work, but something is making me hesitate.

S: How would you like to frame this as a goal, quite specifically, so that we can work on it? Because moving the business to Cape Town includes a lot of things.

Z: I wonder if the goal is to make a decision about moving? To move the business to Cape Town next year, starting with a six-month trial period from 1 January, and see how it goes and track the movement from there. I don't want to be under pressure with a date for moving. Making it a year of transition will let me see how it goes.

S: So, you said, 'I would like to move the business to Cape Town during 2022 starting with a six-month trial period from 1 January.'

Z: That's it.

Step Two: What is your current **Reality**?

S: That's the fastest we have ever created a goal – it took 45 minutes last time. You are getting better at it! In fact, you've been thinking about this for a long time; but you said that if you just think about it, you won't take any action. Let's look at the current reality, and your motivations and assumptions. Tell me about the context now – what you want and why.

Z: Health, wellbeing and mental wellness are the biggest considerations. I'm in my 60s now, but I am not ready to hang up my boots. Health-wise, I feel better than I have felt for ages, but my frustration levels are very high. Jo'burg is quite a wild city, not the place where you think of resting and relaxing. I would like a better quality of life. So, there is a concern around the stress levels in Jo'burg. I have lived here happily, made a lot of friends and most of my business contacts are here. It's an OK city, but I am from the Cape and I need the sea. Two of my siblings live in Cape Town, my business partner is there, and it is a more relaxed city – although they drive like crazy! If I made the decision, I could make it work. The more I procrastinate, the more daunting it becomes.

S: So, you have concerns about health, wellness, and wellbeing. You are from Cape Town, but moving back there is daunting, and by procrastinating it becomes more daunting. Tell me more about the procrastination, what's daunting, and why you need courage.

Z: I'd like to think I am a high-risk-taking individual, but deep down I need a lot of certainty before I make a move like this. Also, I lack the detail orientation to look at the pro's and con's. I am a spur-of-the-moment kind of guy. I make decisions, do it and then think about it. The daunting-ness is that if I lose the business, I lose everything. I would rather keep the revenue and live in Jo'burg than have the lifestyle but struggle to make ends meet.

S: Can I ask a questions about that assumption, that if you lose the business you lose everything?

Z: Sure.

S: Do you think it is true or possibly true, and if so what are your reasons for thinking so?

Z: Yes I think it is true. The reason is that everything I am is in my business, and everything is invested in the IP in the business. I don't know what I would do if I lost it all. However, on the other hand, there is a pipeline of work, it doesn't matter where I live. No one needs to know unless clients need to pay for the flight. My business partner does well in Cape Town, and there is definitely more we can tap into. There is retail clothing, petroleum, insurance, hospitality, and a population of coaches in Cape Town, and I don't see them walking on the beaches in long beards and sackcloth. That is the risk: can I sustain the business? If I had gone to Cape Town last year, COVID would have made little difference. But I need more certainty.

S: Okay. So it's possible that you will not lose everything, but you say very clearly that you want certainty. Do you remember what Nancy Kline says, that certainty is a myth! But the other question is, instead of worrying about losing everything, what is it that you need to think about in terms of how you source your business? What I heard you say was that your business is everything to you. You also said there is business in Cape Town, although we both know Jo'burg is currently a hub for commerce. Where do you source your business now, and what would happen if you were living in another city?

Z: My work comes to me via existing clients and word of mouth. I have a few big clients who constantly give me work, and they inform other people about my services, and I get other work that way. I don't blog, I don't market. I get everything via a phone call saying 'Can you help us, please?' Most people ask me, 'Are you in Cape Town?', because they think I live there. During lockdown I have had only a couple of face-to-face meetings with people. I had dinner with a CEO the other night – but that is a rare occasion. So, how do I source my work and be different? I do want also to build an online business, which would be global. It doesn't matter where people are, they should be able to access the website and my services. That's been on the back-burner for a year. My business partner and I have a very niche business. The business needs to move online anyway, and in fact I have a new website design for it, offering training programmes and consultations. I have subconsciously started moving in that direction; I'm almost talking myself into it.

S: That raises other questions. What impact will the online business have on your work with teams and leadership? Maybe that is a question you cannot answer now.

Z: My sense is that we will keep our existing clients and programmes – there is massive opportunity to tap into or leverage off our current clients in Cape Town and Jo'burg. The other arm of my business will be to sell online courses. It just makes sense.

S: Shall we continue with context and current reality before we look at options?

Z: Yeah.

S: Great. So what would keep you in Jo'burg? In other words, what would have to be there for you to stay?

Z: I would need to have a signature client who needs me – that could be reason enough to stay. The other reason is my daughter, but she is moving overseas next week. For the first time in my life, I can do whatever I like – neither of those reasons has materialised.

S: How likely is it in SA that a client would say they need you to stay in Jo'burg?

Z: Not likely, and anyway most people ask 'When are you coming up to Jo'burg?'

S: You've said you work online mostly. Tell me how you operate. You were talking about going to Jo'burg once a month. How do you communicate with your clients? Do you see them face-to-face, and would that stop you from going to Cape Town?

Z: I am not seeing people every week; 60% to 80% of my work is online coaching and speaking to clients. Every week I spend half a day reaching out to existing clients to see how they are doing. The revenue-generating work is all online. Face-to-face work is less than 10%. I do socialise a lot. During the pandemic I realised a lot of my colleagues were going through trauma, and I became the go-to counsellor for people who needed a sense of comfort. It's also a sense of our collegiality that having time with people has helped me grow cognitively.

It's quite encouraging – not something I do a lot of the time!

S: Would that keep you from moving?

Z: No, it's not a reason to stay here. Not at all.

S: So, the other thing is – you said you're a very sociable person. Do you think you will be less sociable when you are in Cape Town?

Z: No. It's the first thing I do in Cape Town, socialise.

S: Does that mean there isn't anything concrete that will hold you to Jo'burg?

Z: No. I do like the vibe and pace of the city, but I'm not frustrated when I go to Cape Town. I just worry that I might take my foot off the acceleration.

S: What would make you take your foot off the accelerator?

Z: Because my family are there, and retired, and they want to constantly take me on wine farm visits. There is nothing emotional that keeps me in Jo'burg – just my daughter. And I am moving a developing online business; if that is successful I will do 90% of my work online.

S: We seem to have talked about quite a few of your assumptions and clarified that they needn't hold you back. A signature client in Jo'burg would not need you to stay in Jo'burg; you sometimes see clients face-to-face, but that is only 10% of the time, and not something to keep you from going to Cape Town; and you needn't take your foot of the accelerator as most of the business in online?

Z: That sounds right.

Step Three: What are your Options?

S: I'm not hearing that there's anything tying you down. So, is it a possibility to move to Cape Town. If so, shall we look at your Options? We have already worked through your goal and current reality. Shall we just brainstorm and explore all the possibilities?

Z: My objective is that I trial it in January, and ease myself out of my place here and look for a place down there. That's one option. I can just plunge in and do it and start working from down there. I might be more productive there; I think better there.

S: What are the other options?

Z: I could have two places – one in each city. I could get a tiny place here to keep going – a little bedsitter. And I would be only one flight or a two-day drive away. I can have both places operating – it's a business expense. That's the low-risk option – but my sense is that it is a weak action. I need to commit to it and make it work. Those are the two main options. Commit fully or halfway, and by the middle of next year let the Jo'burg place go.

S: What are the options with your business partner in Cape Town – how is that useful to you?

Z: I think it would be useful because we could plan more regular time together to create new work, systems and new products. Also, it's always easier if people are close by – family, and my business partner – and the emotional support would certainly be there.

S: You said you did quite a lot of team coaching together online, and that it worked really well?

Z: Yes, as I am in Jo'burg and he is in Cape Town usually. But I decided to fly down so we could facilitate the sessions physically in the same room; it is very tough to co-facilitate separately. We ran those well, with executive groups in large companies, and the feedback was really positive. That proved to me we can do a lot together from Cape Town.

Step Four: What Will you do?

S: OK, those are two big options with a third area of support in Cape Town. You are talking about hanging onto your unit in Jo'burg till next year. Let's talk about what you will do. What is it you think you need to do to start to put this into place?

Z: I think it would fit more comfortably if I had a discussion with my business partner about the possibilities for work, looking at our shared network and how to tap into that shared network. I would place a lot of weight on what he recommends; I don't like making these decisions on my own. I could gain more certainty that there are marketable opportunities in Cape Town. There are areas we haven't yet explored, and a lot of online teamwork we could be doing. I don't think we have tapped into that local market, let alone the global market. The online business will be revenue-generating, and we will sell online courses. I have already made an unconscious move in that direction without actually formalising it. The other consideration is that I always seem to get more work when I'm in Cape Town. I would tap into those resources to create some certainty. And I need to go down to Cape Town soon to look at property.

S: You said a couple of things: talk to your business partner and make plans, as you each work in both cities. That would give you some certainty if he says there are possibilities. You are building an online business, and you talked earlier about developing products; you have already started moving in that direction. You say that work is primarily online, and most people are communicating online. It sounds like you think this is worth exploring, and you have come up with some concrete ways to do so. Also, you will be going to Cape Town soon to look at properties.

Z: So, now that I am exploring it, it puts things into perspective. Verbalising unspoken thoughts helps put things in boxes and moves things into one direction or another. This conversation has shifted me closer to making a decision moving away from the indecisiveness of the last few years.

S: Do you want to write anything down?

Z: I'll write down the objective and the actions that emanated from that.

S: Do you want me to reiterate your goal?

Z: Yeah.

S: You said, 'I would like to move the business to Cape Town during 2022, starting with a six-month trial period in January.'

Z: And I said I would like to trial it for January – and to do that I would like to find a place in December to rent – and that it may be possible to have two places to start with, Cape Town and Jo'burg.

S: You've said it's low-risk to keep Jo'burg, and by the middle of next year it might be possible to let the Jo'burg one go. You said a couple of other things – I thought they were quite important from the way you emphasised them – that the reason for thinking about this was your health and mental wellness, and that you have a wide network in both cities.

Z: Yeah. So I would like to talk to my business partner about the possibilities for work in Cape Town, and think about my emotional support there. So, the four top things are: (1) talk to my business partner, (2) spend more time getting certainty, (3) build my online business, and (4) travel in December.

S: I think you've got it.

Z: We got that all done in … 62 minutes.

Conclusion

This has been a very practical chapter about the purpose of both coaching and mentoring, as well as looking at how to create goals, and work with the goal-setting model, GROW. To ensure that it works, think about how well you really listen to your direct reports when they come to you for help. How impatient are you to move the conversation along the lines you want it to go? And where do you stop, listen silently, giving the direct report a chance to download how they are, where they are, and what they would like to consider working on – rather than making assumptions or judgments about where they should be going? How often do you let them think deeply through an issue or an objective they are struggling with? GROW will help you to do this.

Chapter 10

Managing people: Delegation

First steps – hiring the right people

Before you can delegate work, you need to have the right people in place. So let's talk about what you should be looking for in your new recruits. One of your first questions is: do I hire for experience, or can I train them to do what I need them to do?

Look for four traits when you are interviewing:

1. *Do they have a positive attitude?* This is important for your and their success. Someone with a positive attitude is much easier to motivate in the future.

2. *What is their energy level?* In our flatter structures in today's workplace, you probably need someone with high energy. Find out what community activities they are involved in outside of work, and what they have done to go beyond the call of duty in previous roles or jobs. This is an indication of someone who is a self-starter and is not short on energy.

3. *What is their sense of enthusiasm?* Ask them, "Of all the jobs you have ever had, which did you like best, and why?" Remember that you are more interested in the enthusiasm you can hear in their voice. Enthusiasm is contagious in the workplace. But be sure it is relevant for your workplace.

4. *Do they sound as if they are a self-starter and self-disciplined, always looking to learn and develop themselves?* They may be involved in team sports or play a musical instrument as a hobby. You are looking for an indication of their self-discipline. In other words, if they have the patience to go through the training and hard work that it takes to be proficient in a team sport, or to play an instrument, then the likelihood is that they are very trainable and will be motivated and willing to always learn something new.

An employee with a positive, can-do attitude, the right amount of enthusiasm and the rigour of self-discipline will be willing to be trained in any new challenge you present them with.[247]

When you are looking for a match between the job and the person, identify those already in your employ who are the right calibre of people you need. In other words, before looking outside, first look inside and see whether there are already individuals within the organisation that match your criteria and whom you think would rank in the top ten per cent of all possible hires.

Activity: Criteria for each job

List the criteria for each job for which you are hiring in terms of the characteristics, competences, skills and experience that you need for the role. This will help you to select the right calibre of person for the job. First identify the staff members you consider to be in the top ten per cent – then list your rationale for putting them there. When you are preparing for your recruitment interview, for internal and external candidates, have a list of the qualities that you have already created.

How to do this?

Make a list of the top performers you now have and write down every quality that caused you to put them in the top 10 per cent. Do that now. Next, create a second list of the qualities you are looking for. For example: willing to take the initiative, handles customer conflict well, is self-disciplined, takes feedback well, is a self-starter, and is willing to learn. Armed with your list of qualities and characteristics that are required for the role, you have a very high chance of hiring the right people. Once they are hired, then is the time to think about their development and growth – and one of the ways to develop them is through delegation.

Delegation is developing your team

Delegation is giving your subordinates the responsibility and authority to carry out a task for which you remain ultimately accountable. In fact, you should be delegating at least ten per cent of your job at all times. All delegation involves risk, as you are letting go of doing what you do well to develop your subordinates or direct reports. Although you cannot avoid the possibility of risk, you can accept it and ensure that you:

- plan delegation;
- demonstrate your belief in your team members;
- explain and brief them on what the task entails; and
- manage and get feedback throughout the entire delegation process.

At some stage you will have to let someone else do your favourite type of task or project. It is important to understand that nobody does a new task or project for the first time at the speed that you currently do it. So, expect to take the time needed to delegate. Plan for it, explain the task or project fully in digestible chunks, and get feedback throughout the process.

Delegation means letting go of direct control – you cannot remain on top of your own job if you touch everything that goes through your team. Take a step back and supervise the staff member, using your new learning as you go to change and adapt your style of delegation. Delegation means handing on part of your job, but it does not mean losing your job. Learn to:

1. *Delegate responsibility* so that your staff member takes responsibility for planning the project, communicating with you and ultimately taking responsibility for what works and what doesn't work. Delegate the entire task knowing they will be doing it instead of you.

2. *Delegate the authority* to do the job, and let others know that the authority sits with the selected team member. This involves decision making power and the authority to seek out resources to complete the job.

3. *Accept accountability.* Know that ultimately the buck stops with you, as you are ultimately accountable if things go wrong. But your job is to lead all your people towards the results that are needed.

4. *Understand that you are motivating your staff* to work with and alongside you in achieving results.

The secret behind delegating effectively

Your motivation to delegate may be inhibited by the following perceived difficulties or disadvantages:

*   I enjoy doing it!

*   I don't want to give it up.

*   Lack of resources.

*   Time.

*   Quicker to do it myself.

*   No time for staff.

*   Fear.

*   Not confident to delegate.

*   It involves risk.

- I will lose control.

- Not doing well.

- It could reflect badly on me.

- Easy to have it done badly.

- The staff member may lack the competence.

- The person may prove to be incapable.

- Lack of trust in team members.

You should nevertheless bear in mind that the following advantages or benefits may be gained from delegating:

- Reduces my workload.

- Delegation is a long-term process.

- Eventually saves time.

- I can get on with other things.

- Quality time for planning and thinking.

- Should reduce my stress level.

- I and everyone else can move on.

- We will all be more effective.

- Creates better understanding.

- Gives ownership.

- Shows trust.

- Motivational tool.

- Motivates a more "cohesive" team.

- Creates promotional opportunities.

- Allows development of others.

- If planned first, it gets easier.

We often know we should be delegating, but we find many reasons not to. The first stumbling block is that you can work faster than they can due to your experience. Let's identify all of the reasons you can find for not delegating to others.

Activity: List every reason why you and other managers don't delegate

You know can do it faster, and you believe that if you do it, it will be done right the first time. Also, if a member of your team makes a mistake, then you are responsible. So your thinking is that if you do it yourself you have better control. Quicker, better, done right – or maybe you just like to do it. Think about something you should have delegated months ago – not only were you comfortable doing it, maybe you even gained kudos for doing it. These are all stumbling blocks to doing what managers are hired to do: to achieve results through the efforts of others.

What are your own reasons for not delegating?

1.
2.
3.
4.
5.

What would have been the advantages and benefits if you had delegated the job?

1.
2.
3.
4.
5.

See the lists of disadvantages and advantages of delegation provided above for ideas.

What are some of the reasons that you should delegate?

- If you do not delegate, you will simply be leading a team of one.
- As a manager you have moved from doing to guiding, mentoring and coaching – you have become a manager of people. And your role depends on getting work done through others.

- As a manager you are responsible for the growth and development of others – and delegation is one of the most powerful tools in your toolbox.

- In terms of managing time, you cannot get everything done yourself. That is the reason why you have been asked to manage a team.

- If you do not delegate, you are making yourself the one person in the team who cannot be promoted. Remember, delegation is also about building your succession so that you can move on.

- As an overseer, supervisor, and guide you have greater control.

- With delegation, you free yourself up to deal with the more important matters for which you are responsible.

- Your role as manager is to prepare the individuals in your team and organisation for their own opportunities and the growth of the organisation.

When to delegate

- When it provides an opportunity to develop and train someone.

- When one member of your team has a higher level of skill than you do.

- When it would offer an opportunity for one of your people to stand out and take the limelight.

- When you have insufficient time and someone else has enough.

- When you wish to motivate your team member and show confidence in them.

Delegation is a powerful people development process, and will help you to learn to work smarter. When planning what to delegate, consider the following four factors:

1. *Your needs* – what skills do you need to pass on to your individual staff or team members that will free you up for other roles?

2. *Team member needs* – what skills do they need to acquire to step more powerfully into their role or to prepare for transition to another role?

3. *Organisational needs* – what areas in your workplace require greater depth and breadth – as well as knowledge and skill? Consider what learning all team members went through during the COVID pandemic to be able to manage meetings remotely. What other new skills are needed for the future?

4. *Match individual and work* – Be sure to plan for a good match between the nature of the work and the staff member's style of working and approaching a project.

How to delegate

When delegating be sure to set specific, clearly stated, measurable goals for the task. This involves four key elements:

1. *An action verb* (e.g. to increase, contact, sell, enrol).

2. *A measurable result* (what your expectation is for the outcome of the project).

3. *The date* by which time the objective is to be achieved.

4. *An agreement* as to when and how the staff member is to check in and follow-up with you.

Activity: Working with delegation

A Human Capital Manager, Laura, is handing over one of her key roles to her 2IC (second-in-command), Rob. She is ultimately responsible for organising the team coaching sessions for all the internal teams within the bank in which she works.

- Write down how you think Laura can go about delegating the role to Rob, before working with the steps in delegation listed below.

Steps in delegation

1. Set and explain a *clear objective*, and involve the delegate in understanding the objective.

2. Assign the task and *agree the milestones* and the completion date with the individual. Provide any necessary advice and guidance, including information and data that may be needed by the individual. Be sure to share the necessary background to help the team member to determine their options in tackling the project.

3. *Suggest approaches but do not be directive* – encourage them to use their own initiative in coming up with new approaches. You may want to suggest an approach to get them started, but it is usually best to help them think through how to approach it. They will think differently from you, and may even have better ideas than you! Be sure to listen to their ideas.

4. Clearly *state the level of authority* assigned and what is allocated to them in terms of resources, control, and authority. You need to give them authority with responsibility and let others in the division or organisation know they have it.

5. *Agree follow-up* or feedback sessions, with any agreements about timing and where your involvement is needed or not.

Example of delegation

Laura usually manages the Monday morning weekly team meetings for her ExCo (Executive Committee) and wants to hand it over to her Deputy, Rob, who will eventually step into her role. This is the first step on the road to slowly handing over her responsibilities to him. How can she go about this first stage?

Step One: Set and explain a clear objective

> "Rob, I want to hand over to you the important task of managing the weekly Monday morning meetings for the internal management team. This is ultimately to prepare you to step into my shoes as I begin to take on more and more work from my boss. These need to be scheduled and put into each team member's diary weekly, but on a rolling twelve-month basis. I would like you to think about planning for the weekly agenda, and to discuss the agenda with me at some point during each week. Although I am open to you changing the way we have structured these meetings to date, I would like to understand your rationale for any new structure."

Step Two: Assign the task, agree milestones and completion dates

> "We have time now for you to share your thoughts about how you might plan to manage those Monday morning meetings. Also, I want to share with you the various people that you need to include when planning the agenda, and the relevant data that will be needed for each meeting. There are a few difficult people in the team with whom you will need to negotiate, so I suggest we also think about how to win them over to you now chairing the weekly meetings. I would also like us to agree when you will share the agenda with me each week and get my input – with the understanding that sometimes I will be able to attend the meeting, and sometimes not."

Step Three: Suggest approaches, but do not be directive

> "I always plan as much as possible in advance, but I would like to hear your thoughts about this and how you will manage this extra responsibility within your role. Also, can you share your ideas about how we might motivate the quieter members of the team to begin to take part in a more constructive and engaging way? You have seen what I have tried to do, but I would like to hear your ideas which may work more practically than mine have to date. Can

you also share any new ideas you have which I may not have thought about yet? The point of handing over this role to you is for your own development and growth, but we also need to keep in mind the objectives of the meetings themselves."

Step Four: Clarify their authority, available resources and control

"Just to clarify, you will have the authority to organise these meetings, bring in the right people and decide what needs to change to make the meetings more effective and inspiring. They have become quite mundane under my leadership, and I am hoping your fresh energy and new ideas will motivate others to engage more positively. You will have my budget for these meetings, and I will expect you to manage and stay within the budget. Also, you will have the authority to invite whoever is needed to these meetings, and you will have my support in ensuring that they respond positively to your taking on this role."

Step Five: Agree follow-up or feedback sessions

"My suggestion, unless you have a better one, is that you check-in with me at our usual weekly meeting on a Friday, which gives some planning time for the Monday, and you can take me through what issues you are experiencing and how you suggest we resolve them. I am very much looking forward to hearing back from you later this week on how the planning for your first meeting is going, and from my side I will email and speak to everyone in the team that you are stepping into this new role."

Activity: Your experience of delegation

1. Describe a delegation process that went very well with a subordinate – and identify step by step what made it work.

2. Describe a delegation process that did not go well – and describe what you could have done differently.

Delegate meaningful and important work to motivate your team

Delegating meaningful and important work achieves higher levels of performance, productivity and motivation. Be sure the task or job resonates with the delegate's intrinsic motivators. Here are four ways in which you can motivate your subordinates and direct reports.

1. Identify your employees' intrinsic motivators

Ask your employees to say what would motivate them – and have a discussion with them so that you can understand what is meaningful to them. Ask them what are those intangibles that resonate with, and have helped, them to achieve new and difficult tasks previously. This helps to create connection and meaning with any work you plan to delegate. As a young manager, I had a boss who continued to give me pay increases, when what I really wanted was acknowledgement for a job well done and ultimately the possibility to step into a more challenging role. In the end I left for another job that offered more of what made work meaningful for me.

Ask, not what would make them happier, but what would make them more effective and efficient. It is important to understand that often organisations throw external motivators at employees which do not tap into their own internal motivators. You are looking for their own intrinsic motivators that are the reason they stay late for a job, or make them leap out of bed on a cold, dark morning in winter and arrive at work upbeat and ready to roll up their sleeves.

Are you listening when they tell you what would motivate them? Extrinsic motivators such as salary increases, bonuses, job security, and promotions are important, but they tend to be given to employees before finding out if those motivators would ensure that individual would work more productively. You are looking for intrinsic motivators such as a sense of belonging, community, acknowledgement, understanding and empathy, and a sense that they are being heard in the team and in the workplace.

Activity: Identifying motivators

Identify and rank the motivators for each member of your team which you think will increase their individual performance and motivation.

2. Help your team members find meaning and connection to their work

If you and your people do not understand what that single, powerful statement is that identifies what you and they do for a living – then it is difficult to stay positive and motivate others. When my clients ask me what I do as an executive coach and a team coach, my answer always is: I help people to think and to treat people well. That is how I ultimately see what I do in working with my clients. (Of course, there is a lot within that, such as helping them to build self-awareness, growing and stretching their capacity as leaders and managers in difficult situations and times, managing conflict, and working with complex decision making processes.)

Activity: Define the essence and positive impact of your work

1.   **You, the team leader**

Write a statement that defines the essence and positive impact of what you personally do for a living.

For example, such a statement could be:

- "To create a positive and inspirational working environment with a focus on employees and customers"; or

- "Providing connections between the community and the organisation to provide jobs and sustainability for the families living in the community"; or

- "Helping the company to maintain profitability to provide sustainable employment in the community"; or

- "Creating an environment which is inclusive and diverse offering equal opportunities for all."

Only after you have found meaning and connection to your work can you help your employees to do the same for themselves. You first need to identify the impact of what you do for a living, and only then can you help them.

2.   **Your team members**

Have a discussion with each member of your team to ask them to write one statement that answers the question: What is the positive impact and essence of what they do for a living?

Let them figure out their own impact. Or you can conduct a survey, collect all the impacts, and publish the list without their names, to help motivate people within your team or division.

3.   **Help them set and achieve goals**

Control your own expectations regarding their goals, and help them to get consistent results before setting higher expectation goals. *Rule Number One in setting goals with a direct report is to discuss it with them and get their buy-in to the agreement*:

"I had a boss when I was moving up the ladder as a manager to become a director, and every year my boss insisted on passing his goals on to me. Each year I explained exactly what targets were realistic and motivational for myself and my division of 250 people – and each year my personally set targets were reached. I insisted that I could never achieve the targets that my boss's boss set out for him."

By setting the goals together with your team members you can build rapport with them and inspire confidence in what is possible to be achieved. Most importantly, hear what their rationale is while setting their targets.

4. Appropriately correct the individual's behaviour when needed

If the individual goes off target or does not show signs of aligning with the targets that have been set for a task or project – speak with them privately. *Rule Number Two is to praise in public and criticise in private*. Correct behaviour in private and discuss the issue and the behaviour, not the person. Also, plan your timing for the conversation so that you create a supportive environment and do not get hooked by your own dismay or anger.

Creating your delegation plan

Finally, you need to think about creating an overall delegation plan, as follows:

1. *Decide what can be delegated and write out a plan*:

   - Set out the main objectives of the job.

   - Conduct a time audit (brief) for the duration of the project.

   - List the actual expected activities compared with the objectives.

2. *List what cannot be delegated*:

   - Tasks beyond the skills or competences of others.

   - Rituals such as retirement presentations, long service awards, project management successes.

   - Confidential and security matters such as performance appraisals, promotions and dismissals.

   - Policy making such as formulation of appraisals and important policy documentation.

   - Crises – you need to shoulder the problem, help others to problem solve, and involve the people necessary to find solutions.

3. *Decide to whom to delegate*:

   - Who has the time and appropriate skills and competences?

   - Who is ready for a new challenge which will stretch them to learn and grow?

   - What training will be needed for them to complete the project?

   - Who must you inform that this team member will have the authority to carry out the job?

4. *Brief the team member*:

   - Define the task or project.

   - Establish with them the problems and pitfalls of the task.

   - Define together any additional authority they need.

   - Establish the authority and inform the relevant people.

   - Explain the task and discuss the pitfalls and good points.

   - Ask them to come back to you with a plan.

   - Set report-back targets.

   - Establish supervision and feedback sessions.

5. *Your delegation brief*:

   - Give the global picture.

   - Why them?

   - Define the task or project?

   - How does it affect them?

   - Define the boundaries of their authority.

   - Tell them the advantages and pitfalls.

   - Agree the time boundaries.

   - Discuss the resources needed.

   - Agree monitoring and check-ins.

   - Establish any training required.

   - Ensure they have enough training for the job.

Activity: Deciding who to delegate to

1. Make a list of tasks to be delegated.

2. Review the personal skills and attributes of each team member.

3. Place the name of an appropriate team member by each task, matching skills and attributes.

4. Make a list of all the details and instructions to help the team member accomplish each task.

5. Decide on the appropriate monitoring and evaluation controls.

Conclusion

In Part Three we have begun to take a look at motivation and delegation. As managers we want our staff to be happy and to perform to their utmost ability. If they are able to work more effectively and efficiently, they become our strongest competitive edge. Being employed yourself, you know what a difference motivation makes in your own work – and if is good for all employees, it is good for the company.

We explored some of the new research in understanding our notions of motivation, looking at the work of Edward Deci and Richard Ryan, and at the importance of delegation and how to make it work. Most managers find it easier to do the work themselves, rather than to pass it on to their direct reports. The consequences of this is that you do not uplift the skills and competence of those you manage, and ultimately risk losing them to another organisation which values what they have to offer.

Importantly, successful delegation develops the maximum potential of each individual within your team. The beauty of delegation is that your own work forms the main source of responsibilities to be delegated. However, be sure to set specific, clearly stated, measurable goals, and create a delegation brief that covers all the bases we have discussed so far.

We now move on in Part Four to discuss the importance of how you communicate as a leader-manager – and some of the benefits and pitfalls of becoming a skilled communicator.

Part Four – Becoming a skilled communicator

The aim of this section is to improve your confidence and ability to convey your meaning powerfully, without infringing the rights of others. And to be able to handle difficult people and difficult situations with greater ease.

Chapter 11: Managing difficult people and situations

Chapter 12: Assertive communication skills to negotiate behaviour change

Chapter 11

Managing difficult people and situations

Improving the effectiveness of your communication skills

It is important to negotiate and deal more effectively with difficult situations and difficult people in your role as a leader-manager. As we go through this chapter, start to think about the various situations where you have found yourself trying to manage difficulties with your direct reports, team, colleagues or customers, and when you have found yourself floundering for the right approach and the right words.

Think about what difficult people do, the type of behaviour they display, and learning how to describe specific behaviours that you find difficult to manage. The more clearly we can define our own behaviour and theirs, the more able we are to manage the situation. Just making general personality statements does not help us to resolve the issues at hand. Be careful of labels, as they can become descriptions of personality. Let us first look at the difference between personality and behaviour.

What is the difference between personality and behaviour?

While personality is what you are like as a person, behaviour is how you behave, including what you say and do. Although it is difficult to change who you are, you always have a choice as to how you want to behave and what you want to say or do in a particular situation. Personality refers to the combination of characteristics or qualities that form an individual's distinctive character.

Personality focuses on two comprehensive areas: One is understanding individual differences, and in particular *personality characteristics*, such as sociability or irritability. The other is understanding how the various parts of a person come together as a whole. If we do not specifically describe what the person says and does, we often resort to labelling them with personality difficulties rather than specific behaviours. An individual can choose to change by changing their behaviour.

According to *The Encyclopaedia of Psychology*,[248] *personality* indicates the constant and stable self of an individual, which makes them unique and different from other people. From a person's personality, we can predict their behaviour in each situation. Personality is usually divided into components known as the Big Five or CANOE (Conscientiousness, Agreeableness, Neuroticism, Openness to experience, and Extraversion). An individual's genetics or environment may play a crucial role in making them what they are:

> The humanistic approach to personality attempts to understand personality and its development by focusing on the positive side of human nature and self-actualisation, or people's attempts to reach their full potential. According to Rogers,[249] the key to becoming self-actualised is developing a healthy self-concept. The primary road-blocks are conditions of worth – criteria that we must meet to win the positive regard of others. Although the humanistic approach emphasises the positive dimension of human experience and the potential that each of us has for personal growth, it has been faulted for being unscientific.[250]

Behaviour, in contrast, defines a person's conduct, what they say and do, and is learned over their life stages of development. The way a person expresses their emotions reveals their behaviour. Where behaviour is transient, personality is constant and long-lasting. Your personality travels with you wherever you go, but your behaviour depends on the environments in which you grew up and have lived throughout your life.

While you may act very professionally in a business meeting, with a degree of self-awareness about how people are experiencing you, your behaviour may completely change in a social environment where you may be more spontaneous and relaxed with friends or family. Where some of us are appreciative and tolerant of others, some of us may be more critical and judgmental. Your behaviour is all about how you present yourself. Your behaviour may change throughout your life as you mature and develop self-awareness, and it is also influenced by your family, education, workplace, and social and cultural background.

Sometimes it is difficult to comprehend the difference between personality and behaviour. Where personality defines you, behaviour simply defines your reactions to the environments and situations in which you find yourself. Sometimes we confuse personality with how people behave – that is their actions in terms of what they say and do.

Although many employers require personality tests in the recruitment process, it is also important to find out how new hires will behave in a working environment. This is because we engage with people in the workplace, and it is important to be able to manage our interactions with them. The working environment has its own culture, ethics, and mores, accepted or appropriate ways of behaving. The workplace is a network of systems of relationships at all levels.

As individuals we begin to develop our personality at an incredibly early stage in life, where our behaviour is underpinned by our own values and mores, and how we feel. According to Kazdin,[251] everyone's personality is an internal combination of the mind, individual will and energies, as well as heart and consistency. We display our behaviour externally in the world and it is self-constructed; personality is natural.

As Table 5 indicates, personality is determined by an individuals' essential characteristics, where behaviour is underpinned by our thinking and feeling.

Table 5: Personality compared with behaviour

Personality	Behaviour
An individual's essential characteristics contribute to their overall personality.	The way someone organises their thinking and actions define their behaviour.
Personality remains stable.	Behaviour keeps changing depending upon age and intelligence.
Personality is permanent.	Behaviour is temporary and situation based.
Personality can be evaluated by observing someone's behaviour.	Behaviour cannot be judged according to someone's personality.
Personality is who you are as a person.	Behaviour is how you express yourself. It is what you say and do, and what you do not say and do.
Personality is not something unique to humans as recent research into animal behaviour shows.[252]	Behaviour can relate to humans, animals, etc.

Source: Kazdin.[253]

To help understand the difference, Table 6 provides some specific examples of personality versus behaviour.

Table 6: Examples of personality versus behaviour

Personality	Behaviour
Stubborn.	Unwilling to acknowledge another person's point of view.
Defensive.	Puts blame on someone else and denies culpability.

Personality	Behaviour
Not a team player.	Speaks aggressively; constantly interrupts; talks over you; refuses to join in social or leisure activities; refuses to take part in meetings or discussions; disagrees constantly.
Persistent.	Consistent dissatisfaction at appraisals and performance reviews, especially for a salary increase.
Manipulative.	Keeps their own views hidden; finds out yours and then asks you to do something they want.

What do difficult people do?

Let us look at what difficult people actually do that relates to behaviour. Figure 14 illustrates some examples of how people can behave when being difficult.

Figure 14: What do difficult people do?

Activity: Descriptions of behaviour

1. What is it that you find difficult people do – what behaviours do they tend to display?

2. Describe specific behaviours that you have encountered as a manager that you have found difficult to manage.

Note: If you find yourself giving descriptions of personality rather than behaviours in answer to the above questions, just rework them and turn them into descriptions of behaviour.

Activity: Your difficult people

Consider the people with whom you work and manage (e.g. your direct reports, staff and team members, peers and colleagues, other supervisors and managers, and other stakeholders in the business). Choose a few people and describe how each is *difficult* in terms of their behaviour and the language that they each use. Include examples of phrases each one uses.

	Behaviour	*Language they use*
1.		
2.		
3.		

Activity: How do you respond?

On a scale of 1 to 10, how stressed do you feel when dealing with the difficult people with whom you work? What is your usual response pattern to the behaviours that you listed in the Activity above?

1. What do you say and what do you do?

2. What could you say and do differently?

Three quick steps to deal with difficult behaviour

There are three quick steps to deal with difficult behaviour:

1. Listen and acknowledge what the other person is saying or doing, being careful not to interrupt too soon.

2. Use a transition word such as "and", "however", "also", "yet" to make a link. This transition links what they are saying to what you think and are going to suggest as a way forward.

2. Suggest a potential way to move forward, think about or resolve the situation, and listen to their response.

As an example, here is a suggested reply if someone says to you, "I cannot take on this work project due to everything you have already loaded me with."

1. **Listen and acknowledge**

    Listen carefully to them and let them know that you have not only heard them but be clear in expressing your acknowledgement of what they have said:

    > "John, I understand that you are frustrated by the amount of workload with which you are currently juggling. And I also realise that you have been putting in extra hours to get through your work."

2. **Make a link and make your point**

    Make a link to your acknowledgement by using a word such as: and, however, also – try to avoid the word "but" which is a "contradictory" word rather than a linking word:

    > "However, the reason I have chosen you for this role is because you have the experience and the network of relationships to fulfil it. This also means that you will complete the job in half the time of any of the others in the team."

3. **Suggest action**

    The third step is to suggest a possible way forward. It opens the conversation to move you forward to a solution rather than deeper into disagreement or conflict:

    > "My suggestion is that you take me through what projects you are currently working on, and we can prioritise them and look at what could be delegated

to someone else in order for you to take this on. Shall we do it right now as we are together?"

These three steps can also look like this:

- "I appreciate how important it is; what your thoughts are on this; how do you feel about the situation ..."

- "Also, I feel (or think) ..."

- "What I suggest is / What I would like us to do is ..."

Changing behaviour

What is important if we are going to gradually shift people's inappropriate behaviour, is that we need to change their reward, or the reinforcement of why their behaviour needs to change. We cannot know what is going on in their thoughts and feelings. We can only deal with their behaviour, i.e. what they say and what they do. If we change *our* behaviour, chances are that they will change theirs.

How do you typically respond, and what could you do differently?

1. Use humour where it is appropriate.

2. Try and keep calm yourself.

3. Listen and acknowledge them.

4. Ask questions – but be careful not to interrogate them.

5. Describe and praise their value and good points.

6. Empathise, sympathise, and recognise their side of the problem.

Traditional ways managers have dealt with people problems

1. Deny that the problem is their responsibility, and say it is the other person's problem. This rarely works.

2. Behave aggressively or passively back to the employee – not to be recommended!

3. Give the person a "pep talk" – which can work if it is done immediately or with persistent behaviour.

4. Coaching or counselling – if there is impatient or inappropriate behaviour and coaching the employee would help to resolve the issue or motivate them; or suggesting counselling if there is some healing that is required due to an issue in their current life that they may need help with.

5. Performance appraisals and training – can help if the behavioural response seems to have become a pattern of which the employee may not be conscious.

6. Disciplinary reviews – following the appropriate steps for performance management with your Human Capital Division.

7. Get rid of them – this is very often what managers feel is necessary with persistent, inappropriate behaviour. However, be sure to take them through a disciplinary review process if possible before you decide to fire, transfer, or promote them. The behaviour may be underpinned by limiting assumptions on the part of the difficult person which may be untrue and may be possible to explore.

Understanding the brain

As Ingra Du Buisson-Narsai points out in Chapter 6, a theory still widely held within psychology and society views the human brain as composed of three layers (the so-called "triune brain"):

1. an instinctual brain, the "brainstem" or "primitive brain" composed of a "reptile brain" and a "mammalian brain", supposed to have developed first and to be focused on *survival*;

2. an impulsive or emotional brain, the "limbic brain", supposed to have developed second, which is focused on *feeling*; and

3. a neo-cortex which supposedly developed last and is focused on complex problem-solving, reasoning and self-governance involving *thinking*.

This "triune brain" is supposed to have evolved in stages, with each new processor being loaded on top of the previous ones. One of the implications of this theory is that it is supposedly possible for the cortical brain to be bypassed or hijacked by the "primitive brain" or the "limbic brain", causing you later to regret how you reacted or behaved.

In fact, as Cesario, Johnson and Eisthen[254] point out, in a journal article appropriately titled "Your brain is not an onion with a tiny reptile inside", this belief has long been invalidated by neurobiological research. This means that the use of disruptively rude, aggressive or otherwise antisocial modes of expression by an individual can no longer be blamed on the hijacking of their "logical" brain by the intervention of a "primitive" or "limbic" brain system. It nevertheless remains essential for leader-managers to learn to how to deal with such unhelpful behaviour, whatever psychological factors may be motivating it, and to avoid such behaviour being triggered in themselves.

Trigger, behaviour, reward or desired outcome

Your goal when dealing with difficult situations and people is to stay out of an unhelpfully emotive response and have an understanding for those apparently lacking more mature emotional intelligence. We need to learn how to cope with emotion and irrationality which can disrupt any business environment through temperamental bosses, moody colleagues and power struggles.

We need to understand what is triggering our own behaviour so that we can adapt a more appropriate series of behaviours. It could be that you are faced with a difficult staff member, or someone is behaving more aggressively than usual – or there is conflict in the situation which you do not feel you are trained to handle. It is important to understand your triggers, and to identify the types of behaviour you display when triggered. And it is also important to try to identify the triggers of the other person, or persons, and be able to speak to them about their resulting behaviour.

A trigger could be a problem to solve or an attempt to delegate a task or project to a team member. The resulting behaviour, when you try to discuss it with a member of your team, may be an aggressive or challenging questioning style, fighting back, or trying to force irrelevant facts onto the table. One reward or desired outcome could be the ability to encourage the person displaying difficult behaviour to respond in a more appropriate way. This would lead to the ultimate reward of solving the presenting problem.

Activity: Trigger, behaviour and reward or desired outcome

1. Think of a recent situation where you behaved inappropriately. What was the trigger and how did you behave as a result? What did you do or say that was slightly off-base or inappropriate? What was the ultimate outcome that you were seeking, and what was the outcome that was ultimately achieved? Did you change your behaviour to achieve this outcome, and if so, how?

    Trigger:

    Behaviour:

    Reward or desired outcome:

Activity: Trigger, behaviour and reward or desired outcome (continued)

2. Think of a recent situation where you were faced with someone who did not want to take on your task or project, and who fought back verbally and perhaps inappropriately. What do you think was their trigger? How did you behave to deal with it (what did you do or say that was encouraging to them), and what was the ultimate reward or outcome they were seeking? In the end, what was achieved? Did they or you change behaviour to achieve your or their outcome, and if so, how?

    Trigger:

    Behaviour:

    Reward or desired outcome:

Case study: Matthew's behaviour

Background

Matthew (not his real name) has been the CEO of a successful company for the last year. He is 45 years old, and has very firm ideas on how to best manage people – in general terms, he believes that people respond best when the pressure is on. Matthew has tremendous energy: he arrives at work at 07h00 most mornings and stays late till 19h30 every evening.

In his own eyes, he works extremely hard, and expects others to do the same. He is a stickler for detail, and frequently sends managers and directors scurrying back from meetings to collect more facts. Face-to-face meetings with him are more like inquisitions. He adopts an overly aggressive questioning style and "bawls people out" when he discovers mistakes. He prides himself on his ability to move heaven and earth to "fix" problems, and his grasp of both legal and financial problems is very impressive. This means that he interferes a great deal. As soon as he suspects a deficiency, he "pounces" on the person concerned and sorts it out himself.

When there is a problem to be solved, Matthew is very fond of gathering all the involved parties together in one room and trying to force the facts out onto the table. To bring out the facts, he adopts a very challenging approach, style and tone.

The results of Matthew's behaviour

Theresa (not her real name), the Director of Marketing, reports to Matthew, and particularly resents this treatment. She is also seriously concerned about the effects of Matthew's behaviour on others, having noticed that her colleagues are beginning to show signs of stress. They are putting in enormously long hours trying to keep up with him, and are also becoming more competitive and less co-operative towards one another.

This preoccupation with Matthew has reached absurd proportions – the team spends unproductive time talking about him in his absence and trying to anticipate his next move. Another alarming effect of Matthew's behaviour is that directors and managers spend inordinate amounts of time getting the details right for all their cases, so that his probing will not catch them out.

Directors and managers who were previously willing to delegate are now less inclined to do so. They feel that the only way they can really know what is going on is to involve themselves. This attention to detail means they spend all their time on day-to-day issues, finding themselves not included in any forward planning, management of people, or development of the company's business.

Furthermore, Theresa notices that too many managers are less willing to admit mistakes than previously. They increasingly try to contain problems and conceal them from Matthew. Ironically, he has complained to Theresa that too many managers are "fire-fighting instead of doing what they are paid to do, which is to think". He told Theresa that he could not understand why people thought he was such a hard man:

> "Don't they understand that conflict management is all about stimulating alternative courses of action? When I go for them, what I really want is for them to go away, think again, then come back and tell me about it."

Activity: Finding a solution to Matthew's behaviour

In the case study described immediately above:

1. What behaviour does Matthew display? Try to describe his behaviour very specifically.

2. What are the rewards for his behaviour?

3. What are Matthew's triggers?

Activity: Finding a solution to Matthew's behaviour (continued)

4. How can Theresa solve this problem with Matthew's behaviour? This might even mean trying to identify a new trigger and brainstorming several alternative solutions.

Solving people problems: a step-by-step approach

1. List the unwanted behaviours, then delete either of the two following items:
    *   personality traits; or
    *   anything that is not related to the task at hand.
2. Select the most significant behaviour, and specifically define it.
3. Identify the "rewards" which encourage this behaviour.
4. Identify the "triggers" that precede this behaviour.
5. Decide which new "behaviour" you wish to replace the old behaviour with.
6. Work out how to alter the trigger in order to:
    *   encourage the desired behaviour; and
    *   discourage the unwanted behaviour.

Mediating conflict and building alignment

Webster's dictionary defines alignment as "Bringing parts into proper relative position; to adjust, to bring into proper relationship or orientation".[255] Alignment is always possible to the extent that people will avail themselves of it. This is not the same as agreement or harmony. Alignment is about consciously agreeing to move in the same direction, and has to do with serving common goals. To the degree that alignment is present within a relationship, it can take place on different levels. You can be in alignment about getting a job done together, while disliking a lot about one another, or disliking how the job is executed. You can be in alignment about growing your relationship, while having battles about some aspect thereof. To the extent alignment becomes conscious, it becomes the bridge partners can utilise to create alignment to move in a common direction.

Mediation research has found that one of the most effective ways to create alignment is to not engage with the *positions* (the solutions advocated for by one partner), but to find the *common interests* that lie behind the positions. Even when the positions are locked, the interests or values behind the positions may be aligned. For example, team members may be aligned about a merger but in disagreement about the best way to go about it. The common interest is the merger; the positions are how to accomplish it. A couple may have different positions on how to discipline their child, but they hold a common value of wanting the best for their child. The alignment skills to build relationships are drawn from mediation techniques and adjusted to be more appropriate for leader-managers being able to develop a coaching style in mediating conflict.

Alignment coaching is combined with managing conflict. Conflict is a signal that something new is trying to happen. When handled skilfully it is the transition to constructive change. But toxic conflict can paralyse a team, increase job turnover and absenteeism, and reduce productivity. Alignment is a way to manage conflict in a constructive way.

For you as the facilitator of the conflict, introduce the process and make it clear that each person involved is to communicate to you as the facilitator, and not to speak to the person with whom they are in conflict. This is a way of managing an escalation of the conflict. Further, set the ground rules in terms of behaviour if there are certain behaviours you want to introduce (such as not interrupting the other person, adhering to the timing that you set, giving fully-present attention to whomever is speaking, and committing to the ground rules). As the facilitator you need to time each person for each round that you introduce with each of the items below. I would suggest two or three minutes for each person to answer each of the questions that you ask as the Facilitator. Timing is equal – everyone has equal time.

1. Introduction, Context and Process – Facilitator introduces why are we here and why it is important.

2. Creating a Designed Alliance – "How do we want to have this conversation?" The facilitator asks this question and hears from everyone equally, asking for specific behaviours. Give 15 seconds for each, and go round a few times to elicit all the behaviours. With them reduce the list down to no more than 10 behaviours.

3. Introducing these core principles for the session – summarise the core behaviours, and ask each person in a round if they are willing to commit to working in this way.

4. Resolving issues without blame – ask each person whether they are willing to share the impact this conflict has had on them personally, and whether they are willing to hear the other participants' perspectives without judgement or prejudice. Be clear that you will stop them if they start to work with blame.

5.   Ask each person one at a time, and set equal time for each person to answer, usually four or five minutes: "What is the issue or issues that are causing the problem from your perspective, and what impact has this issue had on you?" You can do as many rounds as needed in order to hear each person out. Keep going until all the heat seems to be spent and everyone has been heard.

6.   Suggest to them that they think about the issue sitting between them, with them sitting next to each other. Ask them to imagine putting the problem out in front of them so that they are sitting next to each other looking at the problem. Then have them speak to what they see from each of their perspectives, to see the problem from different viewpoints.

7.   Ask each participant, "What do you need and from whom to go forward?" Hear from each of them and they may need to vent. Just be sure you have set the guidelines for there to be no swearing and no shouting.

8.   Ask each of them – "What do you think are your areas of commonality – what are the common interests or points behind which you are united?" Summarise those common interests that they seem to align on.

9.   Ask each of them – "What are you personally prepared to concede or do to reach a compromise that would facilitate better engagement and relationships between you?" Everyone needs to be equally willing to give up something to resolve the conflict.

10. Next steps and closing.

Understanding how you react in difficult situations

Changing behaviour means developing an understanding of how you react in difficult situations and taking responsibility to change your behaviour:

> All human beings have an inner stream of thoughts and feelings that include criticism, doubt and fear. We see leaders stumble not because they have undesirable thoughts and feelings but because they get hooked by them, like fish caught on a line. They treat them like facts (I've been a failure my whole career) and avoid situations that evoke them (I'm not going to take on that new challenge). Effective leaders do not buy into or try to suppress their inner experiences. Instead, they approach them in a mindful, values-driven, and productive way, developing emotional agility. To get unhooked: recognise your patterns; label your thoughts and emotions, accept them, act on your values to expand your choices – and understand your commitment to solving the problem.[256]

Strategies you can develop are:

1. *Take response-ability*:

    • Develop the ability to respond.

    • Go back to look at your role to see how you can change the interaction.

    • Notice your own style of communication and what needs to change.

2. *How do you react physically when stressed, and what can you replace it with?*

    • Inappropriate body language – replace it with …

    • Go red, then white – replace it with …

    • Clench your fists – replace it with …

    • Cross your arms – replace it with …

    • Wag your finger (dominant parent) – replace it with …

    • Breathing too quickly or too shallowly – change it to …

    • Shouting at the person (not to be recommended) – change it to …

3. *Physical and mental strategies*:

    • Keep your body relaxed – deepen and lengthen your breathing.

    • Breathe deeply – it helps you to relax.

    • Exercise every day to relieve adrenalin and stress!

    • Use a mental phrase or an affirmation, such as: "I can handle this with composure."

    • Exercise daily in order to manage your adrenalin and stress in a pressurised workplace.

Conclusion

It is important to think about how to manage difficult people and situations as they can cause stress for everyone involved – including the team. One of the first steps is to understand how you react when facing difficult people or situations – and once you understand yourself you can begin to manage others who are struggling to deal with difficulties as they arise. In the next chapter we will look at communication skills, and at negotiating behaviour change by using a direct assertive approach.

Chapter 12

Assertive communication skills to negotiate behaviour change

What is assertiveness?

One of the most critical communication skills for leader-managers today is the ability to use an assertive style to get your message across. Many people misunderstand the use of assertive communication, often thinking that it means being aggressive. Assertiveness is confidently expressing what you think, feel, and believe – standing up for your rights while respecting the rights of others. Another way to define assertiveness is that it is a way to express your thoughts directly, but in a way that is respectful of the opinions and feelings of others.

In this chapter we will look at four styles of communication from which to choose when communicating as a manager:

1. *Passive* – self-protection through avoidance.

2. *Aggressive* – using anger to get results.

3. *Passive-aggressive* – avoiding direct confrontation.

4. *Assertive* – expressing your thoughts directly, but in a way that respects the opinions and feelings of others.

Assertive communication is tailored to the person and the situation. If you stick to your own thoughts, feelings and beliefs, and avoid direct or implied criticism of the other person's thoughts, feelings or beliefs, you are more likely to generate the respect of the person to whom you are speaking. A tip is to communicate in terms of "I" messages rather than "You" messages. An "I" message is honest and is a statement that best describes you. It expresses your thoughts and feelings and is not confrontational. Let us look at three different situations, thinking about how you might have responded in each one.

Our responses often depend on how we are feeling in that moment or on that day. There is a difference in how you respond, depending on whether it was an easy day or a difficult day. If things are going well and you feel calm, you might respond differently than if you had had a particularly difficult conversation with someone or are simply stressed and tired. In the situation below, note the different communication styles available to you.

Situation One: Chaos in Finance

In this situation, you noticed that no one had stepped into the Finance Manager's shoes while she is on holiday. As a result, chaos is taking place, with a plethora of email messages and telephone calls from suppliers who cannot get confirmation on orders, are not getting paid, and are threatening to stop supplying your organisation if something isn't sorted out right away.

You thought you had already dealt with this, but had not handled it in a direct way. You told your team at your last management meeting to sort it out so that the phone calls and email queries from disgruntled suppliers to the Finance Division would be taken care of while the Finance Manager is on holiday. But you were not specific about who should handle what, and did not directly address the people to whom you were delegating a role. Let us look at the replies below, and think about what is different about each style:

1. *To a couple of customers* – "I am sorry; I thought I had let my team know what to do to sort this out. I should have done it myself."

2. *To your team* – "What were you guys thinking!!! Our suppliers are about to cut us off as they are frustrated about not getting paid."

3. *To your suppliers* – "I cannot believe this is happening. For some reason, my team are just not up to scratch – I need to investigate this."

4. *To your team* – "Look, it seems I was not specific or direct enough about what I needed done while the Finance Manager is away. Sally, I need you to redirect all phone calls for the Finance Division to your PA. Have her redirect the calls as needed until the Accounts Manager is back a week from Monday. Daniel, I need you to ring all of the suppliers on this list that have rung me, and reassure them that they will be paid – then go down to the Finance Division and work with them to find a solution to make sure it doesn't continue. And team, next time I ask for something to be done and I am not clear, please ask me to be more specific."

Now let us look at these responses.

Passive response

"I should have done it myself." This message is sending a message of powerlessness. It is passive and implies that you cannot manage your team. Also, it does not express what the Manager (you) will do next to sort out the situation, which means it might happen again.

Aggressive response

"What were you guys thinking!" This is aggressive, as it is blaming, and is probably being said with a raised voice. The next sentence continues to blame: "Our suppliers are about to cut us off as they are frustrated about not getting paid." There is no accountability assigned, as no one is specifically delegated a specific task. Yet the tone and behaviour are accusatory, with no accountability explained.

Passive-aggressive response

"I cannot believe that this is happening." This is passive – implying that the Manager has no control here. And then aggressive and blaming: "For some reason, my team are just not up to scratch – I need to investigate this."

The Manager is admitting to her suppliers that she has no control over her team – and cannot get them to work properly. Using passive-aggressive behaviour, the team might try to get even and sabotage what the Manager wants next time.

Assertive response

"Look, it seems I was not specific or direct enough about what I needed done while the Finance Manager is away. Sally, I need you to redirect all phone calls for the Finance Division to your PA. Have her redirect the calls as needed until the Finance Manager is back a week from Monday. Daniel, I need you to ring all of the suppliers on this list that have rung me, and reassure them that they will be paid – then go down to the Finance Manager and work with them to find a solution to make sure it doesn't continue. And team, next time I ask for something to be done and I am not clear, please ask me to be more specific."

How does the Manager feel about herself now – and how will the others feel? She probably feels more in control, and comfortable acting as a line manager harnessing the team spirit to solve a problem. And her team are now clear on who should be accountable for what. Her message is direct and clear, establishes accountability, and makes it evident that the problem needs to be resolved – while she is respectful in how she communicates with them. Being assertive is making a specific and direct request, making it clear who is accountable for what.

Understanding the four communication styles

1. *Passive* – Reluctance or inability to confidently express what you think and feel.

2. *Aggressive* – Expressing yourself in ways that intimidate, demean, degrade, or blame another person.

3. *Passive-aggressive* – Avoids direct confrontation but opens the door for others to get even later.

4. *Assertive* – Confidently expressing what you think, feel, and believe – standing up for your rights while respecting the rights of others.

Situation Two: Presentation to the ExCo

The presenter, Marianne, asks when concluding her presentation: "If anybody has any questions, I am happy to answer them." The Manager immediately jumps in and shouts, "This is the worst presentation you have ever made! When I hear from my team, I expect more than unsubstantiated opinion."

Marianne, thinking to herself, feels that her Manager has not only attacked her work, but has also attacked her identity in front of the entire ExCo. Marianne's feelings are probably showing up in her body language. She may be shaking slightly, or even be perspiring more than usual. She may feel humiliated, but is unsure what next to expect from her Manager, or what she should now say. She has four possible choices:

*   Passive.
*   Aggressive.
*   Passive-aggressive.
*   Assertive.

Suggestions

Passive

Marianne could apologise, but she may not know what she is apologising for because the Manager was not clear on what he meant by "unsubstantiated opinion". Marianne could say she will go back and rework the presentation, but she is not yet clear about what needs to be reworked. Apologising and not knowing what you are apologising for is a passive response. Marianne could completely lose credibility in front of the team, who may well be embarrassed for her anyway. She could also damage her own self-confidence and self-respect. She needs to find a way to stand up for herself that keeps her confidence and integrity intact, yet does not attack the other person.

Aggressive

Marianne could attack back, "You cannot speak to me like that!" By attacking back, the Manager could do the same, but having more power and authority the Manager could escalate the situation out of control.

Passive-aggressive

Marianne could choose to be silent (behaving passively), or say that she will go back and rework the presentation (which is also passive). But in her own mind she is thinking, "Just you wait. I will alter one of the models we are presenting and remix your presentation, and you will end up being the most embarrassed in front of the client" (aggressive). However, this kind of response sets up future conflict with her Manager, does not restore Marianne's own self-belief and self-confidence, and neither does it increase the Manager's confidence in her.

Assertive

Marianne could give a direct and specific response. She could explain that it is based on the data produced by the entire team and approved by the Manager a week ago. She could directly ask the Manager to clarify what part of the presentation he is unclear about. What is important is that Marianne does not automatically assume her presentation was incorrect, and to be willing to ask for accountability from the Manager. The assertive response is specific, and quotes direct facts. This will show Marianne to be competent, and her colleagues may well feel confident and might back her. Also, Marianne is respectful of the Manager's opinion, but needs clarity on the facts.

An assertive response is direct, corrects any false assumptions or errors, and does not accept inappropriate behaviour. An assertive response also asks for accountability.

Being clear about the four styles

- A *passive* response indicates to the other person that you are not their equal; and worse, that they can always get their way when dealing with you. It also does not let the other person know what your needs are – and we cannot expect the other person to figure them out or to read your mind. Passive people often do not feel they have the power to respond assertively – but they often get fed up and ultimately get even.

- An *aggressive* response violates the rights of another, and indicates that you want your needs to be met at their expense. Aggressive behaviour indicates that you do not care about the other person's thoughts or feelings. It can work in the immediacy of the situation, as people are mostly not inclined to take on a bully or an aggressive person. The aggressive stance tends to attack the person and not the issue. It means possibly undermining or humiliating the other. An aggressive tone of voice may be loud, inflammatory, and threatening.

- A *passive-aggressive* response first indicates that you are rolling over and letting their opinion take dominance. However, when you later do something aggressive, it can only escalate the conflict between the two parties. An aggressive person may behave passively if they do not feel they can take on the situation then and there. But they will get even later. Also, passive-aggressive behaviour can include indirect eye contact and lack of response. The later aggressive behaviour may be sarcastic, with indirect criticism lobbied through other parties.

- The *assertive* response means standing up for your right to be heard without violating the rights of another person. It means everyone's rights are equal. An assertive response gives you confidence in your own stance, and means that you have made a choice that is direct, respectful of both parties, and assigns accountability. It means being clear, direct, stating the facts, and being unemotional. Your tone of voice is evenly modulated, and your voice is at a normal conversational level. It is neither too fast nor too slow, but firm. An assertive person values not just their own needs but the needs of others. They not only ask for accountability from others, but believe they also must be accountable and ask for what they need. In terms of body language, an assertive person will sit or stand tall, respect the space of others, use direct eye contact to indicate equality and confidence, and not show any anger (although they may be firm). An assertive stance gives others confidence in you, and indicates that you deal fairly and respectfully with others. It gives you the confidence to handle any difficult situation with greater ease.

Blocks to communication

What keeps us from being assertive is unclear communication. For example, you are the Manager, and you say to your team. "OK, I have given you the brief – get ready to launch our new app next week. The final steps are to test the app with a random sample of our clients before the end of next week, and to be careful that the colours match not just our company logo, but resonate with our company values. Let me know when the testing is done, and you are ready to go. Any questions?"

The team goes away, and immediately start to debate what the Manager means by "match our company logo" and "resonate with our company values" – what does that mean? And how many participants for random testing are necessary? And what are the criteria to know that we are ready to launch? The message was not entirely clear, and no one had the courage to question the Manager. So, will they be ready with so many uncertainties?

With every message that is communicated, there is an intention on the part of the message giver, and the receiver must decode the message to understand that intention. But decoding a message goes through the filters and experience of the decoder. If the message does not sit well with their experience, then the message will be misunderstood. An assertive message would give more clarity. There are three blocks to clear communication:

- fear;

- role patterns; and

- limiting assumptions about the other party.

Fear

There are essentially certain blocks to hearing the message, and the receiver of the message can interpret only through their own experience, which might be quite different from the experience of the sender. The first block is fear: "What if I get it wrong – what will happen to me and my job?" Fear can block your ability to hear the message. And that may include the fear of failure: "What if I think I understood the message correctly, but somehow I am unclear about exactly what is the intended outcome?"

Role patterns

Another block to being assertive is to do with our social and behavioural development. We carry certain roles in our lives from family members, our position at work and in the community in which we live. With each of the roles we carry we have certain assumptions that empower us, and certain assumptions that limit us. If you have been brought up in a hierarchical society, you may feel hesitant to speak up if you are not an elder in the family or community.

We have certain blind spots about the roles we play at work, at home, and in our social and faith communities. Limiting assumptions can hold us back from speaking clearly and assertively if we do not feel we have the power in our position to do so. One positional role is that of trying to please others. This is often developed from childhood, and can carry on into adult life. Pleasing behaviours include how we should speak, dress, act, behave – and whether we should be pleasing others without taking ourselves into consideration. Our choices and options can be self-limiting, and may mean that we need to embrace new ways of engaging with others.

Limiting assumptions

We make a lot of assumptions about people every day. It is critically important to pay attention to our assumptions as we listen to the other person in any given situation. This means making eye contact neutrally, not interrupting the other person to put them off track, and listening without judgement. It is also important to understand your own biases and triggers. Start to be aware of how you are experiencing other people – but also how they may be experiencing you. What does your body language convey – and what do you see and hear that is causing difficulty for you? If you are simply in "reaction mode", you may miss both listening to and hearing their message. Be aware of the assumptions you are making about their message and their behaviour – and be aware of how you sound to them. In other words, how are they experiencing you?

Give attention to what you see them doing. Maybe they are reacting to your body language. And unless you set aside your own assumptions, you may never find out what is going on. Ask yourself, how do I look to other people? What do I sound like – people make assumptions based on what they hear. What do you hear them saying and what do you see them doing that causes difficulty? Your reaction may be preventing you from really hearing what they are saying. How do I sound to them, and what assumptions are they making about me?

Developing an assertive style of behaviour

The easiest way to remove some of the blocks that prevent us from communicating clearly is to develop an assertive vocabulary and style of behaviour. This means assessing the risk and responding in a way that addresses the facts of the situation. It means determining which battles are worth fighting, and those we can simply walk away from. Most important is to respond to the facts in the situation.

An aggressive person tends to want to win every argument or discussion. In contrast, a passive person will avoid the situation – especially if it means engaging with conflict. Sometimes the assertive choice is not to assert yourself; sometimes it means asserting yourself and asking for accountability from all parties. Assess the risk – what will I lose and what will I gain if I assert myself? Will my speaking up mean I could risk a promotion – is it worth the risk? If I do not speak up, does it mean that I could be looked over for a promotion?

Activity: Ask yourself the following questions

1. What do I want from this communication, i.e. what is my intention?

2. If I continue with the same behaviour, will the situation change?

3. What will I give up if I do not respond assertively?

4. What is the worst that can happen if I behave assertively?

Activity: Changing your behaviour

It is often a good idea to prepare what you want to say and do. Think of a current situation coming up where you may need to change your usual behaviour.

1. What is the situation?

2. What has happened previously?

3. What is your intention?

4. What is the outcome you would like to happen?

5. What is the risk to you by changing your behaviour? Is there a security or a self-esteem risk?

Five key assertiveness techniques

Based on the original work of Carol Price,[257] there are five useful key techniques:

*   *declaration;*
*   *assertive confrontation;*
*   *compromise;*
*   *camouflage;* and
*   *accountability.*

Declaration

Declaration uses direction or explanation of what you want or think – and it is optional whether you give reasons. It may also use escalation if necessary.

"Thank you, Nomsa, for completing the draft budget. It looks alright; however, we need an extra column, 'Performance to Budget,' which will be a calculation of total spend to date subtracted from a *pro rata* apportionment of the annual budget to date."

Declaration is an "I" statement which clearly and specifically says what you want. It is not necessary to include a reason, although as a manager you may wish to. Your approach in using declaration is to ask in a direct, courteous, calm, and specific manner: "I will need this before lunch time today to present to the Chief Financial Officer."

Assertive confrontation

Assertive confrontation describes unacceptable behaviour and gives expectations for future behaviour. This is done in three steps:

1. Describe the unacceptable behaviour (what just happened).

2. Assign consequences.

3. Give expectations of future behaviour.

In this example, one of your direct reports has been asked to co-ordinate all the presentation material to present the advertising strategy to the Executive Committee that you chair. Your original message was noticeably clear to your direct report:

"Vusi, I need you to compile all the slides for the advertising strategy in the order we agreed this morning in our meeting – that means chronologically as the campaign is to be rolled out. I then require them to be loaded onto my computer ready for my presentation at 10h00 tomorrow morning."

The next morning, the slides are not on your computer as you begin to set up the meeting room at 09h00. You call Vusi in, and use Assertive Confrontation to manage the situation:

"Vusi, yesterday afternoon I made it clear what was needed for the presentation at 10h00 today. The slide presentation is not on my computer" (*unacceptable behaviour*).

Vusi replies:

"I did not have time to get to it, as Themba asked me to help with her presentation."

Your reply:

> "Themba's presentation is not until tomorrow morning. Please get my slides in order within the next 30 minutes – no need to take my computer. Go back to your office and work with the slides on your computer. It means my presentation will be late, which will be very embarrassing to the team (*consequences*). So, get started right now, and drop everything else you are doing. Email me the slides by 09h45 this morning, and make sure this does not happen again" (*expectations of future behaviour*).

What is most important is that only facts were addressed. The direct report was neither humiliated nor called lazy or incompetent. By being clear about the facts, it is less likely that the direct report will want to get even. And the goal of the manager was to get the job done as quickly as possible before it was too late. Next time Vusi will think twice about not doing what his line manager has asked.

Compromise

Compromise means coming to an agreement that satisfies the basic needs of both or all parties involved in the negotiation or communication. But compromise is about defining the expectations for both parties and then trying to satisfy those needs. It might be a win–win, but that is not always the case.

One of your direct reports, Caroline, speaks to another of your direct reports, Jenny, and asks for help on a project:

> "Jenny, the CEO has asked me to help him design his lecture and slides for his presentation to the School of Business tomorrow. But he still wants his other speech to the Minister of Health to be edited by tomorrow noon. You are a whizz at editing, and fast. Can you edit his other speech for me by noon tomorrow? That way I can help the CEO with his lecture and slides."

Jenny's reply:

> "I cannot help you, as the Chief Financial Officer (CFO) and I are in back-to-back meetings trying to finalise the budget before the CFO's meeting with the Minister at the end of the week. Sorry."

Caroline's response:

> "OK, I tell you what. I will ask the CEO to give the CFO and you another day to complete the budget for the Minister, on the understanding that you will edit the School of Business speech. That gives you even more time for the CFO, and it will make you look good to the CEO."

To compromise, there are three steps:

1. *Stating what you want* – "You are a whizz at editing, and fast. Can you edit his other speech for me by noon tomorrow?"

2. *Listening to the concerns of the other* – "The CFO and I are in back-to-back meetings trying to finalise the budget before the CFO's meeting with the Minister."

3. *Offering solutions to the problem* – "I will ask the CEO to give the CFO and you another day to complete the budget for the Minister, on the understanding that you will edit the School of Business speech. That gives you even more time for the CFO, and it will make you look good to the CEO."

Caroline offered solutions to Jenny's problem and made those solutions conditional on Jenny helping Caroline ("That gives you even more time for the CFO"). It did mean extra work for Jenny, but she gained extra time to work on the other project. The key is for both parties to be able to give and to receive. You do not always get everything that you want – but by listening to the concerns of the other and finding a solution to both problems, both are able to complete their two projects. They each walk away with their needs satisfied.

Camouflage

Camouflage means responding to another person in such a way that they have no idea what you just said or meant. There are three levels of camouflage:

- *non-response*;
- *limited response*; and
- *clouding*.

Non-response – first-level camouflage

Using non-response is a way to regain your composure. It might mean making eye contact but not speaking, or it could be sarcasm which side-steps the issue. I would, however, not recommend sarcasm. If you do not respond you are simply waiting for the other person to fill the gap. You must be at ease to use non-response.

Limited response – second-level camouflage

For example, you are late to a meeting and the Chair of the meeting asks why you are late when you finally arrive. You can either use non-response as in the above scenario, or you could use limited response.

Limited response is particularly useful if the Chair is sarcastic or somewhat aggressive in their address to you. Such as, "Oh, I see you decided to grace us with your presence. Is there a particular reason why you are late?" Limited response could be: "I am late. Do you need to know why I am late right now?" without responding to the sarcasm in the Chair's comment. It shows you might be willing to give a reason after the meeting, and it puts the responsibility for the conflict on the Chair.

Also, with limited response you are changing the tone of the conflict from a personal attack to a more neutral conversation that can take place outside of the meeting. It is important that your tone stays neutral with limited response. What is important is that even if the Chair is not in control of their emotions, you remain in control of yours, and you move the conflict away from the meeting.

Clouding – third-level camouflage

Clouding is responding without any logical connection to what was just said – and sometimes the more bizarre the better.

In this situation, the Chair asks you, "Why are you late?" And your response could be "I see you have a new haircut; it suits you." This is not logically connected to the question but puts the spotlight back onto the Chair who would probably just move on. Or a more bizarre response might be, "The news just came in that we are moving to Level Zero of Lockdown within two weeks' time." It catches the other person off guard, and it is unlikely they will escalate.

However, sometimes clouding is not in your best interest. For example, if the other person has no sense of humour; or if you find yourself in a threatening situation where you may need to protect yourself; or if the Chair is someone that you have never met or do not recognise. The main purpose of clouding is to create a grudging kind of respect, and to momentarily protect yourself.

One of the benefits of clouding as an assertive technique is that it usually wins over others who are in the room, and it puts the other person right into the middle of the interaction with the focus off you.

Accountability

Accountability is holding the other person accountable for their inappropriate behaviour, especially if that behaviour involves one of the "isms" (e.g. sexism, racism, nationalism). Assess the risk before using accountability, as its usefulness will vary from one situation to another. Determine what are the consequences before trying to use accountability. To use accountability, be sure of the facts and understand where responsibility lies.

For example, if you are female and you walk into a situation with four men, and one of them makes a very inappropriate comment (e.g. "Oh, hello, Sexy. I love seeing you in that short skirt with your gorgeous long legs"), but no one else says anything. You may choose non-response as a first-level reply, but if the comments continue you will need to escalate to asking for accountability. In this case, the comment is entirely inappropriate, and the person needs to be held accountable. And often, if you hold them to account, they back off.

An accountability reply could be: "If you continue along these lines I and my team will immediately withdraw from helping you with this project." This response moves you from victim to a person who is worthy of respect. "If you continue along these lines" means that you have called them to account, and may need to continue to do so if they persist. Most people who make comments like this are used to no one responding to their bullying or aggressiveness, and when called to accountability will usually back down. If not, you may need to take the matter to HR.

Once when working in London, I was about to start a workshop with 30 senior managers, and one of the last ones to enter the room said to me, "Oh, no, you're an American. And a woman." My reply was, "Nice to meet you, and I am happy to re-register you on a future workshop with another facilitator." He did not apologise, but sat down somewhat nonplussed. In a coffee break I approached him and had a chat with him, reiterating that I was happy to enrol him on another workshop and at another date. He had calmed down and did not create any further difficulties that day. One of the reasons he did not pursue the issue was that none of his colleagues supported him.

Working with the five techniques

There are never easy answers to any difficult situation. What is useful about assertiveness is that it is a choice whether, when, and how to be assertive. You do not need to take on every situation as one in which there is a potential fight. Be strategic about how you use assertiveness. It always depends on the individuals who are involved, and what are the various personalities and relationships in the situation. What is clear is that you can stand up for your own rights while still respecting the rights of others.

Activity: Your volatile situations

Think of one or two situations which you faced recently and did not feel that you handled as well as you could.

- Write down a few sentences about the potential disagreement or conflict that arose.

- Write out which assertiveness skill you could have used for each situation: *declaration, confrontation, compromise, camouflage* or *accountability.*

If you are heading into a situation that might be volatile, think about which of these five techniques might be applicable.

Conclusion

In Part Four we looked at managing difficult people and difficult situations – improving the effectiveness of your communication skills by understanding the difference between personality and behaviour. If we are to gradually shift our own and other people's inappropriate behaviour, we need to understand how the brain works, which will help us to identify triggers and desired outcomes. It is important to identify the triggers to inappropriate behaviour if we are to negotiate behavioural change.

When finding yourself in a tricky situation, identify the limiting assumptions you are making about yourself and the other person, and whether there is an alternative assumption that will help you to understand their message and their behaviour. At the same time, be aware of how you sound and look to them. This will help you to assess the situation more clearly.

We also looked at four styles of communication: passive, aggressive, passive-aggressive and assertive. These are four possible choices in communicating and negotiating. And we worked with five techniques of assertiveness which can help you to convey your message directly when dealing with difficult situations: declaration, confrontation, compromise, camouflage and accountability.

Part Five – Next-level leadership

Chapter 13

Understanding next-level leadership

Introduction

> The illiterate of the twenty-first century will not be those who cannot read and write, but those who cannot learn, unlearn, and relearn – Alvin Toffler, *Future Shock*.[258]

My first experience of management was when I was working for a multinational pharmaceutical company during my late 20s, and was promoted to a management position in Human Resources. Although there were none of today's sophisticated online tools and techniques, I witnessed line managers struggling with the demands of new roles; and while many would make the transition with some bumps and scrapes, others would crash and burn.

Even though our organisation was regarded as one of the forerunners in innovative training and development practices, I clearly remember the lack of transition management support, and the feeling that, as a manager, you had to make it up as you went along. The reality was that there was no clear definition (and even less understanding) of high-potential leadership, and the unique challenges managers face in their career aspirations.

And now, many years later, it still surprises me to see so many managers grappling with similar questions, such as:

- "What skills do I need to excel in my next-level leadership role?"

- "Will a professional business school qualification help me develop the necessary skills?"

- "Why am I constantly being overlooked for promotion? It feels personal."

- "My manager seems to lack the language and social intelligence to engage in a mature conversation about my development."

- "My development plan is vague, and there is very little support for my career progression."

Strikingly, research conducted with over 600 managers over a four-year period reported that less than five per cent of managers have mastered the level of skill and agility needed for sustained success in today's turbulent business environment.[259]

Why read this chapter?

If you are a leadership development professional, or a line manager looking for guidance, and you sense that you require a refreshing of your personal and leadership capacities, this chapter is for you. It provides an in-depth examination of the concept of next-level leadership. It also describes the distinct transitions that leaders make, in their quest for personal and leadership mastery. We offer a context, definition, and some guidelines for the development of next-level leadership. We provide a guide to the fundamental steps of next-level leadership, and ten insightful questions to be used for your personal development journey.

But to start with, let us explore the shifting context in which modern leaders must operate, and how next-level leadership is positioned as a critical capability set required in a new and ever-changing world of work.

The volatile environment and its impact on leaders

Context

The year 2020 showed that innovative leadership solutions do not occur in a vacuum. They are the result of the efforts of highly adaptable leaders who are committed to solving difficult, and often intractable, problems in an ever-changing context. The defining factor is the way in which these leaders approach problems and collaborate to find solutions:

> In his book, *The Age of the Unthinkable*, Joshua Ramo describes how Danish theoretical physicist, Per Bak, developed a theory about sand running through an hourglass.[260] As the sand went through, it organised itself into a cone that from the outside looked quite stable, but in reality was deeply unstable. Every grain of sand was connected by invisible pressures and tensions, so the internal dynamics of the sand pile were unknowable and totally unpredictable. You never knew which grain of sand would cause the sand pile to collapse. Stability, he argued, was the passing phase; instability was the constant.
>
> Ramo believed the sand pile represented our world – increasingly granular (more players entering every day) and increasingly interdependent (more unknowable connections between them). Think about it: In 2001 there were 500 million people online. Today the number is 3.5 billion (40 per cent of the world's population) and growing. They send about 200 billion emails a day. There are more than seven billion cellphone subscribers today – more than the population of the world. They are using those devices to connect in ways

that could not have been imagined a decade ago. Facebook has over 1.8 billion users; 75 per cent of them are outside the United States. Twitter has more than 650 million users, 75 per cent of them outside the United States. Today information is available 24 hours a day, seven days a week, binding us all together and creating a 'global awakening in expectations'.[261]

We live in a connected but unstable world, and complexity is accumulating. Our world, like the sand pile in an hourglass, is volatile – things change, change quickly, and for reasons beyond our control. It is uncertain – gaining conviction about future outcomes is ever more challenging. It is complex – we can never know the interaction of the multiple variables we must consider, let alone how to integrate them effectively, and it is also ambiguous – the same data can yield multiple and often competing interpretations.

Leadership in a global pandemic

Nothing could have prepared us for the COVID-19 coronavirus pandemic. I have personally witnessed organisations, management teams and brave individuals who, when lockdown happened, rose to the challenge of redefining and remodelling their businesses within hours, and conversely, those who, 12 months later, are still debating issues and searching for consensus on who is right. Many of these latter organisations might struggle to survive.

An example of reactive and indecisive leadership came recently from Johannesburg, at the point where the official death toll from COVID-19 had just exceeded 50 000. There were reports that government officials had refused calls early in 2020 to order vaccines. Then, scrambling to make up for lost time, one million AstraZeneca vaccines were ordered from the Serum Institute of India. They arrived amid much fanfare, with the state president and his ministers providing a public relations spectacle by arriving in a cavalcade on the airport runway to welcome the arrival of the life-saving vaccines.

Shortly afterwards, studies revealed that the AstraZeneca vaccine had, according to the World Health Organisation, disappointing results for the South African variant of the virus. The government immediately suspended its vaccination roll-out plan, and raced to source other vaccines from elsewhere. In addition, the imminent expiry date of the vaccines was apparently discovered only on the day of their arrival, highlighting a lack of planning and preparation potentially endangering the lives of many citizens.

Activity: Question for reflection

Do you believe the leaders in government and business worldwide have the necessary skills and resilience to tackle the complexity and volatility of the current challenges we face? Give reasons for your answers.

Acquiring the mind-set of a next-level leader

Are great leaders born or made?

The age-old question: nature *versus* nurture? Where does talent come from? Are great men and women born or made?

Research conducted by leading psychologist Carol Dweck shows that regardless of the baseline ability nature bestows on an individual, nurture (effort and attitude) can produce extraordinary gains in ability. Dweck, a Stanford University psychology professor, has demonstrated conclusively that nurture can indeed trump nature. This does not necessarily mean that with enough effort one can become the next Serena Williams or Mozart. Williams would naturally have always been a much better player than most, but she never would have been the great player she became without her legendary attitude and effort. The media often showcases the great performers and recounts their beginnings as child prodigies (e.g. Mozart composing symphonies at the age of six). However, the less fantastic, but more important reality, according to Dweck, is that *attitude toward success* plays a far greater role in long-term success than raw talent itself.[262]

In one particularly intriguing series of studies, Dweck discovered that student attitudes toward their own learning can be shifted by as little as a word or sentence of feedback from an authority figure. Students praised for their *effort* took on greater challenges and performed better than their classmates over time, while those praised for their *ability* avoided more difficult assignments and performed worse on subsequent testing. Leaders who understand learning can consider what kind of climate they encourage in their organisations, and what values they model, when it comes to the respective merits of hard work and effort.[263]

Nancy Kline's work on creating thinking environments is also instructive. She states that people are likely to accelerate their thinking capability in the *absence of fear and judgement,* and suggests a ratio of five instances of appreciation to every instance of criticism, which helps people think for themselves.[264] This would be a useful (and challenging) benchmark for managers to align with.

The character of next-level leadership

We are observing an emerging consensus regarding the definition of effective next-level leadership. Leaders who successfully make the transformation tend to be more agile, versatile and adaptive, demonstrating agile behaviours when responding to the complex, paradoxical and ever-changing situations that confront them. The ability of a leader to use their behavioural skillset to improvise in meeting the demands of their constantly changing environment becomes a distinctive leadership competence.[265] The willingness to be open to learning in new and different situations is vital.

Next-level leaders are agile and adaptive

Many business leaders describe the current business climate as managing in a continual state of organisational paralysis. While some political leaders have excelled during these times of crisis, others have found that their traditional approaches are no longer appropriate. *Times of crisis expose weak leadership* – they illuminate the fault lines within those who think arrogance, dogma and ego will carry the day. The leadership that will take us through these tough times requires courage beyond bluster, compassion beyond patronisation, and authenticity that is borne of emotional maturity and profound wisdom.[266]

Leadership agility

Leadership agility is the capability of a leader to sense and respond to changes in the business environment with actions that are focused, fast and flexible. It is about a leader's ability to prepare all employees for a volatile and uncertain world that enables them to shift their mind-sets and supporting skills from: "I know change is coming, but I can't really see the potential changes that might impact our organisation" to: "I see change coming and am prepared and already doing something about it." In short, we must anticipate.[267]

As senior leaders, our primary responsibility is to create hope in times of uncertainty and fear. The way to do this is through articulating an inspiring and positive vision of the future, interpreting this vision in functional teams, and ensuring effective and efficient execution.

Many of us will have witnessed narcissistic leaders who use fear mongering, lies, disinformation and conspiracies to stay in power. Feeding their followers a diet of dystopian negativity to keep them angry and distracted, this toxic brand of leadership can lead only to conflict, social upheaval, and the destabilisation of even the greatest of democracies.

Radical change is holding leadership practices to the fire, and many countries, organisations and individuals are found to be wanting. In this environment of volatility and uncertainty, developing agile and adaptive leaders is an organisation's best strategy for risk management and survival.

Next-level leaders are resilient

It is relatively easy to swim with tides of negativity, pessimism and popularism, but far more challenging to stand up and courageously do what is needed to lead people and organisations, not only to survive, but also to heal and to thrive. This is the mental and emotional resilience required from every individual tasked with the responsibility of leadership.[268]

We need to build mental and emotional resilience *in our workplaces*, especially during these tough times, when markets crash, revenues are under pressure, consumers are cash-strapped, and political and social paranoia become norms.

Resilience is the ability to design – and redesign – organisations, institutions and systems to better absorb disruption, operate under a wider variety of conditions, and shift more fluidly from one circumstance to the next.[269]

Resilient leaders maintain their core purpose and integrity in the face of dramatically changed circumstances.[270] Resilience is what makes the difference between those who succumb to problems and the pressures of change, and those who fight through them. Resilient people can use difficult situations as a motivator to try harder. This requires being able to absorb great pressure, and to build the necessary courage and resilience. Some individuals seem to flourish and take stress in their stride, while the same situation can cause mental and physical anxiety in others.[271]

The difference between these two types of people lies in their psychology, i.e. their mental hardiness and emotional resilience. There is a strong correlation between mental and physical wellbeing and a person's ability to manage their thoughts and beliefs during stressful periods in their lives.[272]

In the wake of the global COVID-19 outbreak, change is ongoing, plans unravel, and expectations aren't always met. People who are dogmatic, and can't handle ambiguity or uncertainty, are less likely to feel motivated at work and more likely to become overwhelmed.[273]

That is why resilience – maintaining equilibrium under pressure – is one of the most important skills for leaders at all levels to master. The question isn't how you can avoid difficulty and stress – that is nearly impossible. The question is, "How do you face difficulty and stress?" We can all benefit from improving our leadership resilience – making us better able to deal with crises, recover, and adapt.

Reflection and journaling

One way to improve leadership resilience is to reflect on your experiences. Learning or reflection journals can be used as tools for gaining insight into your leadership experiences. The process of writing and reflection builds self-awareness, encourages learning, and opens the door to adaptability.

It is important to emphasise that learning leadership resilience doesn't come from the doing, but from the *reflection on* the doing.

Activity: Reflect on the doing

To foster your reflection, even if you do not journal, just spend some time thinking. Recall a time in your personal or professional life when you were able to rise above a difficult situation. Then ask yourself:

1. What happened?
2. What was I thinking and feeling at the time?
3. What did I do that helped me get through that situation?
4. What did I learn from the experience and my reaction to it?

You have the resources within you to become more resilient. But it does take some effort to learn what will work best for you, and it requires making time for yourself.[274]

Next-level leaders are emotionally mature

Emotionally mature individuals have the innate ability to handle crises without unnecessarily escalating or exacerbating them. Instead of looking to apportion blame to someone else for their problems or behaviour, emotionally mature people seek to *fix* the problem or behaviour. They accept responsibility for their own actions. They collaborate with those who disagree with their own point of view in order to find solutions to problems.[275]

As part of the research for my Master's degree at Stellenbosch Graduate School of Business in 2010–2011, I studied with Professor David Kolb at Case Western University in Cleveland, Ohio, the expert on experiential learning theory. I also spent time with Dr Bill Joiner at Harvard University in Boston, Massachusetts, whose work on leadership agility is profound and increasingly relevant. Both these experts have been instrumental in shaping the thoughts and opinions outlined in this chapter. Joiner, in particular, has been researching the behavioural characteristics of next-level leaders in their journey from functional (expert) manager to next-level (catalytic) leader for the past 20 years. His work is most important at this defining and historic time, as we grapple with a global pandemic and unstable democracies, with little conventional wisdom to guide us.

Two core questions guided Joiner's research:

- What is it, exactly, that changes as a person grows from one stage of development to another?

- How do leaders become more effective as they grow into more advanced stages of development?

Research suggests that, as managers advance from one development stage to another, they *develop a distinct set of mental and emotional capacities* that enable them to respond more effectively to change and complexity. That is, *their level of leadership agility increases*. These are the next-level leaders.[276]

There is an increasing realisation that we need more catalytic leaders, with their openness to change, their willingness to rethink basic assumptions, and their visionary orientation. They represent the beginning of an advanced level of authentic leadership agility, capable of sustained success in today's highly complex, constantly changing business environment.[277]

Catalytic leaders are the embodiment of emotional maturity. They have a deeper capacity for empathising with others because they can imagine accurately what it is like to be another person, facing whatever situation they're facing. They develop a real curiosity about frames of reference that differ from their own, and they listen to other views because they genuinely want to consider new possibilities. In responding to people whose views differ from their own, they move more fluidly between assertiveness and accommodation.

A lack of mental and emotional maturity could originate from parental neglect, poor schooling, inappropriate role models, or societal and environmental challenges. This is clearly seen in the manifestation of dysfunctional behaviours such as bullying, anger, aggression, dogma, manipulation and narcissism, which are often compensators for a lack of emotional support and development so crucial in our formative years of emotional growth and development. Importantly, advancing the career of an individual who is emotionally immature can have debilitating consequences for their teams and their organisations, and especially for themselves as individuals.

Emotional self-awareness is key

Our initial reaction to unforeseen change is generally a mix of fear and overreaction. No one *wants* to fail. If we can learn to understand our own unique fears, and not project them onto others, we will discover that team members who are fully engaged are far more creative and productive than those who are frightened and insecure.

Self-awareness means having a deep understanding of one's emotions, strengths, weaknesses, needs, and drives. People with strong self-awareness are neither overly critical nor unrealistically hopeful. Rather, they are honest – with themselves and with others. People who have a high degree of self-awareness recognise how their feelings affect them, other people, and their job performance. Self-awareness extends to a person's understanding of their values and goals. Someone who is highly self-aware knows where they are headed and why. A highly self-aware leader has a greater likelihood of successful transitioning, than one who is low on self-awareness. Without self-awareness, learning and development strategies translate into mindless reactions to the environment. A lack of self-awareness is *the* single biggest factor in leadership derailment.[278]

Activity: Your learnings

1. Who have been your role models, and what have been your learnings from these experiences?

2. Have you asked for feedback about your leadership style from those you manage and influence?

3. What have you learned and changed as a result?

High performers versus high potentials

Many organisations develop and promote their *high performers* without realising that high performance in one situation does not guarantee high performance in a different situation elsewhere. Learning from experience and learning new skills (or honing current ones) to perform in *first-time situations* is how we demonstrate *high potential*.[279] Few would argue that potential can be detected from current performance in an area the person already knows well. The word "potential", according to Webster's dictionary[280] means "existing in possibility; capable of developing into actuality".

So, it cannot be fully detected from what a person already demonstrates – it requires the person do something new or different.[281]

Activity: Question for reflection

1. How does your organisation identify and develop high-potential leadership candidates?

2. How individualised is the programme – is it customised to the unique needs of each individual?

3. Is learning agility a measurement of potential where you work?

Lessons from executive derailment

Leaders typically transition through a series of career passages which are challenging and developmental. In such circumstances, people are faced with unique situations that make existing leadership practices inadequate and obsolete.

Research into leadership derailment was conducted at the Centre for Creative Leadership. These studies compared successful versus derailed executives. Derailed executives were individuals identified as having high potential, who were promoted but who ultimately failed. Research found that both successful and derailed executives:

*   were very bright;

*   had been identified as high potentials early in their career;

*   possessed outstanding records of achievement;

*   were ambitious and willing to sacrifice; and

*   possessed very few personal flaws.[282]

However, one derailment factor was repeatedly observed: *derailed executives were unable or unwilling to change or adapt*. They relied too much on a narrow set of work skills. Successful and derailed executives also differed in the way they managed hardship and mistakes. Executives who were successful overwhelmingly handled failure with poise and grace. They admitted mistakes, accepted responsibility and acted to correct the problems. In contrast, leaders who derailed were defensive about their failures, attempted to keep them hidden, or blamed others.[283]

When investigating derailment in a group of global executives working in foreign cultures, researchers observed that many global executives failed for seemingly contradictory reasons. For example, some executives were perceived as too autocratic, while others delegated too much. Some executives were viewed as too detail-oriented and tactical, while others were too visionary and strategic. Some executives failed because they were too brash, while others failed because they were too unassuming. The underlying problem was that a strength in one culture could become a fatal flaw in another culture (for example, confidence being perceived as arrogance, or decisiveness being perceived as not listening). These findings clearly indicate that global leadership requires leaders to learn and adapt to local customs and cultures.[284]

Activity: Your derailers

1. What are the areas that you might regard as possible derailers in your career?

2. How are you overcoming these?

The learning and development challenge

Chamorro-Premuzic stated that, while leaders are responsible for driving employee engagement, only 30 per cent of employees are actively engaged, costing the U.S. economy 550 billion US dollars a year in productivity loss. Moreover, a large global survey of employee attitudes toward management suggests that a staggering 82 per cent of people do not trust their manager. You need only to Google "my boss is ..." or "my manager is ..." and see what the auto-complete text is to get a sense of what most people think of their leaders.[285] Over 50 per cent of employees leave their jobs because of their managers. The rate of derailment, unethical incidents and counterproductive work behaviours among leaders is so high that it is hard not to be shocked by a leader's dark side.

As leadership and behavioural coaches, we are often called upon to provide remedial assistance to managers who are struggling to cope with the demands of a next-level role. Generally, this is because they have been incorrectly identified as suitable for the role, or are poorly supported and developed. They are typically promoted for their functional and technical expertise, or because they have a reputation of being a leader people fear. None of these factors are indicators of high-potential leadership, and are often contra-indicators for catalytic next-level leadership.

It is easy to become overwhelmed by the transformative shift that needs to be made to operate effectively at a next level of leadership mastery. Managers should not be exposed to *yet another* training course that will "fix" their lack of emotional intelligence. We need a new level of understanding and interpretation of the science underpinning next-level leadership. Organisations need to learn to understand how people learn, then design highly individualised strategies for their high potentials. They need to assess the core dimensions of learning agility, identifying individuals with the potential for future leadership positions. This approach differs from many traditional practices found in organisations today.

The career progression ladder

Transitions in management

To articulate the steps to next-level leadership, the illustration of a management career progression ladder in Figure 15 shows the transitions that are made in a typical corporate career. Each of these levels has a unique transition behavioural makeup or "DNA" that increases in complexity and ambiguity. Of importance is the *capability compounding effect,* where the leader needs to have acquired the capabilities at the current level, before making a smooth and effective transition *to the next level.*

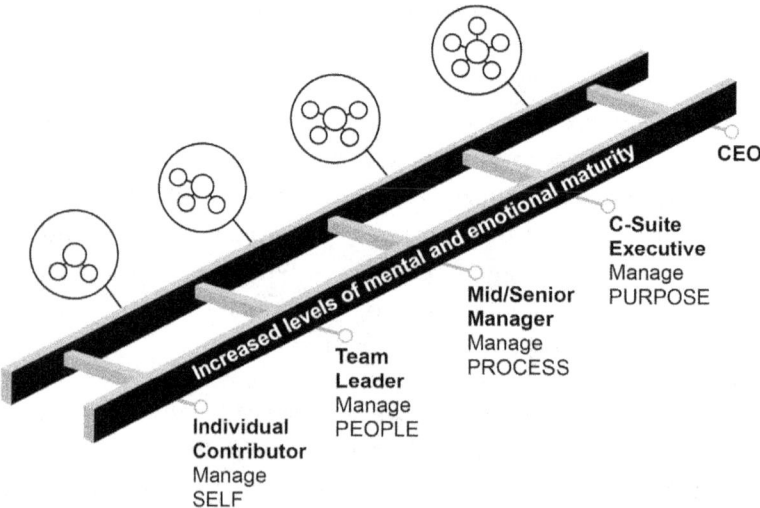

Figure 15: The management career progression ladder

Source: Taylor.[286]

Three factors influence making successful transitions:

1. The *level* at which the progression is applicable. The higher the level, the greater the complexity and capability required.

2. The *speed* at which the transformation is made to the next level. Being an agile learner is key.

3. The *context* in which the leader is asked to contribute, i.e. the industry, the regulatory environment, competitive activity, corporate culture and leadership values.

Table 7: The key leadership capability shifts required at every career step

Step	Key leadership capability shifts
Step 1: Individual contributor – managing self	• Provide professional expertise to the organisation in your area of speciality, not only completing your assigned work, but also learning to work with others collaboratively.
	• Show up to work on time, getting along with your co-workers, managing your time and priorities.
	• Keep your line manager informed, and following basic workplace etiquette.
	• Learning how to solve problems, making decisions, using good judgement, and controlling your emotions.
Step 2: Team leader – managing others	• Let go of work which defined your previous successes as an individual.
	• Effectively manage the performance of other people. Create a climate in which people want to do their best.
	• Motivate many kinds of direct reports and team or project members.
	• Determine each person's "hot button" and use it to get the best out of them.
	• Delegate tasks and decisions to your direct reports.
	• Empower others, and encourage open dialogue.
	• Invite input from each person, and share ownership and visibility.
	• Make each individual feel their work is important.
	• Create strong morale and spirit in the team, sharing wins and successes.
	• Define success in terms of the whole team.
	• Create a feeling of belonging within the team.
	• Learn how to coach people to realise their potential, and hold people to account.

Step	Key leadership capability shifts
Step 3: Middle or senior manager – managing process	• Continue developing the abilities rooted in the previous level. • The integration of functions is now what is important. • The biggest shift is looking at plans and proposals functionally to identify a profit perspective and a long-term view. • Stop the frenetic "doing" and reserve time for reflection and analysis. • Learn about and tap into everyone's values, goals, hopes, dreams, and fears. • Getting to know each team member, learning how to inspire commitment, energise, and harness the individual and collective passion of the team. • Leadership of others and teams requires transforming yourself into a next-level leader. • Learn how to coach clever people, using more advanced techniques of development.
Step 4: C-Suite – managing vision and purpose	• At this level, leadership becomes more holistic and strategic. • Transition from running your own show to running a variety of shows. • Value the success of other people – not just your own. • Shift thinking from a functional perspective to profit generation. • Communicate a compelling and inspired vision or sense of core purpose. • Talk optimistically about possibilities in the future. • Create mileposts and symbols to rally support behind the vision.
	• Make the vision sharable by everyone. • Inspire and motivate entire units or organisations. • Build strategic alliances with key stakeholders.

Source: Charan, Drotter and Noel[287]; Lombardo and Eichinger[288]

In Table 7, you will see the critical behavioural shifts required for each step in the career management ladder. When individuals do not fully acquire the necessary specific competences, the leadership pipeline quickly becomes clogged with managers who operate at a level or two below where they should be. This can create *structural compression*, a situation where the organisational design hierarchy becomes unstable. In dysfunctional organisations, the capability structures collapse as a result, with inevitable dire consequences for the business.

By clarifying and understanding the concepts outlined in this section, managers will not only receive targeted training and be coached into their level-specific roles, but will start preparing themselves for the next-level career role and skill set required. This accelerates the talent and succession management process, and is at the heart of high-performing organisations.

Activity: Your development strategy

1. Where are you at in your leadership career?

2. What observations have you made regarding where you might have missed some developmental aspects of these steps?

3. Has this affected your ability to perform in your current role?

4. Having read this chapter, are there any changes you would make to your personal development strategy?

The journey to next-level leadership

The aspiration to a C-Suite position or higher is the dream of many ambitious managers. But the journey requires careful planning, hard work, patience, study and reflection to develop complex skills and capabilities. Often, timing and a stroke of luck work in your favour. It is helpful to partner with a wise mentor and an experienced executive coach to take the journey with you. An independent sounding board makes all the difference in avoiding derailment traps.

Fundamental steps to next-level leadership: the ten clarity questions

There are ten questions, often incorporated into our coaching work with leaders, that create a platform for next-level leadership, and will help you start your journey:

Role clarity:

1. What is the scope of the role, and what has been contracted?

2. Is there clarity and a mutual understanding of the purpose and accountabilities required in your role?

3. How will you sell yourself and your contribution to your key stakeholders?

The context:

4. What are the cultural dynamics at play in this organisation?

5. What seems to be valued in this organisation? Are there blind spots?

6. Do your personal values align with the organisation and its leadership?

Success measures:

7. Who is key to your success in this role? Do you have a healthy and mature relationship with them?

8. How will you contract the measures of success in your role?

Next-level platform:

9. What is your next level of growth? Can it be accommodated where you are?

10. Based on 360° feedback received:

    • What strategic, conceptual and perspective skills do you require?

    • What EQ and SQ (emotional and social skills) do you require at the next level?

    • Where are your blind spots?

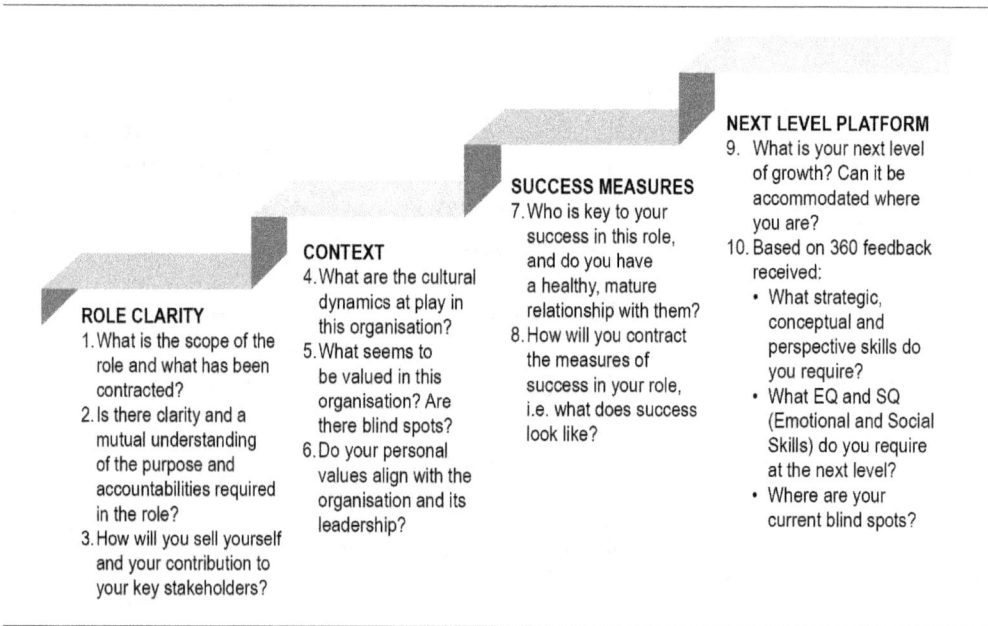

ROLE CLARITY
1. What is the scope of the role and what has been contracted?
2. Is there clarity and a mutual understanding of the purpose and accountabilities required in the role?
3. How will you sell yourself and your contribution to your key stakeholders?

CONTEXT
4. What are the cultural dynamics at play in this organisation?
5. What seems to be valued in this organisation? Are there blind spots?
6. Do your personal values align with the organisation and its leadership?

SUCCESS MEASURES
7. Who is key to your success in this role, and do you have a healthy, mature relationship with them?
8. How will you contract the measures of success in your role, i.e. what does success look like?

NEXT LEVEL PLATFORM
9. What is your next level of growth? Can it be accommodated where you are?
10. Based on 360 feedback received:
    • What strategic, conceptual and perspective skills do you require?
    • What EQ and SQ (Emotional and Social Skills) do you require at the next level?
    • Where are your current blind spots?

Figure 16: The fundamental next-level leadership steps

Source: Taylor.[289]

Conclusion

Hooijberg and Watkins indicate that the pandemic has accelerated a pre-COVID-19 shift in how individuals and teams do intellectual work. "Companies have learned that routine tasks involving transactions and co-ordination can be done virtually, while work requiring true team collaboration (collective learning, innovation, building a shared culture) is still best face-to-face. They envision the post-pandemic future of teamwork will be a purposeful hybrid combination of virtual co-ordination and in-person collaboration".[290]

This will require the skills and capabilities of next-level leadership as outlined in this chapter. Start your journey with confidence.

Chapter 14

Conclusion

This first book in our *Management Mastery and Practice* series has been an introduction to the core principles of managing people and teams. Beyond that, it aims to provide practical steps to foster an understanding that we cannot manage others without identifying our own motivators, subconscious limiting assumptions and overt behaviours. I hope that this series has introduced you to the essential principles of managing people – and that it will also provide you with a clear map to manage yourself: a life-long process which, if you follow it effectively, can lead to enriching your proficiency in all spheres.

At every moment in our life, at work and at home, we are faced with choices, and this is especially true today with the ever-faster pace of business decision making. This is why it is vital for managers and supervisors at all levels to develop themselves and their ability to deal with different new challenges. Keys to acquiring that crucial competence are developing real self-awareness and assimilating a deeper understanding of our own potential and that of our teams. It is only by starting with ourselves, expanding our personal wisdom and emotional capabilities, that we can manage others in their path to grow and develop.

The choice is simple: if you cannot manage yourself you will not manage people properly. If you can develop self-awareness and manage yourself effectively, you are on your way to being a successful manager. It is all about developing self-mastery. Managers need to continually develop the skill, *competence*, and capacity to lead and manage. And within the component of management there is a deep level of leadership.

This book offers you a way to think about what you are doing – helping you to *understand* what you are thinking and feeling and how you are behaving in each difficult situation, and to see and *appreciate* people from their perspective. Within your management team, this book can be used to create a common language and a common perspective to develop yourself and others. Without a common language and common purpose it will be difficult manage the business, develop a new strategy, or create a new culture.

Most managers are task-oriented and work extremely hard. But what might you be missing in terms of understanding others, reflection and mindfulness – ticking off tasks but not understanding what you want to achieve for yourself, your team and the business? Now, having looked at the intrinsic motivators of yourself and your team members, as well as the values and experience they bring, what conversations are not taking place? This book offers you an opportunity to have the conversations that will take you to the next level of leading and managing people.

Bibliography

Adair, J. (1973) *Action-Centred Leadership*. New York, NY: McGraw-Hill.

Adolphs, R. (2009). The social brain: Neural basis of social knowledge. *Annual Review of Psychology*, 60:693–716.

American Manufacturing Association (AMA) (2008). *Coaching: A global strategy of successful practices*. New York, NY: AMA.

Barrett, L.F., Adolphs, R., Marsella, S., Martinez, A.M., and Pollak, S.D. (2019). Emotional expressions reconsidered: Challenges to inferring emotion from human facial movements. *Psychological Science in the Public Interest*, 20(1):1–68.

Bennis, W.G., and Nanus, B. (2003). *Leaders: Strategies for taking charge*. Third edition. New York, NY: HarperCollins.

Blake, R.R., and McCanse, A.A. (1991). *Leadership Dilemmas: Grid solutions*. Houston, TX: Gulf Publishing.

Blake, R.R., and Mouton, J.S. (1964/1994). *The Managerial Grid*. 1994 paperback re-release of 1964 first edition. Houston, TX: Gulf Publishing.

Bolman, L.G., and Deal, T. (2001). *Leading With Soul: An uncommon journey of spirit*. Second Edition. San Francisco, CA: Jossey-Bass.

Boyatzis, R.E., and McKee, A. (2005). *Resonant Leadership: Renewing yourself and connecting with others through mindfulness, hope and compassion*. Boston, MA: Harvard Business School.

Boyatzis, R.E., Smith, M.L., and Blaize, N. (2006). Developing sustainable leaders through coaching and compassion. *Academy of Management Learning and Education*, 5(1):8–24.

Bressler, S.L., and Menon, V. (2010). Large-scale brain networks in cognition : emerging methods and principles. *Trends in Cognitive Sciences*, 14(6):277–290.

Buckingham, M. (2012). Leadership development in the age of the algorithm. *Harvard Business Review*, 90(6):86–94.

Busse, R., and Warner, M. (2017). The legacy of the Hawthorne experiments: A critical analysis of the Human Relations School of Thought. *History of Economic Ideas*, 25(2):91–114.

Caldari, K. (2007). Alfred Marshall's critical analysis of scientific management. *European Journal of the History of Economic Thought*, 14(1):55–78.

Carlson, N.R, Miller, H.L., Heth, D.S., Donahoe, J.W., Lee, B. (2014). *Psychology: The Science of Behaviour*. Seventh edition. Harlow, Essex: Pearson Education.

Casey, G.W. (2017). *Leading in a VUCA World*. SC Johnson Graduate School of Management, Cornell University. Webpage: www.johnson.cornell.edu/wp-content/uploads/sites/3/2019/04/Cornell-Executive-Education-VUCA-Leadership-February-2017.pdf. Retrieved 30 July 2020.

Cavanagh, M.J., and Grant, A.M. (2002). *Coaching Psychology: A solution-focused, cognitive-behavioural approach*. Sydney, NSW: University of Sydney: Coaching Psychology Unit.

Centre for Creative Leadership (CCL) (2020). *Leadership Resilience: Handling stress, uncertainty, and setbacks*. Greensboro, NC: CCL. Webpage: www.ccl.org/articles/leading-effectively-articles/leadership-resiliency-handling-stress-uncertainty-and-setbacks/. Retrieved 2 March 2021.

Cesario, J., Johnson, D. J., and Eisthen, H. L. (2020). Your brain is not an onion with a tiny reptile inside. *Current Directions in Psychological Science*, 29(3):255–260.

Chamorro-Premuzic, T. (2016). What science tells us about leadership potential. *Harvard Business Review*, September. Webpage: hbr.org/2016/09/what-science-tells-us-about-leadership-potential. Retrieved March 2020.

Charan, R, Drotter, S., and Noel, J. (2001). *The Leadership Pipeline: How to build the leadership powered company*. San Francisco, CA: Wiley.

Chemers, M.M. (2001). Leadership effectiveness: An integrative review. In Hogg, M.A., and Tindale, R.S. (eds), *Blackwell Handbook of Social Psychology: Group processes* (pp. 376–399). Oxford: Blackwell.

Clipartkey.com (2021). *Clipart Motivation Concept – Maslow's Hierarchy of Needs*. Webpage: www.clipartkey.com/view/himiTJ_clip-art-motivation-concept-maslows-hierarchy-of-needs/. Retrieved 14 March 2021.

Cohen, S.L. (2009). *Four Key Leadership Practices for Leading in Tough Times*. Burlington, MA: Right Management.

Csikszentmihalyi, M. (1990). Literacy and intrinsic motivation. *Daedalus*, 115–140.

David, S., and Congleton, C. (2013). Emotional agility: How effective leaders manage their negative thoughts and feelings. *Harvard Business Review*, November.

De Meuse, K.P., Dai, G., and Hallenbeck, G.S. (2010). Learning agility: A construct whose time has come. *Consulting Psychology Journal: Practice and Research*, 62(2):119–130.

Deci, E.L., and Ryan, R.M. (1985). *Intrinsic Motivation and Self-Determination in Human Behaviour*. Perspectives in Social Psychology series. Boston, MA: Springer.

Deci, E.L., and Ryan, R.M. (1990). A motivational approach to self: Integration in personality. *Nebraska Symposium on Motivation*, 38:237–288.

Di Domenico, S.I., and Ryan, R.M. (2017). The emerging neuroscience of intrinsic motivation: A new frontier in self-determination research. *Frontiers in Human Neuroscience*, 11(March):1–14.

Du Buisson-Narsai, I. (2020). *Flight, Fight or Flourish: How neuroscience can unlock human potential*. Randburg: Knowres.

Eichinger, R.W., and Lombardo, M.M. (2004). *The 6 Qs of Leadership: A blueprint for enduring success at the top*. Lominger In Focus paper. Minneapolis, MN: Lominger Limited.

Energy Resourcing (2021). Introducing Generation C. Webpage: energyrsourcing.com/blog/6-ting s-you-need-to know-about-generation-c/. Retrieved May 2021.

Fayol, H. (1949). *General and Industrial Administration*. Translated by C. Storrs. New York, NY: Pitman.

Fisher, A. (1998). Success secret: A high emotional IQ. *Fortune*, 26 October, 293–298.

Feldman-Barrett, L. (2018) *How Emotions Are Made: The Secret Life of the Brain*. London: Pan Macmillan.

Fiske, S.T., and Taylor, S.E. (2013). *Social Cognition: From brains to culture*. Thousand Oaks, CA: Sage.

Gardner, H. (1995). *Leading Minds: An anatomy of leadership*. New York, NY: Basic Books.

Garms, E.T. (2013). Practicing mindful leadership. *Training and Development*, March, 32–35.

Garrick, L. (ed.) (2006). *Supporting Guide – Hay Group Inventory of Leadership Styles Diagnostic*. Report for Senior Careers Development Service. Philadelphia, PA: Hay Group.

George, B., Sims, P., and McLean, A. (2007). Discovering your authentic leadership. *Harvard Business Review*, 85(2):129–138.

Gillison, F., Osborn, M., Standage, M., Skevington, S. (2009). Exploring the experience of introjected regulation for exercise across gender in adolescence. *Psychology of Sport and Exercise*, 10(3):309–319.

Goleman, D. (1996). *Emotional Intelligence: Why it can matter more than IQ*. London: Bloomsbury.

Goleman, D. (1998). *Working with Emotional Intelligence*. New York, NY: Bantam Dell.

Goleman, D. (2000). Leadership that gets results. *Harvard Business Review*, 78(2):78–90.

Goleman, D., Boyatzis, R., and McKee, A. (2002). *Primal Leadership: Learning to lead with emotional intelligence*. Boston, MA: Harvard Business School.

Gordon, E., Barnett, K.J., Cooper, N.J., Tran, N., and Williams, L.M. (2008). An "Integrative Neuroscience" platform: application to profiles of negativity and positivity bias. *Journal of Integrative Neuroscience*, 7(3):345–366.

Gove, P.B. (ed.) (2018). *Webster's Third New International Dictionary Unabridged*. Revised edition. Springfield, MA: Merriam-Webster.

Griffiths, K.E., and Campbell, M.A. (2008). Regulating the regulators: Paving the way for international, evidence-based coaching standards. *International Journal of Evidence-Based Coaching and Mentoring*, 6(1):19–31.

Gross, J.J. (ed.) (2007). *Handbook of Emotion Regulation*. New York, NY: Guilford.

Hart, A. (2014). Is personality unique to humans? *BBC News*, 10 December. Webpage: www.bbc.com/news/science-environment-30395493. Retrieved April 2021.

Hayes, S.C., Strosahl, K.D., and Wilson, K.G. (1999). *Acceptance and Commitment Therapy: An experimental approach to behaviour of change*. New York, NY: Guilford.

Herzberg, F.I. (1966). *Work and the Nature of Man*. Cleveland, OH: World.

Hicks, M.D., and Peterson, D.B. (1999). The development pipeline: How people really learn. *Knowledge Management Review*, 9:30–33.

Hooijberg, R., and Watkins, M. (2021). The future of team leadership is multimodal. *MIT Sloan Management Review*, 9 February. Webpage: sloanreview.mit.edu/article/the-future-of-team-leadership-is-multimodal/. Retrieved March 2021.

Horney, N., Passmore, W., and O'Shea, T. (2010). Leadership agility: A business imperative for a VUCA world. *People and Strategy*, 33(4):32–38.

Howell, J.P. (2013). *Snapshots of Great Leadership*. Hove: Routledge.

Joiner, B. (2009). Creating a culture of agile leaders: A developmental approach. *People and Strategy*, 32(4):28–35.

Joiner, W.B., and Josephs, S.A. (2007). *Leadership Agility: Five levels of mastery for anticipating and initiating change*. San Francisco, CA: Jossey-Bass.

Judge, M. (2017). Why emotional maturity and emotional intelligence are important for healthy relationships. *TheRoot.com*, 5 December. Webpage: www.theroot.com/why-emotional-maturity-and-emotional-intelligence-are-i-1821030316. Retrieved December 2020.

Kabat-Zinn, J. (1994). *Wherever You Go There You Are: Mindfulness meditation in everyday life*. New York, NY: Hyperion.

Karlin, D. (2011). *Leaders: Their Stories, Their Words: Conversations with Human-Based Leaders™*. Ottawa, ON: A Better Perspective.

Kazdin, A.E. (ed.) (2000). *The Encyclopaedia of Psychology*. Washington, DC: American Psychological Association and New York, NY: Oxford University Press.

Kerpen, D. (2019). *4 Key Generational Trends in the Workplace*. Inc.com, 25 July. Webpage: www.inc.com/dave-kerpen/4-key-generational-trends-in-workplace.html. Retrieved 10 January 2021.

King, S.N., Altman, D.G., and Lee, R.J. (2011). *Discovering the Leader in You: How to realise your leadership potential*. San Francisco, CA: Jossey-Bass.

Kleckner, I. R., Zhang, J., Touroutoglou, A., Chanes, L., Xia, C., Simmons, W.K., Quigley, K.S., Dickerson, B.C., and Barrett, L.F. (2017). Evidence for a large-scale brain system supporting allostasis and interoception in humans. *Nature Human Behaviour*, 1(5):1–14.

Klenke, K. (1996). *Women and Leadership: A contextual perspective*. New York, NY: Springer.

Kline, N. (1999/2004). *Time To Think: Listening to ignite the human mind*. London: Cassell.

Kline, N. (2005). *The Thinking Partnership Programme: Consultant's Guide*. Wallingford: Time to Think.

Kline, N. (2017). *The Transforming Meetings Programme*. Wallingford: Time to Think.

Kline, N. (2020). *The Promise That Changes Everything: I won't interrupt you*. London: Penguin Life.

Kross, E., and Ayduk, O. (2011). Making meaning out of negative experiences by self-distancing. *Current Directions in Psychological Science*, 20(3):187–191.

Lacida, K. (2012). *Toxic Leadership*. Lead Change Group, 17 August. Webpage: leadchangegroup. com/toxic-leadership/. Retrieved January 2021.

Lewin, K., Lippitt, R., and White, R.K. (1939). Patterns of aggressive behaviour in experimentally created "social climates". *Journal of Social Psychology*, 10:271–299.

Lieberman, M.D. (2007). Social cognitive neuroscience: A review of core processes. *Annual Review of Psychology*, 58(1):259–289.

Lipkin, N. (2013). *What Keeps Leaders Up At Night? Recognising and resolving your most troubling management issues*. New York, NY: AMACOM.

Lohr, D. (1988). *How to Delegate Work and Ensure It's Done Right*. Audio cassette book. Boulder, CO: Career Track.

Lombardo, M.M., and Eichinger, R.W. (2000). High-potentials as high learners. *Human Resource Management*, 39(4):321–330.

Lombardo, M.M., and Eichinger, R.W. (2009). *FYI: For Your Improvement: A guide for development and coaching for learners, managers, mentors, and feedback givers*. Fifth edition. Los Angeles, CA: Lominger.

Mandela, N.R. (1994). *Long Walk to Freedom*. Edinburgh: Little, Brown.

Maslow, A. (1968). *Toward a Psychology of Being*. New York, NY: Van Nostrand.

McClelland, D.C. (1961). *The Achieving Society*. Princeton, NJ: Van Nostrand.

McClelland, D.C. (1987). *Human Motivation*. New York, NY: Cambridge University.

McGregor, D. (1960). *The Human Side of Enterprise*. New York, NY: McGraw-Hill.

McWhinney, W. (1993). *Paths of Change: Strategic choices for organisations and society*. Thousand Oaks, CA: Sage.

Mind Tools (2018). *The Blake Mouton Managerial Grid*. Webpage: www.mindtools.com/pages/ article/newLDR_73.htm#. Retrieved 16 January 2021.

Miner, J.B. (2002). *Organisational Behaviour: Foundations, theories, and analyses*. New York, NY: Oxford University Press.

National Research Council (1994). Self-confidence and performance. In *Learning, Remembering, Believing: Enhancing human performance* (pp.173–206). Washington, DC: The National Academies Press.

Neider, L.L., and Schriesheim, C.A. (eds) (2010). *The "Dark" Side of Management. Research in Management Series*. Miami, FL: University of Miami.

O'Neill, M.B. (2000). *Coaching with backbone and heart: A systems approach to engaging leaders with their challenges*. San Francisco, CA; Jossey-Bass.

Peltier, B. (2001). *The Psychology of Executive Coaching: Theory and application*. New York, NY: Brunner-Routledge.

Pentland, A.S. (2012). The new science of building great teams. *Harvard Business Review*, 90(4):60–69.

Peters, J., and Büchel, C. (2010). Episodic future thinking reduces reward delay discounting through an enhancement of prefrontal-mediotemporal interactions. *Neuron*, 66(1):138–148.

Peterson, D., and Goldsmith, D. (2020). *Journey to Mastery*. PowerPoint slides in the ACE Programme: Accelerating Coach Excellence. London: WBECS Group.

Price, C. (1994). *Assertive Communication Skills for Professionals*. Workbook and audio cassette. Boulder, CO: Career Track.

Purdue Global University (2020). *Generational Differences in the Workplace [Infographic]*. Purdue Global University. Webpage: https://www.purdueglobal.edu/education-partnerships/generational-workforce-differences-infographic/. Retrieved 15 January 2021.

Ramo, J.C. (2009). *The Age of the Unthinkable: Why the new world disorder constantly surprises us and what we can do about it*. New York, NY: Little, Brown.

Rogers, C. (1959). A theory of therapy, personality and interpersonal relationships, as developed in the client-centred framework. In Koch, S. (ed.), *Psychology: A study of a science. Volume 3: Formulations of the person and the social context* (pp.184–256). New York, NY: McGraw Hill.

Rosenthal, S.A., and Pittinsky, T.L. (2006). Narcissistic leadership. *The Leadership Quarterly*, 17(6):617–633.

Rumsey, M.G. (ed.) (2013). *The Oxford Handbook of Leadership*. Oxford: Oxford University Press.

Russell, J.A., and Barrett, L.F. (1999). Core affect, prototypical emotional episodes, and other things called emotion: dissecting the elephant. *Journal of Personality and Social Psychology*, 76(5):805–819.

Ryan, R.M. (2013). *Self-determination*. Notes compiled by Stout-Rostron, S., from presentation to Coaching in Leadership and Healthcare Conference 2013, Harvard / McLean Medical School, Cambridge, MA, 28 September.

Ryan, R.M., and Deci, E.L. (2000). Intrinsic and extrinsic motivations: Classic definitions and new directions. *Contemporary Educational Psychology*, 25(1):54–67.

Schacter, D.L., Benoit, R.G., and Szpunar, K.K. (2017). Episodic future thinking: Mechanisms and functions. *Current Opinion in Behavioural Sciences*, 17: 41–50.

Siegel, D.J. (2009). Mindful awareness, mindsight, and neural integration. *The Humanistic Psychologist*, 37(2):137–158.

Smuts, J. (1926). *Holism and Evolution*. New York, NY: Viking.

Spearhead Training Group (2017). *Management Development Programme*. Participant workbook. Chipping Norton: Spearhead Training.

Spinelli, E. (1989). *The Interpreted World: An introduction to phenomenological psychology*. London: Sage.

Sporns, O. (2013). Structure and function of complex brain networks. *Dialogues in Clinical Neuroscience*, 15(3):247–262.

Stagen, R., and Thomas, B. (2006) *Learning to Learn*. Unpublished paper. Dallas, TX: Stagen Leadership Institute.

Stout Rostron, S. (2006). The history of coaching. In: M. McLoughlin (Ed.), *Sharing the Passion: Conversations with Coaches* (pp. 16–41). Cape Town: Advanced Human Technologies.

Stout-Rostron, S. (2012). *Business Coaching Wisdom and Practice: Unlocking the secrets of business coaching*. Second edition. Randburg: Knowres.

Stout-Rostron, S. (2014a). *Business Coaching International: Transforming individuals and organisations*. Second edition. London: Karnac.

Stout-Rostron, S. (2014b). *Leadership Coaching for Results: Cutting-edge practices for coach and client*. Randburg: Knowres.

Stout-Rostron, S., and Taylor, M. (2019). Three studies on new approaches to leadership development. *The Corporate Report*, 9(2):9–19.

Stout-Rostron, S., and Taylor, M. (2020). Building emotional and mental resilience in tough times. *SA Coaching News*, May.

Stout-Rostron, S., and Taylor, M. (2021). Challenges to coaching and mentoring in a hybrid environment. *Coaching News Africa*, 3(7):4–7.

Sunday Times (2013). Mandela. *Sunday Times*, 8 December.

Tarver, E. (2020). *11 Types of Motivation: What they are and how to use them*. Webpage: https://www.evantarver.com. Retrieved 13 October 2021.

Taylor, F.W. (1919). *The Principles of Scientific Management*. New York, NY: Harper and Brothers.

Taylor, M. (2021a). Personal interview, 8 January 2021.

Taylor, M. (2021b). *The Management Career Progression Ladder*. Unpublished diagram.

Taylor, M. (2021c). *The Fundamental Next-Level Leadership Steps*. Unpublished diagram.

Terrapinn Training (2006). *Women in Management*. Participant workbook. Bryanston: Terrapinn Training.

Toffler, A. (1970). *Future Shock*. New York, NY: Random House.

Triola, V. (2021). *The four forms of Motivation*. Retrieved 13 October 2021. Webpage: https://vincenttriola.com/blogs/ten-years-of-academic-writing/the-four-forms-of-motivation-are-extrinsic-identified-intrinsic-introjected.

TutorRoom (2018). Best learning motivation for learners. *TutorRoom*. Webpage: tutorroom.net/en/education-platforms/best-learning-motivation-learners/. Retrieved 24 January 2021.

Uzuegbu, C.P., and Nnadozie, C.O. (2015). Henry Fayol's 14 Principles of Management: Implications for libraries and information centres. *Journal of Information Science Theory and Practice*, 3(2):58–72.

Ward, J. (2016). *The Student's Guide to Social Neuroscience*. London: Psychology Press.

Weber, M. (1978). *Economy and Society: An outline of interpretive sociology*. Berkeley, CA: University of California Press.

Wheatley, M.J. (2006). *Leadership and the New Science: Discovering order in a chaotic world*. Third edition. San Francisco, CA: Berrett-Koehler.

Whitecloud, W. (2010). *The Magician's Way: What it really takes to find your treasure*. Novato, CA: New World Library.

Whitmore, J. (2002). *Coaching For Performance: Growing people, performance and purpose*. Third Edition. London: Nicholas Brealey.

Wilber, K. (2006). *Integral Spirituality*. Boston, MA: Integral.

Wilson-Starks, K.Y. (2003). Toxic leadership. *Transleadership Inc.* Webpage: www.transleadership.com/ToxicLeadership.pdf. Retrieved January 2021.

Yalom, I.D. (1980). *Existential Psychotherapy*. New York, NY: Basic.

Yerkes, R.M, and Dodson, J.D. (1908). The relation of strength of stimulus to rapidity of habit-formation. *Journal of Comparative Neurology and Psychology*, 18:459–482.

Zenger, J.H., and Folkman, J. (2003). The leadership tent. *Executive Excellence*, 20(2):5–5.

Zolli, A., and Healy, A.M. (2012). *Resilience: Why things bounce back*. New York, NY: Simon and Schuster.

Endnotes

1   Stout-Rostron, S., and Taylor, M. (2020). Building emotional and mental resilience in tough times. *SA Coaching News*, May.

2   Stout-Rostron and Taylor, 2020

3   Stout-Rostron, S., & Taylor, M. (2021). Challenges to coaching and mentoring in a hybrid environment. *Coaching News Africa*, 3(7):4–7.

4   Joiner, W.B., and Josephs, S.A. (2007). *Leadership Agility: Five levels of mastery for anticipating and initiating change*. San Francisco, CA: Jossey-Bass.

5   Joiner, B. (2009). Creating a culture of agile leaders: A developmental approach. *People and Strategy*, 32(4):28–35.

6   Goleman, D. (2000). Leadership that gets results. *Harvard Business Review*, 78(2):78–90.

7   Garrick, L. (ed.) (2006). *Supporting Guide – Hay Group Inventory of Leadership Styles Diagnostic*. Report for Senior Careers Development Service. Philadelphia, PA: Hay Group.

8   Goleman, 2000: 81–86.

9   Stout Rostron, S. (2006). The history of coaching. In: M. McLoughlin (Ed.), Sharing the Passion: Conversations with Coaches (pp. 16–41). Cape Town: Advanced Human Technologies.

10 Stout-Rostron and Taylor, 2020.

11 Joiner, W.B., and Josephs, S.A. (2007). *Leadership Agility: Five levels of mastery for anticipating and initiating change*. San Francisco, CA: Jossey-Bass: p8.

12 Stout-Rostron, and Taylor, 2020: 3

13 Klenke, K. (1996). *Women and Leadership: A contextual perspective*. New York, NY: Springer, p7.

14 Gardner, 1995: 6.

15 Bolman, L.G., and Deal, T. (2001). Leading With Soul: An uncommon journey of spirit. Second Edition. San Francisco, CA: Jossey-Bass, p11.

16 Stout-Rostron, S., and Taylor, M. (2019). Three studies on new approaches to leadership development. *The Corporate Report*, 9(2):9–19.

17 Stout-Rostron and Taylor, 2019.

18 Fayol, H. (1949). *General and Industrial Administration*. Translated by C. Storrs. New York, NY: Pitman.

19 Taylor, F.W. (1919). *The Principles of Scientific Management*. New York, NY: Harper and Brothers, p140.

20 Caldari, K. (2007). Alfred Marshall's critical analysis of scientific management. *European Journal of the History of Economic Thought*, 14(1):55–78.

21 Fayol, 1949.

22 Uzuegbu, C.P., and Nnadozie, C.O. (2015). Henry Fayol's 14 Principles of Management: Implications for libraries and information centres. *Journal of Information Science Theory and Practice*, 3(2):58–72, p70.

23 Weber, M. (1978). *Economy and Society: An outline of interpretive sociology*. Berkeley, CA: University of California Press.

24 Weber, 1978.

25 Busse, R., and Warner, M. (2017). The legacy of the Hawthorne experiments: A critical analysis of the Human Relations School of Thought. *History of Economic Ideas*, 25(2):91–114.

26   McWhinney, W. (1993). *Paths of Change: Strategic choices for organisations and society.* Thousand Oaks, CA: Sage, p126.

27   McWhinney, 1993: 45.

28   Smuts, J. (1926). *Holism and Evolution.* New York, NY: Viking.

29   McGregor, D. (1960). *The Human Side of Enterprise.* New York, NY: McGraw-Hill.

30   McGregor, 1960: 43–82.

31   McGregor, 1960: 43–58.

32   McGregor, 1960: 59–82.

33   Kerpen, D. (2019). *4 Key Generational Trends in the Workplace.* Inc.com, 25 July. Webpage: www.inc.com/dave-kerpen/4-key-generational-trends-in-workplace.html. Retrieved 10 January 2021.

34   Energy Resourcing (2021). Introducing Generation C. Webpage: energyrsourcing.com/blog/6-ting s-you-need-to know-about-generation-c/. Retrieved May 2021.

35   Kerpen, 2019.

36   Kerpen, 2019.

37   Energy Resourcing, 2021.

38   Purdue Global University (2020). *Generational Differences in the Workplace [Infographic].* Purdue Global University. Webpage: https://www.purdueglobal.edu/education-partnerships/generational-workforce-differences-infographic/. Retrieved 15 January 2021.

39   Purdue Global University, 2020.

40   Purdue Global University, 2020.

41   Energy Resourcing, 2021.

42   Peterson, D., and Goldsmith, D. (2020). *Journey to Mastery.* PowerPoint slides in the ACE Programme: Accelerating Coach Excellence. London: WBECS Group.

43   Blake, R.R., and Mouton, J.S. (1964/1994). *The Managerial Grid.* 1994 paperback re-release of 1964 first edition. Houston, TX: Gulf Publishing.

44   Miner, J.B. (2002). *Organisational Behaviour: Foundations, theories, and analyses.* New York, NY: Oxford University Press, p713.

45   Miner, 2002.

46   Stout-Rostron, S. (2014b). *Leadership Coaching for Results: Cutting-edge practices for coach and client.* Randburg: Knowres, p23–24.

47   Blake and Mouton, 1964/1994.

48   Blake and Mouton, 1964/1994.

49   Blake, R.R., and McCanse, A.A. (1991). *Leadership Dilemmas: Grid solutions.* Houston, TX: Gulf Publishing.

50   Mind Tools (2018). *The Blake Mouton Managerial Grid.* Webpage: www.mindtools.com/pages/article/newLDR_73.htm#. Retrieved 16 January 2021.

51   Spearhead Training Group (2017). *Management Development Programme.* Participant workbook. Chipping Norton: Spearhead Training.

52   Spearhead Training Group, 2017.

53   Spearhead Training Group, 2017.

54   Spearhead Training Group, 2017.

55   Spearhead Training Group, 2017.

56   Gove, P.B. (ed.) (2018). *Webster's Third New International Dictionary Unabridged.* Revised edition. Springfield, MA: Merriam-Webster.

57   Gove, 2018.
58   Terrapinn Training (2006). *Women in Management*. Participant workbook. Bryanston: Terrapinn Training, p8–10.
59   Spearhead Training Group, 2017.
60   Adair, J. (1973) *Action-Centred Leadership*. New York, NY: McGraw-Hill.
61   Stout-Rostron, 2014b: 13.
62   Bennis, W.G., and Nanus, B. (2003). *Leaders: Strategies for taking charge*. Third edition. New York, NY: HarperCollins, p4.
63   Stout-Rostron, 2014b: 4.
64   Stout-Rostron, 2014b: 4.
65   Chemers, M.M. (2001). Leadership effectiveness: An integrative review. In Hogg, M.A., and Tindale, R.S. (eds), *Blackwell Handbook of Social Psychology: Group processes* (pp. 376–399). Oxford: Blackwell, p376.
66   Stout-Rostron, 2014b: 14–15.
67   Karlin, D. (2011). *Leaders: Their Stories, Their Words: Conversations with Human-Based Leaders*. Ottawa, ON: A Better Perspective, px.
68   Goleman, D., Boyatzis, R., and McKee, A. (2002). *Primal Leadership: Learning to lead with emotional intelligence*. Boston, MA: Harvard Business School, p54–59.
69   Wheatley, M.J. (2006). *Leadership and the New Science: Discovering order in a chaotic world*. Third edition. San Francisco, CA: Berrett-Koehler, p130.
70   Buckingham, M. (2012). Leadership development in the age of the algorithm. *Harvard Business Review*, 90(6):86–94.
71   George, B., Sims, P., and McLean, A. (2007). Discovering your authentic leadership. *Harvard Business Review*, 85(2):129–138.
72   Lipkin, N. (2013). *What Keeps Leaders Up At Night? Recognising and resolving your most troubling management issues*. New York, NY: AMACOM, p135.
73   King, S.N., Altman, D.G., and Lee, R.J. (2011). *Discovering the Leader in You: How to realise your leadership potential*. San Francisco, CA: Jossey-Bass.
74   Boyatzis, R.E., and McKee, A. (2005). *Resonant Leadership: Renewing yourself and connecting with others through mindfulness, hope and compassion*. Boston, MA: Harvard Business School, p4–5.
75   Goleman, D. (1998). *Working with Emotional Intelligence*. New York, NY: Bantam Dell, p3–5.
76   Chemers, 2001.
77   Eichinger, R.W., and Lombardo, M.M. (2004). *The 6 Qs of Leadership: A blueprint for enduring success at the top*. Lominger In Focus paper. Minneapolis, MN: Lominger Limited, p1.
78   Eichinger and Lombardo, 2004: 3.
79   Fisher, A. (1998). Success secret: A high emotional IQ. *Fortune*, 26 October, 293–298.
80   Eichinger and Lombardo, 2004: 3.
81   Zenger, J.H., and Folkman, J. (2003). The leadership tent. *Executive Excellence*, 20(2):5–5.
82   Eichinger and Lombardo, 2004: 20.
83   Eichinger and Lombardo, 2004: 21.
84   Eichinger and Lombardo, 2004.
85   Goleman, 1998: 318.
86   Goleman, 1998.

87   Goleman, D. (1996). *Emotional Intelligence: Why it can matter more than IQ*. London: Bloomsbury.

88   Stout-Rostron, 2014b: 61–63.

89   Stout-Rostron, 2014b: 62.

90   Stout-Rostron, 2014b: 62.

91   Stout-Rostron, 2014b: 62.

92   Stout-Rostron, 2014b: 63.

93   Goleman, 1996.

94   Wilber, K. (2006). *Integral Spirituality*. Boston, MA: Integral.

95   Stout-Rostron, 2014b: 111.

96   Stout-Rostron, 2014b: 110.

97   Rumsey, M.G. (ed.) (2013). *The Oxford Handbook of Leadership*. Oxford: Oxford University Press, 68.

98   Rumsey, 2013: 27.

99   Howell, J.P. (2013). *Snapshots of Great Leadership*. Hove: Routledge, p23.

100 National Research Council (1994). Self-confidence and performance. In *Learning, Remembering, Believing: Enhancing human performance* (pp.173–206). Washington, DC: The National Academies Press, p174.

101 National Research Council, 1994: 174.

102 Rumsey, 2013: 27.

103 Howell, 2013: 4.

104 Mandela, N.R. (1994). *Long Walk to Freedom*. Edinburgh: Little, Brown.

105 Mandela, 1994: 19–20.

106 Mandela, 1994: 20–21.

107 Mandela, 1994: 6–7.

108 Mandela, 1994: 522–524.

109 *Sunday Times* (2013). Mandela. *Sunday Times*, 8 December.

110 *Sunday Times*, 2013.

111 Stout-Rostron, 2014b: 32–34.

112 Lewin, K., Lippitt, R., and White, R.K. (1939). Patterns of aggressive behaviour in experimentally created "social climates". *Journal of Social Psychology*, 10:271–299.

113 Miner, 2002: 40.

114 Miner, 2002: 40.

115 Miner, 2002: 40.

116 Miner, 2002: 40.

117 Goleman, 2000.

118 Garrick, 2006.

119 Goleman, 2000: 81–86.

120 Stout-Rostron, 2014b: 29–30.

121 Cohen, 2009: 3–5.

122 Cohen, 2009: 5.

123 Neider, L.L., and Schriesheim, C.A. (eds) (2010). *The "Dark" Side of Management. Research in Management Series*. Miami, FL: University of Miami, p29.

124 Rosenthal, S.A., and Pittinsky, T.L. (2006). Narcissistic leadership. *The Leadership Quarterly*, 17(6):617–633, p629.

125 Rosenthal and Pittinsky, 2006: 617.

126 Lacida, K. (2012). *Toxic Leadership*. Lead Change Group, 17 August. Webpage: leadchangegroup.com/toxic-leadership/. Retrieved January 2021, p1.

127 Wilson-Starks, K.Y. (2003). Toxic leadership. *Transleadership Inc*. Webpage: www.transleadership.com/ToxicLeadership.pdf. Retrieved January 2021.

128 Wilson-Starks, 2003.

129 Stout-Rostron and Taylor, 2020.

130 Stout-Rostron and Taylor, 2020.

131 Taylor, M. (2021a). Personal interview, 8 January 2021.

132 Garms, E.T. (2013). Practicing mindful leadership. *Training and Development*, March, 32–35.

133 Stout-Rostron, 2014b: 37–38.

134 Kabat-Zinn, J. (1994). *Wherever You Go There You Are: Mindfulness meditation in everyday life*. New York, NY: Hyperion.

135 Siegel, D.J. (2009). Mindful awareness, mindsight, and neural integration. *The Humanistic Psychologist*, 37(2):137–158, p146.

136 Garms, 2013: 34.

137 Garms, 2013: 34–35.

138 Stout-Rostron, 2014b: 40–41.

139 Di Domenico, S.I., and Ryan, R.M. (2017). The emerging neuroscience of intrinsic motivation: A new frontier in self-determination research. *Frontiers in Human Neuroscience*, 11(March):1–14.

140 Adolphs, R. (2009). The social brain: Neural basis of social knowledge. *Annual Review of Psychology*, 60:693–716.

141 Fiske, S.T., and Taylor, S.E. (2013). *Social Cognition: From brains to culture*. Thousand Oaks, CA: Sage.

142 Lieberman, M.D. (2007). Social cognitive neuroscience: A review of core processes. *Annual Review of Psychology*, 58(1):259–289.

143 Barrett, L.F., Adolphs, R., Marsella, S., Martinez, A.M., and Pollak, S.D. (2019). Emotional expressions reconsidered: Challenges to inferring emotion from human facial movements. *Psychological Science in the Public Interest*, 20(1):1–68.

144 Gross, J.J. (ed.) (2007). *Handbook of Emotion Regulation*. New York, NY: Guilford.

145 Du Buisson-Narsai, I. (2020). *Flight, Fight or Flourish: How neuroscience can unlock human potential*. Randburg: Knowres.

146 Cesario, J., Johnson, D. J., and Eisthen, H. L. (2020). Your brain is not an onion with a tiny reptile inside. *Current Directions in Psychological Science*, 29(3):255–260.

147 Ward, J. (2016). *The Student's Guide to Social Neuroscience*. London: Psychology Press.

148 Cesario, Johnson and Eisthen, 2020: 255.

149 Cesario, Johnson and Eisthen, 2020: 259.

150 Barrett et al., 2019.

151 Kleckner, I. R., Zhang, J., Touroutoglou, A., Chanes, L., Xia, C., Simmons, W.K., Quigley, K.S., Dickerson, B.C., and Barrett, L.F. (2017). Evidence for a large-scale brain system supporting allostasis and interoception in humans. *Nature Human Behaviour*, 1(5):1–14.

152 Russell, J.A., and Barrett, L.F. (1999). Core affect, prototypical emotional episodes, and other things called emotion: dissecting the elephant. *Journal of Personality and Social Psychology*, 76(5):805–819.

153 Feldman-Barrett, L. (2018). *How Emotions Are Made: The Secret Life of the Brain*. London: Pan Macmillan, p74.

154 Sporns, O. (2013). Structure and function of complex brain networks. *Dialogues in Clinical Neuroscience*, 15(3):247–262.

155 Bressler, S.L., and Menon, V. (2010). Large-scale brain networks in cognition : emerging methods and principles. Trends in Cognitive Sciences, 14(6):277–290.

156 Bressler and Menon, 2010.

157 Bressler and Menon, 2010.

158 Gordon, E., Barnett, K.J., Cooper, N.J., Tran, N., and Williams, L.M. (2008). An "Integrative Neuroscience" platform: application to profiles of negativity and positivity bias. *Journal of Integrative Neuroscience*, 7(3):345–366.

159 Yerkes, R.M, and Dodson, J.D. (1908). The relation of strength of stimulus to rapidity of habit-formation. *Journal of Comparative Neurology and Psychology*, 18:459–482.

160 Csikszentmihalyi, M. (1990). Literacy and intrinsic motivation. *Daedalus*, 115–140.

161 Boyatzis, R.E., Smith, M.L., and Blaize, N. (2006). Developing sustainable leaders through coaching and compassion. *Academy of Management Learning and Education*, 5(1):8–24.

162 Hayes, S.C., Strosahl, K.D., and Wilson, K.G. (1999). *Acceptance and Commitment Therapy: An experimental approach to behaviour of change*. New York, NY: Guilford.

163 Kross, E., and Ayduk, O. (2011). Making meaning out of negative experiences by self-distancing. *Current Directions in Psychological Science*, 20(3):187–191.

164 Peters, J., and Büchel, C. (2010). Episodic future thinking reduces reward delay discounting through an enhancement of prefrontal-mediotemporal interactions. *Neuron*, 66(1):138–148.

165 Ryan, R.M., and Deci, E.L. (2000). Intrinsic and extrinsic motivations: Classic definitions and new directions. *Contemporary Educational Psychology*, 25(1):54–67.

166 Schacter, D.L., Benoit, R.G., and Szpunar, K.K. (2017). Episodic future thinking: Mechanisms and functions. *Current Opinion in Behavioural Sciences*, 17: 41–50.

167 Whitecloud, W. (2010). *The Magician's Way: What it really takes to find your treasure*. Novato, CA: New World Library.

168 Stout-Rostron, 2014b: 46.

169 Stout-Rostron, 2014b: 46–47.

170 Stout-Rostron, S. (2012). *Business Coaching Wisdom and Practice: Unlocking the secrets of business coaching*. Second edition. Randburg: Knowres, p26.

171 Griffiths, K.E., and Campbell, M.A. (2008). Regulating the regulators: Paving the way for international, evidence-based coaching standards. *International Journal of Evidence-Based Coaching and Mentoring*, 6(1):19–31.

172 Whitmore, J. (2002). *Coaching For Performance: Growing people, performance and purpose*. Third Edition. London: Nicholas Brealey.

173 Ryan, R.M. (2013). *Self-determination*. Notes compiled by Stout-Rostron, S., from presentation to Coaching in Leadership and Healthcare Conference 2013, Harvard / McLean Medical School, Cambridge, MA, 28 September.

174 Ryan, 2013.

175 Ryan, 2013.

176 Ryan, 2013.

177 Ryan, 2013.

178 Stout-Rostron, 2012: 59–60.

179 Stout-Rostron, 2012: 59.

180 Stout-Rostron, 2012: 59–60.

181 Stout-Rostron, 2012: 52–53.

182 Peltier, B. (2001). *The Psychology of Executive Coaching: Theory and application*. New York, NY: Brunner-Routledge.

183 O'Neill, M.B. (2000). Coaching with backbone and heart: A systems approach to engaging leaders with their challenges. San Francisco, CA; Jossey-Bass.

184 O'Neill, 2000.

185 Yalom, I.D. (1980). *Existential Psychotherapy*. New York, NY: Basic.

186 Hicks, M.D., and Peterson, D.B. (1999). The development pipeline: How people really learn. *Knowledge Management Review*, 9:30–33.

187 Spinelli, E. (1989). *The Interpreted World: An introduction to phenomenological psychology*. London: Sage.

188 Kline, N. (1999). *Time To Think: Listening to ignite the human mind*. London: Cassell.

189 Kline, N. (2005). *The Thinking Partnership Programme: Consultant's Guide*. Wallingford: Time to Think, p4.

190 Kline, 1999: 100–1.

191 Stout-Rostron, 2014b: 58.

192 Kline, N. (2017). *The Transforming Meetings Programme*. Wallingford: Time to Think.

193 Yalom, 1980: 319.

194 Stout-Rostron, 2012: 250.

195 Kline, 2017.

196 Kline, N. (2020). *The Promise That Changes Everything: I won't interrupt you*. London: Penguin Life, p214.

197 Pentland, A.S. (2012). The new science of building great teams. *Harvard Business Review*, 90(4):60–69.

198 Stout-Rostron, 2012: 28.

199 Stout-Rostron, 2014b: 70.

200 Stout-Rostron, S. (2014a). *Business Coaching International: Transforming individuals and organisations*. Second edition. London: Karnac.

201 Yalom, 1980: 280.

202 Maslow, A. (1968). *Toward a Psychology of Being*. New York, NY: Van Nostrand, p21.

203 Clipartkey.com (2021). *Clipart Motivation Concept – Maslow's Hierarchy of Needs*. Webpage: www.clipartkey.com/view/himiTJ_clip-art-motivation-concept-maslows-hierarchy-of-needs/. Retrieved 14 March 2021.

204 Maslow, 1968.

205 McClelland, D.C. (1961). *The Achieving Society*. Princeton, NJ: Van Nostrand.

206 McClelland, 1961.

207 Stout-Rostron, 2014b: 21.

208 McClelland, D.C. (1987). *Human Motivation*. New York, NY: Cambridge University, pp303; 318; 348; 355.

209 TutorRoom (2018). Best learning motivation for learners. *TutorRoom*. Webpage: tutorroom.net/en/education-platforms/best-learning-motivation-learners/. Retrieved 24 January 2021.

210 Herzberg, F.I. (1966). *Work and the Nature of Man*. Cleveland, OH: World.

211 Herzberg, 1966.

212 Herzberg, 1966.

213 Herzberg, 1966.

214 Deci, E.L., and Ryan, R.M. (1985). *Intrinsic Motivation and Self-Determination in Human Behaviour*. Perspectives in Social Psychology series. Boston, MA: Springer.

215 Ryan, 2013.

216 Deci, E.L., and Ryan, R.M. (1990). A motivational approach to self: Integration in personality. *Nebraska Symposium on Motivation*, 38:237–288.

217 Ryan, 2013.

218 Ryan, 2013.

219 Ryan, 2013.

220 Ryan, 2013.

221 Ryan, 2013.

222 Ryan, 2013.

223 Ryan, 2013.

224 Tarver, E. (2020). *11 Types of Motivation: What they are and how to use them*. Webpage: https://www.evantarver.com. Retrieved 13 October 2021.

225 Gillison, F., Osborn, M., Standage, M., Skevington, S. (2009). Exploring the experience of introjected regulation for exercise across gender in adolescence. *Psychology of Sport and Exercise, 10*(3): 309–319, p309.

226 cf Deci & Ryan, 1985/1991.

227 Gillison et al., 2009: 309-310.

228 Gillison et al., 2009: 310.

229 cf Mullan, E. & Marland, D. (1997). Variations in self-determination across the stages of change for exercise in adults. *Motivation and Emotion*, 21, 349-362.

230 Gillison, 2009: 310-311.

231 cf Ryan & Deci, 2000.

232 Gillison et al., 2009: 315.

233 Triola, V. (2021). *The four forms of Motivation*. Retrieved 13 October 2021. Webpage: https://vincenttriola.com/blogs/ten-years-of-academic-writing/the-four-forms-of-motivation-are-extrinsic-identified-intrinsic-introjected.

234 Gillison et al., 2009: 310-311.

235 Triola, 2021.

236 Stout-Rostron, 2014a: 16–17.

237 Cavanagh, M.J., and Grant, A.M. (2002). *Coaching Psychology: A solution-focused, cognitive-behavioural approach*. Sydney, NSW: University of Sydney: Coaching Psychology Unit, p4.

238 American Manufacturing Association (AMA) (2008). *Coaching: A global strategy of successful practices*. New York, NY: AMA. (Douglas and McCauley, 1999; cited in AMA, 2008: 8).

239 Stout-Rostron, 2014b: 69–72.

240 O'Neill, 2000:104.

241 Stout-Rostron, 2014b: 80–81.

242 Whitmore, 2002.

243 Whitmore, 2002.

244 Whitmore, 2002: 59.

245 Whitmore, 2002.

246 Whitmore, 2002: 89–90.
247 Lohr, D. (1988). *How to Delegate Work and Ensure It's Done Right*. Audio cassette book. Boulder, CO: Career Track.
248 Kazdin, A.E. (ed.) (2000). *The Encyclopaedia of Psychology*. Washington, DC: American Psychological Association and New York, NY: Oxford University Press.
249 Rogers, C. (1959). A theory of therapy, personality and interpersonal relationships, as developed in the client-centred framework. In Koch, S. (ed.), *Psychology: A study of a science. Volume 3: Formulations of the person and the social context* (pp.184–256). New York, NY: McGraw Hill.
250 Carlson, N.R, Miller, H.L., Heth, D.S., Donahoe, J.W., Lee, B. (2014). *Psychology: The Science of Behaviour*. Seventh edition. Harlow, Essex: Pearson Education, p464.
251 Kazdin, 2000.
252 Hart, A. (2014). Is personality unique to humans? *BBC News*, 10 December. Webpage: www.bbc.com/news/science-environment-30395493. Retrieved April 2021.
253 Kazdin, 2000.
254 Cesario, Johnson and Eisthen, 2020: 255.
255 Gove, 2018.
256 David, S., and Congleton, C. (2013). Emotional agility: How effective leaders manage their negative thoughts and feelings. *Harvard Business Review*, November.
257 Price, C. (1994). *Assertive Communication Skills for Professionals*. Workbook and audio cassette. Boulder, CO: Career Track.
258 Toffler, A. (1970). *Future Shock*. New York, NY: Random House.
259 Joiner, W.B., and Josephs, S.A. (2007). *Leadership Agility: Five levels of mastery for anticipating and initiating change*. San Francisco, CA: Jossey-Bass, p6, 8.
260 Ramo, J.C. (2009). *The Age of the Unthinkable: Why the new world disorder constantly surprises us and what we can do about it*. New York, NY: Little, Brown.
261 Casey, G.W. (2017). *Leading in a VUCA World*. SC Johnson Graduate School of Management, Cornell University. Webpage: www.johnson.cornell.edu/wp-content/uploads/sites/3/2019/04/Cornell-Executive-Education-VUCA-Leadership-February-2017.pdf. Retrieved 30 July 2020
262 Stagen, R., and Thomas, B. (2006) *Learning to Learn*. Unpublished paper. Dallas, TX: Stagen Leadership Institute, p4.
263 Stagen and Thomas, 2006: 4.
264 Kline, 1999: 62.
265 Stout-Rostron and Taylor, 2020: 6.
266 Stout-Rostron and Taylor, 2020: 2.
267 Horney, N., Passmore, W., and O'Shea, T. (2010). Leadership agility: A business imperative for a VUCA world. *People and Strategy*, 33(4):32–38.
268 Stout-Rostron and Taylor, 2020: 3.
269 Zolli, A., and Healy, A.M. (2012). *Resilience: Why things bounce back*. New York, NY: Simon and Schuster, p5.

270 Zolli and Healy, 2012: 7.
271 Stout-Rostron and Taylor, 2020: 2.
272 Stout-Rostron and Taylor, 2020: 3.

273 Centre for Creative Leadership (CCL) (2020). *Leadership Resilience: Handling stress, uncertainty, and setbacks*. Greensboro, NC: CCL. Webpage: www.ccl.org/articles/leading-effectively-articles/leadership-resiliency-handling-stress-uncertainty-and-setbacks/. Retrieved 2 March 2021.

274 Centre for Creative Leadership, 2020.

275 Judge, M. (2017). Why emotional maturity and emotional intelligence are important for healthy relationships. *TheRoot.com*, 5 December. Webpage: www.theroot.com/why-emotional-maturity-and-emotional-intelligence-are-i-1821030316. Retrieved December 2020.

276 Joiner and Josephs, 2007: 8.

277 Joiner and Josephs, 2007: 10.

278 Stout-Rostron and Taylor, 2020: 3.

279 De Meuse, K.P., Dai, G., and Hallenbeck, G.S. (2010). Learning agility: A construct whose time has come. *Consulting Psychology Journal: Practice and Research*, 62(2):119–130, p120.

280 Gove, 2018.

281 Lombardo, M.M., and Eichinger, R.W. (2000). High-potentials as high learners. *Human Resource Management*, 39(4):321–330, p2.

282 De Meuse et al., 2010: 121.

283 De Meuse et al., 2010: 121.

284 De Meuse et al., 2010: 124.

285 Chamorro-Premuzic, T. (2016). What science tells us about leadership potential. *Harvard Business Review*, September. Webpage: hbr.org/2016/09/what-science-tells-us-about-leadership-potential. Retrieved March 2020, p3.

286 Taylor, M. (2021b). *The Management Career Progression Ladder*. Unpublished diagram.

287 Charan, R, Drotter, S., and Noel, J. (2001). *The Leadership Pipeline: How to build the leadership powered company*. San Francisco, CA: Wiley, pp34, 69, 92, 94.

288 Lombardo, M.M., and Eichinger, R.W. (2009). *FYI: For Your Improvement: A guide for development and coaching for learners, managers, mentors, and feedback givers*. Fifth edition. Los Angeles, CA: Lominger, pp163, 258.

289 Taylor, M. (2021c). *The Fundamental Next-Level Leadership Steps*. Unpublished diagram.

290 Hooijberg, R., and Watkins, M. (2021). The future of team leadership is multimodal. *MIT Sloan Management Review*, 9 February. Webpage: sloanreview.mit.edu/article/the-future-of-team-leadership-is-multimodal. Retrieved March 2021, p2.

Index